Erich Hoyt

The Whale Watcher's Handbook

Illustrations by Pieter Folkens

A Madison Press Book
produced for
Doubleday & Company, Inc.
Garden City, New York

For Françoise Roux

Published in Canada by Penguin Books Canada Limited,
2801 John Street, Markham, Ontario, L3R 1B4

Canadian Cataloguing in Publication Data

Hoyt, Erich, 1950–
   The whale watcher's handbook

Bibliography: p.
Includes index.
ISBN 0-14-007064-8

1. Whales—Identification.   I. Title.

QL737.C4H69 1984   599.5   C83-098791-6

Published in the United States by Doubleday & Company, Inc.
Garden City, New York

Library of Congress C.I.P. data applied for

ISBN 0-385-19036-0

Design, layout and assembly: David Shaw & Associates Ltd.
Cover photograph: Erich Hoyt
Editor: Patrick Crean

Produced by
Madison Press Books
40 Madison Avenue
Toronto, Ontario
Canada M5R 2S1

Printed and bound in Canada
by D.W. Friesen Ltd.

overleaf: *Whale watchers peer at a feeding
humpback as a gull snatches up a sand eel
driven to the surface by the whale.*

Acknowledgements

Part of the opening text originally appeared in *Equinox*, which has encouraged and supported me on several whale-watching ventures.

Many biologists and whale watchers from around the world lent their expertise through letters, telephone calls and interviews. From the United States: Stephen Leatherwood, Kenneth S. Norris, Raymond M. Gilmore, Donald M. Robinson, Norm Famous, Ron Naveen, James and Nancy R. Lethcoe, Stephanie Kaza, Victor B. Scheffer, Ronn Storro-Patterson, James G. Mead, Steven L. Swartz, Eleanor M. Dorsey, David K. Caldwell, Robbins Barstow, Bruce R. Mate, William W. Rossiter, Diane Roberts, Christopher W. Clark, Bernd Würsig, Stanley Minasian, Peter O. Thomas, Sara M. Taber, Nancy Wallace, Peter D. Capen, Richard Osborne. From Canada: David E. Sergeant, Randall R. Reeves, Richard Sears, David E. Gaskin, Mimi Breton, Hal Whitehead, William E. McIntyre, Peter Beamish, Sue Staniforth, Jon Lien, James D. Darling and West Coast Whale Research Foundation. Others include: Antonio M. Teixeira (Portugal), Esteve Grau (Spain), Mats Amundin (Sweden), Allan Thornton (United Kingdom), R. Duguy (France), Jean-Pierre Sylvestre (France), W.H. Dudok van Heel (Netherlands), Alan N. Baker (New Zealand), J.D. Ovington (Australia), Ricardo & Victoria Bastida (Argentina), Alejandro Galeazzi (Argentina), Rae Natalie P. Goodall (Argentina), Ricardo M. Mandojana (Argentina), Luis A. Pastene (Chile), Maria C. Pinedo (Brazil), José T. Palazzo, Jr. (Brazil), Ricardo Praderi (Uruguay), Graham J.B. Ross (South Africa), Roy Cruickshank (South Africa), Tas'an (Indonesia).

For their studies on whale watching, I am grateful to: Stephanie Kaza, Michael Bursk, Maxine McCloskey, John Kelly, John M. Olguin, Kieran J. McNamara and Mary B. Harwood. The idea for this book grew out of Hugh Brewster's whale-watching cruise around Baja California with Sven Olaf Lindblad and Special Expeditions. I'd also like to thank James Bird for helping to prepare the species accounts, Denise Hewitt for transcribing the interviews, Patrick Crean, Ramsay Derry and Robert Emmett Hoyt for skillful editing and helpful comments, and David Shaw for his patience and care in designing this book.

For their research and assistance with the illustrations, Pieter Folkens would like to thank Nanette Butler, William Richardson, Wendy Johnston, Jan Sherer, and Kendal Morris.

Finally, a special thanks to Françoise Roux for her fine eye and help in editing the photographs and for her encouragement.

Contents

A killer whale pod surfaces beside the author's boat off northern Vancouver Island.

Part One

Whale Watching: A New Way to Look at Whales

A "Friendly" Killer Whale

Looking through the binoculars was making me feel queasy. The 32-foot sailboat was rolling in the swells. And yet I rolled with it, my curiosity fueled by hope: Please let that strange-looking object be a whale! Some 300 yards off our bow, over toward the northern shore of Vancouver Island, bobbed what seemed the black, broken trunk of a tree.

"Let me look," said Graeme Ellis, grabbing for the binoculars.

We were six whale-watching neophytes sailing through Johnstone Strait on a windy 1973 summer afternoon. Only Ellis had had experience with whales; in the late 1960s, he had been a trainer – one of the first – of captive killer whales. Now he was eager for this chance to work with them in the wild on the first film and photographic expedition in search of killer whales along the British Columbia coast.

"It's Stubbs!" Ellis shouted, thrusting the binoculars toward me. Twice before we'd seen this odd killer whale, but we were not yet used to her log-like demeanor. This old female had a distinctive, sawed-off dorsal fin. Though she regularly travelled with a family group, a *pod* of a dozen or so whales, she often lagged behind, seeming to need more breaths and more rest time.

Later that afternoon, we got our first close-up view of Stubbs. Easing close in a rubber inflatable Zodiac, we studied her misshapen 18-foot length, fat around the middle, bulging, her scarred fin looking like it had had a too-close encounter with a propeller. Yet she showed no fear of us. As we stood off, our engine idling, she suddenly turned toward us, pushed off with her tail flukes, and slid along the surface like a slow-motion torpedo. We scurried to get out of the way. Little as we knew about whales, science knew even less about the species *Orcinus orca* – not much more than facts about feeding habits of these pack-hunting predators who had been known to subdue even the massive blue whale, many times their size. "Orcas" were an unknown quantity and that was why we were trying to learn about them. Yet at this moment we were more alarmed than curious. For weeks we had been trying to approach whales and now this whale was coming on strong. Her move seemed unaggressive. She stopped beside the boat and lay there motionless, certainly aware of us, yet unafraid. My heart was doing double time, never mind my outward calm.

Why was Stubbs trusting us? As she lifted her head, the water rolled off her shiny black torso, and she spouted. The spray drifted toward us; I could feel wisps of it on my face and arms. We were close enough to touch her, though too stunned to move. We felt privileged just to be with her. A few seconds later, as she dove, gliding to join her pod, we returned to our sailboat to sort out what had happened.

Stubbs was a fine introduction to whale watching – my first "friendly". That encounter was the first of many with Vancouver Island orcas that demonstrated to me the growing whale phenomenon termed "friendly" behavior. I have also witnessed it with long-finned pilot whales near Jan Mayen Island, 500 miles northeast of Iceland, and with bow-riding bottlenose dolphins in the Caribbean. It is even more widely documented with gray and humpback whales. I am only

A breaching humpback performs for whale watchers in Stellwagen Bank waters off Massachusetts.

one of thousands who have been peered at by friendly humpbacks around Hawaii and off Cape Cod in the North Atlantic. Many have had their boats nuzzled by barnacled 40-foot gray whale friendlies off Baja California.

It's strange, yet no matter how prevalent friendly behavior becomes, it never fails to impress even veteran whale watchers. And nothing captivates a new whale watcher faster than an encounter with a friendly: something so big and so alive approaching so close. It renders speechless the most verbal human being, or it makes him stutter in amazement.

Who are these friendlies? Like Stubbs, some are oddballs, casualties of one sort or another. Some are "loners", perhaps outcasts. Other friendlies are juveniles, old enough to be free of their mothers, yet young enough to be adventurous. Or perhaps they are looking for mother substitutes. And then there was the gray whale that appeared off the west coast of Vancouver Island late in the summer of 1982. This animal was *big*. It began hanging around the boats, nuzzling the bow, letting people pat its head. This went on for weeks and created a minor tourist boom in the fishing village of Tofino.

Why are these whales friendly? Unlike some wild animals, they're not looking for a food hand-out. Perhaps they enjoy the scratch on the chin or the playful rub beneath the boats or hearing the screams and cheers of whale watchers. Perhaps they are gregarious, as Professor Kenneth S. Norris from the University of California, Santa Cruz, suggests, and seek out human company when no other whales are around.

Or perhaps they're just curious.

Historically, they have little reason to be fond of humans. Until quite recently, the slightest curiosity toward a human earned the whale a sharp piece of steel in its flesh. Whales have not been able to swim from man fast enough, long enough, nor get far enough away. Since the turn of the century, more than 2 million whales have been reported killed for food, oil, cosmetics and other products. What had started off as aboriginal subsistence in early centuries grew into all-out greed: relentless pursuit and slaughter. The last decade or two brought – none too soon – a growing awareness of the near-irreversibility of the slaughter. And with this awareness came a change of heart – an almost reverent attitude toward these who-knows-how-intelligent social mammals, the largest animals ever to live on our planet. This focus of concern started in the 1960s, the decade of increasing environmental awareness, especially in North America. Whales became the most dramatic symbol of the environment. People began to grasp that if we humans couldn't save the great whales, we probably couldn't save ourselves.

Then, as whaling around North America wound down in the 1960s, the unexpected happened: whales began returning to the once bloody inshore waters. With a mixture of curiosity and surprise, people began watching them from the shores and venturing out to meet them. This time the hunters were equipped with cameras and binoculars, not harpoons. In the United States, Canada and Mexico, whale watching soon became a successful commercial enterprise. Today, it is a substantial industry involving hundreds of thousands of whale watchers and millions of dollars in annual revenue. Flip to the back of this book to see the incredible variety of whale-watching opportunities. In California – the world's whale-watching center – the 1981 tour-boat business was valued at more than $2 million. In New England, more than $1 million a year; in Canada, about $1 million. And these figures all appear to be on the rise. The total monetary value of live whales – including whale watching in the wild and in captivity, and as cultural source material for books, films, records and art – has been estimated at $200 million-plus annually.

The money is only part of the picture. It does not measure the unknown value of live whales to the environment – their function in the ecological balance of the world ocean. It does not include the intrinsic value of whales as superb ''examples of living organisms'', as biologist Victor B. Scheffer puts it: ''They have opened our eyes to the far limits of power, beauty, and grace that life can reach.'' This kind of value defies a dollar estimate, yet whalers and whaling countries obviously disagree. The Japanese – the main killers and consumers of whales today – apparently do not share our enthusiasm for live whales, though the numbers show there is probably more money to be made from watching whales – from tourism – than from killing them.

In this context the friendly nature of North American whales does seem to have survival value. Fanatic whale watchers – I've heard them talk – suggest that the friendlies, the ''crowd pleasers'', know their fate rests on humans and that they are on their best behavior with us, putting on one last show as it were, before the big curtain, extinction, falls. It's impossible to prove that whales are ''trying to tell us something'', yet I do recommend that you go out and meet a few whales from one of the many lookouts or on a whale-watching excursion. Decide for yourself whether whales present a powerful enough argument for their own survival.

The First Whale Watchers

The identities of the first whale watchers are lost to pre-history. We can only speculate: Did they chance upon a beached whale and rejoice over the enormous supply of meat? Or were they fishermen watching live whales from shore or primitive canoe? With what mix of surprise, fear, curiosity, or visions of commerce did they view the whales? Did they wonder, perhaps for an instant, what life was like for a whale?

The earliest known cave drawings of whales go back to Norway around the year 5,000 B.C. The Greeks were the first to draw whales with an accuracy that indicated they had had a good look at them – or at least of *Delphinus delphis*, the common dolphin found in the Mediterranean. Even today one can charter a boat from the Greek islands and meet these dolphins as they ride the bow.

The Greeks were also the first to write about whales and dolphins. Their early prose and poetry is the stuff of legends – fabled tales that reveal far more about the observers than about the observed. Yet the tone is significant: the dolphins are described as gentle and friendly to humans.

Aristotle noted the dolphin's fondness for human company. But, more important, he may have been the first dolphin watcher to look at them scientifically. Best known as a philosopher, Aristotle was also an early biologist, and the first one to publish. The marine section of his 4th Century B.C. *History of Animals*, was probably based on dolphins observed in the clear water around Lesbos, the Greek Island off Turkey, where he lived and wrote in his forties.

Aristotle knew that dolphins were mammals, giving birth to live progeny and suckling them. Far ahead of the 18th Century classifier Linnaeus, Aristotle grouped the whales, dolphins and porpoises together as "cetaceans" and suggested remarkably accurate gestation periods and ages for reaching maturity. He made a few gaffes, but there is in his writing one of the most prophetic passages for the modern era of studying whales by watching them:

"The [dolphin's] young accompany it for a considerable period. It lives for many years; some are known to have lived for more than 25, and some for 30 years." How could he know? He goes on to say that fishermen who catch them "nick their tails sometimes and set them adrift again and by this expedient their ages are ascertained."

Whether Aristotle participated in the experiments, or only reported them, is not clear, but he recognized good science when he saw it. In fact, it is not necessary to nick the tail. From marks on their dorsal fins, unique color patterns, and even gross deformities like the dorsal fin of my friend Stubbs, whales can be distinguished. The researcher who watches a species long enough, lives with it, begins to see individual characteristics. Entomologists even recognize individual insects. To watch whales one needs a protected near-shore area, a lot of patience, good eyes and ears and camera skills. Getting the "IDs" – identification photographs – is essential. Not only can a researcher, in time, determine a whale's age – as Aristotle noted – but he can establish local abundance, home range and migratory patterns, birth and death rate.

After Aristotle, watching whales became almost exclusively the province of whalers. Scientists rarely ventured into the field during the "museum era" which began after the Renaissance. Important work was done on the classification of whales, but there was little observation. The study of whales was largely the study of carcasses supplied by whalers or washed up on beaches.

Modern Whale Watching

In the mid-1940s, the modern era of watching whales began in California with Carl L. Hubbs, a professor at Scripps Institution of Oceanography. During his student days, Ken Norris – who would go on to inspire another generation of whale-watching students – remembers Hubbs crawling up on steep shingled rooftops every winter day – wind, rain or hot sun – "to count migrating gray whales." They could be seen from the rooftops of the Scripps campus as, one by one, they filed past the coast of southern California *en route* to the mating and calving lagoons in Mexico. Through binoculars, Hubbs would count the bushy spouts and yell down numbers to his wife Laura, who marked them down in her notebook. Various students, Norris included, took 15-minute turns on "whale watch". Later, a whale-watching shed was built atop Scripps' Ritter Hall, equipped with 18-power Japanese Navy binoculars, an azimuth circle to plot whale positions, and whale-sighting forms to standardize the records.

The winter of 1946–47 Hubbs counted 200 whales. In later years, the figure slowly grew. Hubbs scrounged rides on U.S. Coast Guard planes and even convinced actor Errol Flynn to finance a helicopter reconnaissance down the Baja California peninsula. These aerial surveys were the first population estimates of the Mexican lagoons.

Another member of the gray-whale group at Scripps was Theodore J. Walker, an associate research oceanographer with a far-from-the-sea fresh-water background. Arriving in California from Wisconsin, Ted Walker began spending time in the Mexican lagoons watching the grays. Something of a lone wolf, Walker would argue with Hubbs – and everyone else – about the whales. One long-standing argument was whether the grays were feeding in the lagoons. The conventional wisdom of the day said they were there to mate and calve, and that was it. If they were feeding in Scammon's Lagoon, why would they need to make a 12,000-mile annual round-trip to the food-rich waters around Alaska?

Ted Walker was certain they were eating Mexican food. He saw them sticking their heads out of the water – an action he called "the spar" – and breaching, water streaming from the sides of their mouths. To Walker, it looked like a convenient way to get down a meal. Hubbs and others said they were just looking around, "spy-hopping". Walker said that the sparring – or spy-hopping – whales had their eyes *closed*, not open and, since whales are sonic creatures, they likely didn't need their eyes to navigate anyway. "They're eating!" he claimed.

As it turned out, both men were partly right, partly wrong. Some grays do eat in the lagoon, but they are not sonic like toothed whales, and sometimes the spar is more of a spy-hop than anything else. Yet in the evolution of whale watching both men made vital contributions. The study of whales – because of Hubbs and Walker – was becoming the art of watching them. They helped lead other scientists, like Ken Norris, into thinking about whales as natural creatures. In the process, they were also "saving the whales," making people *care*. And, for the first time (Ken Norris terms it a crucial step) both the public and government agencies got involved. In 1950, Donald M. Robinson, superin-tendent of Cabrillo National Monument in San Diego, converted an old U.S. Army gun station into the first public whale-watching lookout. About 10,000 people came out to meet the migrating gray whales that first winter. The following year, Robinson co-ordinated sightings with Carl Hubbs at Scripps, a few miles up the coast. In 1952, Raymond M. Gilmore of the U.S. Fish and Wildlife Service took over the counting chores, launching the first official government census.

Whales Make a Comeback

The early years of gray whale research were a time of tremendous discovery for everyone. It was a surprise even to learn that there were enough animals left to study. "The large bays and lagoons where these animals once congregated," wrote the whaler Capt. Charles M. Scammon in 1874, "are already nearly deserted. The mammoth bones of the California gray lie bleaching on the shores . . . scattered along the broken coasts from Siberia to the Gulf of California; and ere long it may be questioned whether this mammal will not be numbered among the extinct species. . . . ''

Sightings became rare in the early 20th Century. More than one writer noted that the species was "probably extinct". By 1949, after setting up the International Whaling Commission, the whaling nations gladly agreed to stop killing grays. There weren't enough animals to hunt anyway. Commercially, the gray whale was extinct. But the gray has staged an impressive comeback, though no one knows how low the population dropped. Recent estimates of 16,500 indicate the population now approaches its original abundance.

The gray whale recovery is one of the great success stories of all conservation. California has celebrated it by declaring the gray its state marine mammal. Every year more and more Californians and visitors become whale watchers. In 1959, Raymond Gilmore escorted a total of 330 paying customers on the first naturalist-led day tours out of San Diego. Today, California-based whale watching includes an estimated 120 boats with tours once or twice a day, plus three ships taking whale watchers for extended excursions off the California coast and down to the Mexican lagoons. In all, 235,000 gray whale watchers paid for their thrill in 1981 – according to whale-watching researcher Stephanie Kaza. Many hundred thousand more watched for free from lookout points. The most popular of these is the Cabrillo National Monument at Pt. Loma, San Diego. There, at the spot where three decades earlier Don Robinson invited the public to view the spectacle that so excited the young Carl Hubbs and the other gray whale pioneers, an estimated 300,000 to 350,000 people came last year to watch whales. Few went away disappointed.

Singing Whales
About the time Californians were getting to know their gray whales, Roger Payne was a young zoologist specializing in the bio-acoustics of bats and owls at Harvard, Cornell and later Rockefeller University. He knew of the early gray whale work on the west coast, but it was a late night encounter with a dead porpoise – washed up on a stretch of Massachusetts beach near his home – that triggered his move to the seas. Learning everything he could about whales, Payne wanted to watch them, but there was no mass east coast movement comparable to the west coast gray whale migration. There had once existed a North Atlantic gray whale, but it had gone extinct, probably at least partly because of late 17th and early 18th Century whalers. When Payne met Ken Norris he told the older naturalist, "I want to spend my life studying sperm whales." He was determined "to learn enough about whales," as he put it, "to have some effect on their fate."

Finding no accessible sperm whales, Payne chartered a sailboat in Bermuda in 1967 to look for humpbacks. He talked to Frank Watlington who had recorded them from the Columbia University Geophysical Field Station at St. David's, Bermuda. Humpbacks were an endangered species and only the previous year, in 1966, had officially received worldwide protection from the International Whaling Commission. The best estimate indicated that some 7,000 humpbacks were left – about 7% of the estimated 100,000 that originally lined every continent's shores.

Payne found the whales and recorded them.

"We have become aware of what we believe to be the humpbacks' most extraordinary feature," Payne wrote (with Scott McVay of Princeton University) in the 13 August 1971 issue of *Science*. The whales "emit a series of surpris-

Whale watchers meet a "friendly" gray whale in San Ignacio Lagoon, Baja California.

ingly beautiful sounds . . . repeated with considerable accuracy . . . a long 'song' that recurs in cycles lasting up to 30 minutes. . . . Because one of the character-istics of bird songs is that they are fixed patterns of sounds that are repeated, we call the fixed patterns of humpback sounds 'songs'. Until there is further evidence, we can only guess what function this remarkable series of vocaliza-tions serves."

In 1970, the humpback tape recordings of Payne and Watlington became a long-playing record album produced by CRM Records. Unlikely candidates for musical fame, humpbacks joined the Beatles and the Beach Boys on the Capitol Records label. *Songs of the Humpback Whale* sold more than 100,000 copies. The idea that these ungainly beasts – hunted to the edge of biological oblivion – were singing soulful songs deep in the sea captured the imagination of office workers and politicians, surfers and rock'n'rollers, even crusty labora-tory zoologists. Royalties have helped the whales, through the New York Zoological Society's Whale Fund, and the record was great PR for their cause: Madison Avenue could not have done a better job of selling humpbacks.

In the meantime, Payne had photographed a few distinctive humpback tail flukes, but found the open waters around Bermuda too rough for good whale watching. He headed south to investigate a lead from Ray Gilmore who, the previous year (1969), had combed the Argentine coast aboard the U.S. Antarctic research vessel *Hero*, spotting some rare right whales in a remote Patagonian bay. The reason for the right whales' rarity can be found in their name. Whalers considered them the "right" whales to hunt: they were slow, floated when killed (unlike humpbacks and blues), contained vast quantities of oil – that's what made them buoyant – and they had long, flexible baleen, prized for ladies' foundation garments and umbrella stays.

Payne recorded the bizarre variety of right whale sounds, mostly low frequency belches and moans, but also a tremendous bellow they made with their blowholes above water. It wasn't exactly singing.

The right whales, however, intrigued Payne. From July to November, there was no shortage of rights off Patagonia, southern Argentina. At the mating and calving grounds around Península Valdés, they came so close to shore they could be studied from land. They seemed the "right" ones to watch. Payne moved his wife Katy, already an indispensable part of the research, and their four school-age children to Patagonia. In 1971, they camped out, subject to the windy caprice of southern Argentina on the South Atlantic. Later, they built a primitive but solid block hut, concrete in deference to that wind. Set 150 feet above the sea, it became an ideal observation platform.

The trick was to figure out how much they could learn without harming or disturbing this rare whale. The first thing the Paynes noticed were the callosities, the peculiar whitish growths right whales have on their heads. Whalers called the largest one, on top of the head, the "bonnet" – that's what it looked like. Unique to right whales, callosities are thickened patches of whitish skin, with a rough outer surface, upon which grow whale lice, barnacles and a few scattered hairs. The Paynes soon realized the callosities varied from one individual to the next and that that was the key to individual identification. The study was off and running.

Sponsored by the National Geographic Society and the New York Zoological Society, the Paynes and later associates have spent a decade taking about 20,000 photographs of callosity patterns. From 1971 through 1977, as they identified 557 individuals, they found that many whales were revisiting in successive years, though the "nursery" areas were used on an alternating basis – with females returning every three years to give birth.

The Paynes first thought the callosities were a splash deflector – to prevent water from entering the blowhole, but as they watched more and more, they began to suspect other uses. The males, they found, have more and larger callosities than females and have more temporary scrape marks on their bodies. The Paynes think the scrapes may be caused by the callosities of other males jostling for access to females. Yet the closest the male whales seem to come to aggression is occasional mild pushing, shoving or rubbing. And often it is to no avail. A common sight is a female lying belly up at the surface surrounded by five or six snorting, frustrated males. Eventually, of course, the female must roll over for air, and the males seem to recognize this. But she quickly resumes her position. Another way to say "I've got a headache" is when the female moves into very shallow water and "stands on her head" – her tail sticking out of the water, genitals high and dry.

The Paynes' adventure with right whales in the southern hemisphere was catalytic in the evolution of watching whales. With cover story exposure in *National Geographic* and several television films, the Paynes' research attracted wide interest to the idea of studying whales by watching them.

Hawaiian Humpbacks

Anyone interested in whales in the mid-1970s sought out the Paynes. One who cornered Roger at the 1975 National Whale Symposium in Bloomington, Indiana, was James D. Darling, a young Canadian then studying gray whales off Vancouver Island. His photographic identification work with gray whales interested Payne and he agreed to be on Darling's committee for his master's thesis at the University of Victoria. He invited Darling to visit him at the Payne Lab near Boston and, in 1976 when Darling arrived, Payne mentioned that he wanted to do a detailed study of humpback songs in waters more favorable than Bermuda, perhaps off Maui. Darling volunteered for the job.

Auau Channel, off Lahaina, Maui, was a tropical paradise – warm, little rain, lots of whales. The sea was rarely too rough to record. Fog did not exist. It was mostly a matter of dropping the hydrophone over the side, turning on the tape recorder and lying back to listen to the humpback serenade.

Darling shot a few identification photographs of humpback tails that first year and the following winter, 1978, but in 1979 the census studies really got rolling. Darling's main objective became the whale-identification work, a two-man operation – a friend drove his Boston Whaler while he took photos. At the same time, researcher Peter Tyack – then a graduate student from New York's Rockefeller University – set up a post in the volcanic hills outside Lahaina to watch the whale action across Auau Channel. In constant radio contact with Darling, Tyack and several assistants used a surveyor's theodolite to plot whale movements and interactions.

On a typical day Darling would go out about dawn to find Tyack a singer. A few miles from shore, he would drop a hydrophone into the water and listen, sometimes picking up sounds of whales singing three or four miles away. Usually, there were several singers. He would motor about half a mile, stop to listen, and if one singer came in louder, he was getting warm. Eventually, he would draw within close range and then a knowledge of the song pattern came in handy.

A song has a number of themes, usually eight, and the whales sing them in order, though sometimes skipping one or two. A song generally lasts 10-15 minutes, though the range is 6-30 minutes. The song is repeated over and over again; a "song session" might last for hours.

The whale surfaces during theme two. "When theme two began," recalls Darling, "we knew the next whale that blew would be our singer. Typically, the singer breathes three times in quick succession. On the final breath, before diving, he shows his tail. I would snap the camera the instant the tail came up."

It would take Darling about an hour to "get on" a singer. After he had identi-fied the whale, he would radio to Tyack who would assign a letter name: "That's A as in aardvark." Tyack would then track A while Darling looked for other whales, each to be assigned another letter. Meanwhile, a second boat assisting Darling would move to the site of A's last tail print – the slick or mark on the water where the singer dove – and hang around to record the complete song session.

The Hawaiian songs Darling and his associates recorded from 1977 to 1979 differed from the songs the Paynes had recorded around Bermuda, but followed the same rules of structure and composition. In their 1971 *Science* paper, Payne and McVay had noted that the Bermuda humpbacks sang the same underwater song in a given year, but that it differed from songs of previous years. It was Katy Payne, comparing taped samples from many different years, who discovered a first in animal behavior, something that sets humpback songs apart from the songs of birds and other species: the songs are constantly changing. It's a gradual change. Songs from successive years sound most alike; songs ten years apart are totally different. Were the whales forgetting parts of their songs every summer on the northern feeding grounds where they rarely sing? The Maui recordings of two full winter seasons of songs held the answer: the whales do not forget, for they are singing the previous season's song when they first return to Maui. During the winter the song gradu-ally changes – as it is being sung. Old phrases are modified or dropped until themes begin to sound different. Yet, regardless of the apparent complexity of the changes, all the singers in a given area at a given time sing the same song.

Recording was easy off Maui, but the singers were still "very mysterious characters," recalls Darling. "Were they males or females? We saw them only briefly when they surfaced. We never expected to see a singer down below, much less go down and sex it."

Toward the end of the 1979 season, a film crew came to Maui on a production called *Nomads of the Deep*, and Darling agreed to help them. Getting underwater footage depended greatly on the Nicklins, a father-and-son diving team from California. Handling a massive 312-pound large-frame camera was Chuck Nicklin's task, while son Flip managed the underwater lights and took still photographs.

Auau Channel was flat calm the morning of 10 March 1979 when Darling encountered "F as in Frank", the sixth whale of the day. The film crew, off shooting in another part of the channel, was in radio contact. With Darling on his Boston Whaler were Gregory Silber and Maureen Hoskyn. She had spent days developing ID shots in a cramped darkroom and was being rewarded with a sunny day out in the boat. Darling, listening on the hydrophone and zeroing in on a singer, got close enough to photograph the tail flukes when he noticed that this singer dove in a "peculiar twisting manner" – probably from an injury to its tail stock. As the whale dipped below, Darling cut the engine and coasted into the whale's tail print. The song was coming up through the hull of the boat "*loud* . . . about the level of a stereo with the volume cranked up." Hoskyn was wide-eyed. Looking over the side, she noticed a glimmer of white, turned turquoise through the slick, and asked: "What's that?"

Darling and Silber first concurred: "Ah, just fish," but the glimmering white did not go away and finally Darling shouted, "Hell, that's no fish, it's a whale!"

It was Frank, the white spots his flippers. Darling grabbed his face mask and slid over the side. About 50 feet down was Frank, flippers outstretched yet motionless, wailing away. His head was pointed down, his body slanting toward the surface at a 45° angle – since labeled the classic singing posture.

"It was the first time I'd seen a singer underwater," says Darling. Excited, he radioed the Nicklins and told them: "Get the camera over here!" The Nicklins knew from Darling's voice that something big was happening. They raced to the spot and eased over the side, sliding the massive movie camera off the stern of their boat. Frank kept on singing as Chuck got the film and Flip swam under-

Researchers observe humpbacks at close quarters.

neath the expanse of belly, close enough to count the barnacles. Casually, he took a few flash photographs. Frank did not flinch.

"We stayed with Frank; it was a day in the life of a singer – all on tape and film and plotted from the transit hut." Flip's underwater photographs of Frank included clear shots of the genital region. Frank was indeed a male.

Darling and Nicklin and others would go on to sex eight more singers – all males – and would follow them as they battled other males over females. The battles were mostly show – lots of blowing bubbles at each other, posturing, and blocking access to a female – but sometimes there was tail lashing and body smashing, bloody head knobs and dorsal fins, blood dripping from flukes. By 1981, after five seasons, Darling and his associates no longer thought of humpbacks as "gentle giants" – as they'd been dubbed. Astute whale watching was bringing researchers closer to the real whale.

The Young Science of Whale Watching

With studies like Darling's, the era of learning about whales by watching them is coming of age. Despite the gray whale pioneers of the late 1940s and early 1950s, it is still a young science. Watching whales and dolphins today recalls an earlier time when students of the revitalized science of ethology, the objective study of animal behavior, took to the field to *watch* animals and record their behavior. They journeyed to places like the Serengeti Plains of Africa with its large mammal wildlife parade. The ocean is one vast Serengeti. Yet, compared to land studies, research at sea – with mammals that spend 95% of their time underwater – is more difficult, time consuming, and expensive. The pearls of knowledge, much less wisdom, do not come easily. The measure of success will be not only how much we can learn from watching, but also how much we can learn without disturbing them.

That sentiment was a major theme explored at a whale conference I attended in June 1983 at Boston's New England Aquarium. Dubbed the "Whales Alive Conference", the official billing was "Global Conference on the Non-Consumptive Utilization of Cetaceans".

The "non-consumptive" cetacean uses? Primarily *watching* them: whether for research, education, or entertainment. But also just "having them around"

A research crew get a last look at a diving humpback and its flukes.

Jim Darling / WCWRF

and "knowing they're out there". The conference was sponsored by the International Whaling Commission, the Connecticut Cetacean Society, Greenpeace, the World Wildlife Fund and other environmental groups. The participation of the first sponsor – the International Whaling Commission – was particularly significant, though it took no position on conference recommendations.

An original directive of the IWC, established by treaty among the whaling nations in 1949, was "to provide for the conservation, development and optimum utilization of the whale resources." The IWC wasn't thinking then about live whales as resources, but at its 1982 annual meeting, the 39 member nations voted 25-7 to shut down whaling in 1986. The legalese was "zero quotas" which does not abolish whaling. "A complete scientific review" will be undertaken by 1990 to determine whether sustainable whaling can be re-established. Also, the whaling ban is binding on no country that chooses to file an objection. The good news is that four of the seven current whaling nations will respect the ban. The Soviet Union, Norway and Japan have filed objections and will continue on their whaling course unless U.S. economic sanctions and world opinion change their minds. Meantime, the IWC is promoting inquiries into other "uses" of whales.

The Whales Alive Conference was attended by representatives of most IWC countries, including the whaling nations, excepting only the Soviet Union. Scientists Steven K. Katona, Hal Whitehead, Stephen Leatherwood, and others related what they had learned from watching whales – "benign research" Roger Payne called it – and pointed to how much there is to learn.

Conservationist Sir Peter Scott and various representatives from environmental groups said that cetaceans – a powerful source of inspiration – often provide the "hook" for getting people to care about the whole environment. Some stressed the importance of commercial whale watching, others the need for studies to define whale harassment.

Oceanarium researchers stressed the value of captive work and the good PR captive animals offer. Some environmentalists argued against keeping cetaceans captive; others called it a "low consumptive" use of cetaceans.

Interspecies communication investigators discussed the possibilities of talking to whales and dolphins and even learning from them. John C. Lilly, a dolphin research pioneer, is using computers in his experiments. He believes communication may be possible.

Whale Watching in the North Atlantic
After three days of talk, the conference moved out to sea for some fresh air and sun with the conference guests of honor – the humpback, fin and minke whales of Stellwagen Bank. About 15 miles east of Boston, due north of Cape Cod, the bank is a summertime open-air market for several species of hungry baleen whales and dolphins and a whale-watchers' paradise – the most predictable spot to view large whales in the North Atlantic. With about 40 of us lining the rails of *Dolphin V*, Capt. Al Avellar and crew escorted us out to sea. We got a whale-watching "lecture" from Charles "call me 'Stormy' not Dr." Mayo. Stormy and other naturalists from the Provincetown Center for Coastal Studies accompany the whale-watching tours of *Dolphin V* and sister ship *Dolphin IV*, trading whale expertise for the chance to do research. It's good for Capt. Avellar, good for Mayo and colleagues, and good for whale watchers. But is it good for whales? That's the question of the day.

Some 14 miles out of Boston, the cry goes up: "Whales!" But this humpback mother and calf are busy, and we move on. A 30-foot minke whale glides by, and a sleek 70-foot fin whale, the endless expanse of back followed by the small curved dorsal fin. They're busy, too. We don't bother them. Twenty minutes later we meet Pegasus – a favorite of Mayo and the Stellwagen Bank regulars. This young humpback starts to bother *us* as she breaches, first at a distance, then gradually closer. Leap after flying leap, the water streaming, pouring off her barnacled nose and flippers, she seems to delight in the spotlight. The boat shuts down. We're two and three deep on the starboard rail, cameras loaded, jockeying for position. She comes closer with every breach and every time she goes up Kodak's stock rises with her.

"This is pretty neat stuff," says Jim Darling, as we push against the rail. I am impressed that he is not jaded despite years of watching humpbacks breach, half a world away, off Maui. "There's something about witnessing 30 or 40 tons of pure exuberance," he says.

Stormy Mayo emphasizes that no one really knows how whale watching affects the animals. Aside from the question of affecting survival, there is the thought: would Pegasus do her "show" without an audience? Perhaps. But to the same extent? For better or worse, how much are we changing her behavior?

On the evidence of this day, whale watching would seem a benign enterprise. Most whale watchers are a careful and caring lot, though their numbers must be monitored, their effect on the whales periodically reassessed. It would be a mistake, however, to deny access to the whales. In my mind, the ill-effects of whale watching are – thus far at least – outweighed by the passionate commitment "sold" whale watchers develop, their eagerness to fight on the whales' behalf.

On the final morning of the conference, we drafted pages of resolutions to be offered to the next IWC meeting. The closing statement came from Victor B. Scheffer, author and retired biologist:

"I believe [the IWC] is experiencing a moral change of life. It is becoming less arrogant and secretive. It is searching for a more widely useful role in the conservation of the whales. . . . By sponsoring our meeting here it seems to admit that whales belong to men, women, and children who will never see a real whale, as well as to the few thousands who claim commercial rights in whale products. It seems to demonstrate that it can accept social as well as industrial responsibility for the future of whales. It is at the point of conceding that to kill a whale with a fragmentation bomb is extremely cruel. I believe it is ready to trade its long-standing goal of maximum sustainable yield for that of *optimum sustainable good.*"

Scheffer is encouraged that the momentum of extinction has been slowed and for some species probably reversed, and he has been encouraged watching people's reaction to watching whales. Caring about whales and other animals, he says, is an extension, even an integral part of our attitude toward other humans, and pure sentiment is reason enough to spare the whales. He seems to feel that whale watching makes us better people. Scheffer told us we were "acting in the interest of unborn generations" of whale watchers – a subspecies of *Homo sapiens* that will go extinct, just as the whales, if there are no whales to be watched.

Still full of our day on Stellwagen Bank, I considered how much poorer our world would be, not just without whales, but without certain individual whales like Pegasus, Stubbs, the humpback singer Frank and some of those California grays who come up to get their heads patted. These whales have enriched our lives by allowing us – *encouraging* us – to watch them.

To the delight of whale watchers a humpback whale breaches near Stellwagen Bank.

Part Two

The Species

There are at least 77 species comprising the living members of Cetacea, the animal order of whales, dolphins and porpoises. Those that follow are generally accepted by scientists, though a number of species are still mired in taxonomic controversy and confusion. The bottlenose dolphin, for example, may be several species (or subspecies). But until the taxonomic work has been done and is accepted, it must be considered as one – though certainly with geographical variations.

To identify a particular species in the field, first turn to the places section (Part Three) to find the list of possibilities in your area. Then, look up each species (using the species section number in parentheses), paying close attention to the visual identification keys and the categories for distinguishing features and description. All of the species listed as common in the places section and most of those listed as sporadic should be identifiable. Practice will increase your proficiency. Also, a good photograph taken in the field will allow later close examination of that sometimes "fleeting moment" when a whale or dolphin surfaces. For some species listed as rare, and others such as the many beaked whales that are rarer than rare, field identification may be difficult, even impossible, except through careful examination of a stranded animal by a specialist. Trying to identify a rare species can be frustrating, but it can also be a challenge. Take notes. For some species, few field observations exist, and new species of beaked whales have been found as recently as in the 1950s. You could be watching a new species.

A final note about the species section: scientific and other "whale words" that may be unfamiliar are defined in the glossary found in the back on page 204.

Cetacean Species by Family

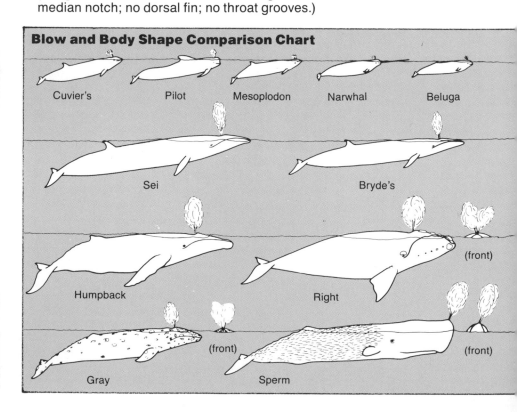

Blow and Body Shape Comparison Chart

Cuvier's   Pilot   Mesoplodon   Narwhal   Beluga

Sei   Bryde's

Humpback   Right   (front)

Gray   (front)   Sperm   (front)

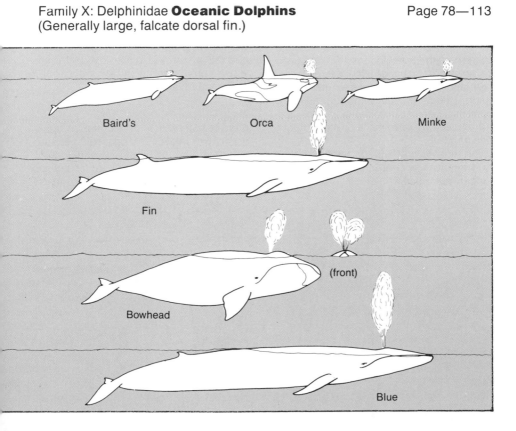

Baird's   Orca   Minke

Fin

Bowhead   (front)

Blue

Gray Whale *Eschrichtius robustus*

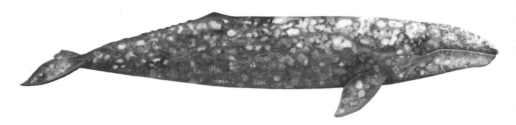

In the 1950s, the gray whale became the first whale to entertain modern whale watchers as it struggled back from near-extinction.

Other names
California gray whale, devilfish, ballena gris (Latin America), seryy kit (Russia).

Distinguishing features
Low hump (instead of dorsal fin) followed by bumpy ridge. Mottled gray coloring.

Description
Length: 40-45 feet; up to 46 feet for females.
Weight: up to about 35 tons.
Baleen: 130-180 yellowish plates on each side, about 1½ feet each in length. Plates on right side are usually shorter and more worn because of predominately right-side bottom feeding (also more scars on right side of head).
Color: mottled gray with barnacles showing white, yellow or orange patches from concentrations of whale lice.

Body: tubular, tapering at both ends. Head is bowed and pointed with straight mouth line curving near gape. Small flippers with pointed tips. Wide flukes separated by median notch. Deep creases (2-5) along throat.
Calves: 12-15 feet and weighing 1-1½ tons. Darker in color with wrinkled skin and no barnacles.

Range and habitat
Nearshore migratory species along the North American Pacific coast. Winters in lagoons of Baja California and mainland Mexico. Feeds in Bering, Chukchi, and western Beaufort seas during summer and fall (a few stop to feed off California, Washington and British Columbia). There is a small Asian population.

Habits
Migrates alone or in fluctuating groups of up to 16 animals. Only cow-calf pairs are constant, and the bond is strong. In the lagoons, females with calves occupy separate parts of the lagoon – away from

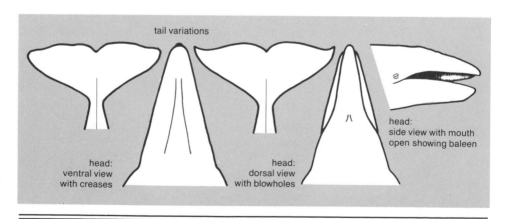

tail variations

head:
ventral view
with creases

head:
dorsal view
with blowholes

head:
side view with mouth
open showing baleen

males. The migration north to the feeding grounds is not as concentrated as the migration south which is faster with speeds over short distances of up to 6½ mph. Average migration speed south has been calculated at just under 2 mph (biologists S.L. Swartz and M.L. Jones based their calculations on peak arrival times at various locations). Feeding gray whales grub along or near the bottom of shallow water sucking up their food and dispersing cloudy trails of mud often visible from the surface.

Diet

Wide variety of invertebrates, especially amphipods, bottom-dwelling isopods, mysids, and polychaetes (tube worms). Because of their feeding methods, gray whales often ingest sand, rocks and other items.

Reproduction

Gestation: 11-12 months. Births occur in winter when grays are at or on the way to the Mexican lagoons. Cows calve every 1-3 years. Calves nurse for about 6-9 months.

Status

Protected since 1946, the gray whales off the west coast of North America have stabilized at about 16,500, according to latest estimates. This number approaches pre-whaling levels. About 180 are taken every year off Siberia. The status of the "Korean" (Asian) gray whale stock is unknown, but probably low in number.

Jay Burdick / Whalewatch Orange County

(Above) *A gray whale breaches off southern California.* (Below) *A feeding gray whale off Vancouver Island.*

Jim Darling / WCWRF

2

Minke Whale *Balaenoptera acutorostrata*

Because of its small size, the minke (pronounced "minky") escaped the whaler's harpoon until recent years. Today, with most large whales endangered, the minke has become the most heavily whaled baleen whale.

Other names

Little piked whale, pike whale, sharp-headed finner, lesser rorqual, little finner, minku or koiwashi kujira (Japan), malyy polosatik or minke (Russia), vaagehval or minkehval (Norway), ballena minke, ballena enana or rorcual pequeño (Latin America).

Distinguishing features

Much smaller than other rorquals. The falcate dorsal fin appears as the minke spouts. The narrow, acutely pointed rostrum is much sharper than a fin whale's (**5**) or a pygmy right whale's (**11**). The diagonal band or patch of white on the flippers of most minke whales is unique among baleen whales.

Description

Length: 20-30 feet, up to 35 feet.
Baleen: 230-360 yellowish plates (white to dark gray in southern hemisphere), usually 300-320, each 11½-21 inches long.
Color: dorsal surface gray to black – lighter on flanks. White ventral surface, including flippers. Underside of flukes is light gray, sometimes bluish gray. White band on dorsal side of flippers, except on some minkes from southern ocean whose flippers are solid black on dorsal side (may be subspecies). Sometimes a light chevron behind the head similar to some fin whales.
Body: streamlined with narrow, pointed head. Single head ridge. Tall, falcate dorsal fin (tallest of all baleen whales in proportion to body length).
Calves: 8-9 feet at birth.

Range and habitat

World ocean to the edge of the ice; most live in cooler waters. Some are migratory.

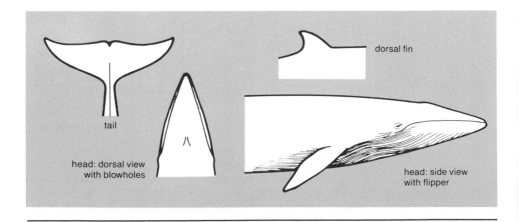

tail

head: dorsal view
with blowholes

dorsal fin

head: side view
with flipper

Habits

Solitary animals, though sometimes in groups of 2-3. Larger groups only on seasonal feeding grounds. Whaler Capt. Charles M. Scammon wrote in 1874 that minke whales could be seen year-round in Juan de Fuca Strait off southern Vancouver Island. It is here that minke photographic identification studies are currently underway. Researchers led by Eleanor Dorsey have found that minkes have unique scarring and color patterns on their backs or unique dorsal fins, and that these individual minke whales have several exclusive but adjoining summer ranges. Minkes can reach speeds of up to 17 mph, though normal swimming speeds are 5-7 mph. They can hold their breath up to about 20 minutes, but normally stay down only 3-8 minutes.

Diet

Krill and small shoaling fish such as capelin, cod, and herring. A "swallower" that sometimes lunge-feeds.

Reproduction

Gestation: 10-11 months. Calves nurse for 6 months or less. Cows may give birth every 1-2 years.

A minke whale pokes its rostrum out of the water, showing its fine ventral grooves.

Status

World numbers unknown. Currently the only baleen whale commercially whaled in the southern hemisphere where the population is estimated at greater than 250,000. The North Atlantic estimate is 130,000.

A feeding minke whale lunges onto its back, pale baleen visible in its open mouth.

3

Sei Whale   *Balaenoptera borealis*

To whale watchers the sei (pronounced "say") is a surprisingly enigmatic whale, considering its large size and substantial world numbers. Identification may be partly the problem. Whalers identified them by their impressive speed and erratic direction changes. By not pursuing them in the same way, whale watchers may observe different behavior.

Other names

Rudolphi's rorqual, pollack whale, Japan finner, iwashi kujira (Japan), ballena boba or ballena boreal (Latin America).

Distinguishing features

Single head ridge distinguishes it from the 3 ridges (usually) found in Bryde's whales(**4**). Gray lower right lip differs from the asymmetrical white of the fin whale.

Description

Length: 45-60 feet, up to 69 feet. Females slightly larger than males.
Baleen: fine texture, dark color with white inner fringes. White plates sometimes at front of mouth. From 219-402 baleen plates on each side. The longest plates measure 2^1/$_2$ feet.
Color: considerable variation. Dorsal surface – dark gray to black, sometimes with bluish tinge extending down the sides. Ventral surface – lighter with sometimes pinkish hue. Random white patches often on body from scars inflicted by lampreys or parasitic copepods.
Body: sleek and streamlined. Flippers are shorter than fin or blue whales'. Dorsal fin is prominent, up to 2 feet high and falcate. Head is slightly arched with downward turn especially to tip of rostrum. 32-60 well-defined throat grooves.
Calves: About 15 feet at birth.

Range and habitat

The world ocean, especially temperate seas. Mainly pelagic in the northern hemisphere, they are also seen around islands and continents in the southern hemisphere. Migrates to cooler feeding areas in summer and warm water in winter.

Habits

Group sizes are usually 2-5, though larger numbers are sometimes seen together on feeding grounds. Possibly the fastest of the large whales with impressive speed bursts of up to 30 mph.

Diet

Euphausiids, copepods, small fish.

Reproduction

Gestation: 11–12 months. Calves nurse for 6–7 months or until about 28 feet long.

Status

World numbers have been estimated at 210,000 with most of those around Australia. Not endangered, but certain stocks have been heavily exploited. The North Pacific stock is protected by the International Whaling Commission.

Peggy L. Edds

Top of a sei whale's head. Note single median ridge.

The Bryde's whale (pronounced "Bree-dahs") is the only rorqual that doesn't migrate to polar or near-polar waters in summer to feed and suckle its young.

Other names
Nitari kujira (Japan).

Distinguishing features
3 (usually) prominent head ridges. Tropical and subtropical range.

Description
Length: 40 feet for males, 43 feet and up to 46 feet for females.
Baleen: coarse, gray. About 300 on each side. Plates up to about 16½ inches long.
Color: smoky gray to black with lighter ventral surface (sometimes white).
Body: sleek and streamlined; closely resembles sei whale. Dorsal fin is prominent, up to 18 inches high, and extremely falcate, often pointed at the tip. The 3 head ridges consist of a large central ridge from the tip of the rostrum to the blowholes with 2 auxiliary ridges on either side. About 45 ventral grooves.

Range and habitat
Tropical and warm temperate waters of the Pacific, Atlantic and Indian oceans.

Habits
In a recent study off Venezuela, group sizes varied by season. Overall, 55% were singles, 27% pairs, and 18% two or more whales. Off South Africa, Bryde's whales were also seen mostly in singles or pairs but seemed to form loose associations with others ½-1 mile apart. Around South Africa there were inshore and offshore populations with different feeding and breeding habits.

Diet
Schooling fish (herring, mackerel, anchovies, sardines); euphausiids, shoaling squid. A "swallower".

Reproduction
Gestation: probably about a year. Calves nurse for about 6 months. In some areas, an unrestricted breeding season.

Status
Numbers about 16,000 in North Pacific; other world areas unknown. Still hunted by whalers. Management is complicated because until recently whalers counted Bryde's whales as sei whales.

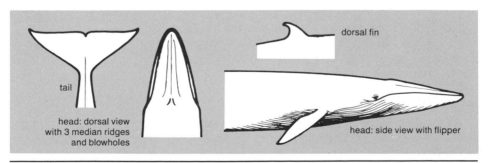

tail

head: dorsal view with 3 median ridges and blowholes

dorsal fin

head: side view with flipper

Sleek, fast-swimming and second in size only to the blue whale(**6**), the ''finback'' has an intriguing asymmetry: the right lower portion of its head is white.

Other names
Finback, finner, razorback, rorqual (France), finhval (Norway), sel'dyanoi kit or finval (Russia), nagasu kujira (Japan), ballena de aleta or rorcual cummun (Latin America).

Distinguishing features
Right lower lip (occasionally upper too) and right front baleen are whitish; pale chevron sometimes visible on the back which is ridged toward tail stock.

Description
Length: up to 88 feet, usually 60-70 feet, with females slightly longer than males (as with all baleen whales).

Weight: up to 50 tons.
Baleen: about 2 feet long; number of plates varies (260-480) with most whales having 350-400 per side.
Body: slender, elongated; generally dark on dorsal side, white on ventral side, but asymmetrical – more white on right side, especially around the head. Dorsal fin up to 24 inches and falcate. Up to 100 ventral grooves.
Head: narrow and V-shaped with sharp, pointed rostrum; single median head ridge.
Calves: 20-21 feet at birth; weight 2 tons.

Range and habitat
Distributed over the world ocean, fin whales prefer deep water. They feed in colder water in spring and summer, migrating to warmer water for calving and breeding during fall and winter.

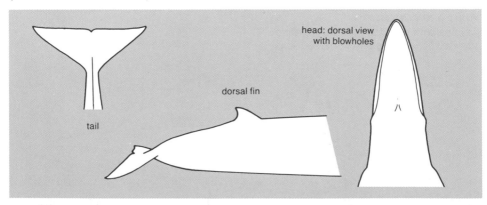

head: dorsal view with blowholes

dorsal fin

tail

Habits

Fin whales travel in pods, usually 6 or 7, but are often seen singly and in pairs. On the feeding grounds, groups often spread out. Radio-tracking studies in southeast Alaska and off Greenland have helped determine respiratory characteristics and movement patterns. One fin whale was followed for about 1,300 miles between Greenland and Iceland. During the long journey, the whale made more long dives during the day, spending more time on the surface at night. Fin whales produce loud low-frequency sounds; at 20 Hz, they are pitched near the lower limit of human hearing. Fins are one of the fastest baleen whales, attaining estimated speeds of 20 mph.

Diet

An opportunistic feeder, "gulps" wide variety of fish including sand lance, herring, capelin, cod and pollock; also euphausiids such as krill, pelagic crustaceans.

Reproduction

Gestation: about 11-12 months. Calves nurse for about 7 months before weaning.

Status

The world population estimated at 200,000; most live in the southern ocean, though considered numerous over most of their range.

(Above) A fin whale surfaces off Massachusetts. (Note white lower right jaw.) (Below) The fin whale's back has light chevron markings. (Note the two blowholes, characteristic of all baleen whales.)

Jane M. Gibbs

Jane M. Gibbs

Blue Whale *Balaenoptera musculus*

Believed to be the largest animal ever to have lived, the blue whale expands when feeding to as much as 6 times its size in total volume (as do other rorquals). At full expansion, the pouch or "cavum ventrale" of a 100-foot-long blue whale might hold almost 1,000 tons of water and food.

Other names
Sulphur-bottom, baleine bleu (France), blaahaval (Norway), ballena azul (Spain), shiro nagasu kujira (Japan), blyuval or goluboy kit (Russia).

Distinguishing features
Much longer than sei or fin whales. Head is broader (more U-shaped than V-shaped). Dorsal fin is much smaller. Flukes, sometimes raised on final dive, have straight rear edge. Head is uniformly colored, unlike fin whale.

Description
Length: 70-85 feet, up to about 100 feet for record Antarctic female blues.
Weight: 90-125 tons, up to more than 150 tons.
Baleen: 270-395 black plates on each side; each plate up to 3 feet long.
Color: mottled bluish gray.
Body: long and streamlined, 1-foot-high dorsal fin varies in shape and is set far back on dorsal surface. Broad straight-edged flukes. Broad, flat rostrum with single median ridge. Long pointed flippers. Two blowholes protected by large, fleshy "splash guards".
Calves: about 23 feet long and 5,500 pounds at birth.

Range and habitat
World ocean, offshore to pelagic; migratory.

Habits
Solitary animals; sometimes encountered in pairs with larger though well-spaced concentrations on feeding banks. Blue whale researcher Richard Sears and his colleagues working in the Gulf of St. Lawrence in Québec have photographically identified individual blue whales by mottled pigmentation patterns on their backs. The same whales returned in successive years, yet seemed to range over wide areas in search of food.

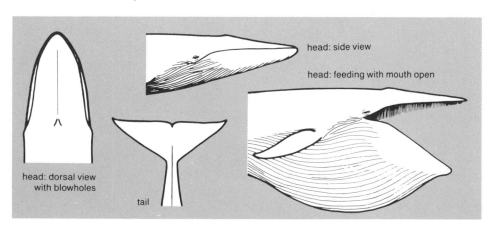

head: side view

head: feeding with mouth open

head: dorsal view with blowholes

tail

(Above) *A blue whale raises its flukes in the Gulf of St. Lawrence, Quebec.* (Below) *A blue whale swims at the surface in the Sea of Cortez, Mexico.*

Richard Sears / MICS

Ronn Storro-Patterson

Diet

Various species of krill. An average-size blue might eat 4 tons of krill a day during the summer.

Reproduction

Gestation: about 12 months. Calves nurse for about 8 months, taking more than 50 gallons of milk a day and adding about 8 pounds of weight per hour (200 pounds a day). When weaned, the calf is 50 feet long and about 50,000 pounds. Cows become sexually mature at about 10 years and may give birth once every 2-3 years.

Status

Endangered. World population estimated at 11,200, a tiny fraction of their original abundance. (9,000 in southern ocean; 1,700 in North Pacific; 500 in Northwest Atlantic.) Protected by the International Whaling Commission since 1966, they are believed to be recovering slowly in some areas.

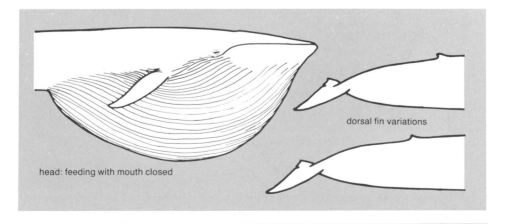

head: feeding with mouth closed

dorsal fin variations

Echoing through the depths of the tropical seas, where humpbacks come to mate and raise their calves, the melodious sounds of the male humpback are considered the longest and most complex songs in the animal kingdom.

Other names
Jorobada or yubarta (Latin America), zatō kujira (Japan), gorbatyi kit (Russia).

Distinguishing features
Head knobs; long, up to 16-foot flippers; flukes (displayed when diving) have black and white color patterns on ventral surface.

Description
Length: up to 53 feet, usually from 38-43 feet. Females 2-3 feet longer than males.
Weight: up to about 40 tons.
Baleen: 2-2 1/2 feet long, 300-400 plates per side.
Body: robust, narrowing quickly after dorsal hump and fin, with wing-like flippers up to 1/3 of body length.
Color: black with white patches of various sizes on flippers and on ventral surface of flukes and body.
Head: somewhat flattened with head knobs of varying size.
Calves: about 15 feet long and 1 1/2 tons at birth. Newborn calves have wrinkly appearance; usually do not lift their flukes.

Range and habitat
Worldwide, with open ocean migrations from cold feeding waters to warmer near-shore breeding and possibly calving areas where they spend the winter.

Habits
Humpbacks have been observed in large groups of 200 or more on feeding grounds. On the mating grounds the only long-term group is the cow and calf sometimes accompanied by a third animal termed an escort. Recent research off Hawaii has determined that escorts are males who seem to be waiting for the

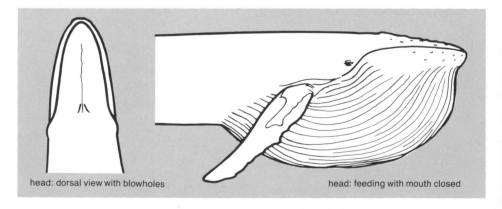

head: dorsal view with blowholes   head: feeding with mouth closed

Baleen plates and head knobs of a feeding humpback whale. The plates are used to strain fish and tiny marine crustaceans.

A humpback named Sirius identifies itself by its unique tail pattern to a group of whale watchers off Plymouth, Massachusetts.

female to come into estrous. When other males challenge an escort for his position, a "surface-active group" is formed. These temporary groups of 4 or more race around at the surface, with males blowing bubble streams and directing tail lashes at each other, some of which result in bloody head knobs and dorsal humps. Studies have shown that the great humpback singers are also males and that the singers sometimes take part in these surface-active groups, fighting to become escorts.

Diet
Schooling fish, including herring, sand lance, capelin, mackerel, cod fish, and salmon. Also euphausiids and crustaceans. Some reports of birds, most likely ingested while lunge-feeding. Humpbacks use bubbles to concentrate their food in bubble nets or clouds.

Reproduction
Births: none observed, but may occur around Nov. in eastern North Pacific, just before arrival on winter breeding grounds. Australian studies indicate that cows give birth every 2-3 years, but Hawaiian studies have found some cows with new calves in 3 successive years. Gestation: 11-12 months. Calves sometimes nurse beyond the first year after birth.

Status
Current estimates for Northwest Atlantic are 3,000. Northeast Pacific: 2,000. Worldwide estimates: 8,000–10,000. An endangered species, humpbacks have been protected worldwide since 1966. A few are taken each year by native whalers off Greenland and Bequia, a small island near St. Vincent's in the Caribbean.

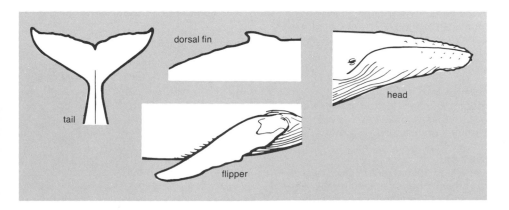

dorsal fin

tail

flipper

head

Reduced by heavy whaling to no more than a few hundred individuals in the North Pacific and Northwest Atlantic, the once numerous "northern" right whale is the large whale closest to extinction.

Other names
Northern right whale, black right whale, Biscayan right whale, nordkaper (Norway) ballena or ballena franca (Latin America), semi kujira (Japan).

Distinguishing features
No dorsal fin. Whitish callosities on the head. Smooth massive black back. Large spatulate flippers.

Description
Length: 35-50 feet, up to 60 feet. Females longer than males.
Weight: up to about 50 tons.
Baleen: 206-268 on each side up to 8 feet long.
Color: black, occasionally mottled with white patches on belly. Callosities on head range from white to pink.
Body: large and stocky with a huge head. Long, narrow, highly arched upper jaw and bowed lower jaw.
Calves: 15-20 feet at birth.

Range and habitat
Near-shore and offshore cooler waters of the northern hemisphere; now reduced to remnant populations. Migratory.

Habits
Little studied, but recent discovery of summering population in the Bay of Fundy has prompted several studies.

Researchers led by Scott Kraus have used photographs of callosity patterns and other marks to individually identify more than 60 whales. In 1980 there were 4 cow-calf pairs in the Bay of Fundy; in 1981, 7; in 1982, 4. Since calves may remain with their mothers for more than a year, successive-year sightings of calves may be redundant. Researchers also note extensive apparent courtship behavior which tends to challenge the absoluteness of the winter mating/summer feeding pattern.

Diet
Planktonic copepods; euphausiids (krill).

Reproduction
Gestation: about a year.

Status
Numbers estimated at 220 for the North Pacific and 200 in the North Atlantic. Have been close to extinction since the 1920s and though protected for many years have not thus far recovered.

Jane M. Gibbs

A right whale shows its long baleen plates.

Note: drawing of right whale (**8**) also illustrates southern right whale (**9**).

Studied intensively since 1970 in the waters around Península Valdés, Argentina, southern right whales congregate close to shore for half of every year to mate, play, and raise their calves.

Other names
Ballena or ballena franca (Latin America).

Distinguishing features
See right whale (**8**).

Description
See right whale (**8**).

Range and habitat
Near-shore and offshore cooler waters of the southern hemisphere; now reduced to remnant populations. Migratory.

Habits
The studies of Roger Payne and his colleagues around Península Valdés were some of the first in the new era of studying whales by watching them. The callosities have been used for individual identification. From 20,000 aerial photographs, 557 whales were identified, 411 of which were seen repeatedly (up to 18 times). Males have more and larger callosities than females – and more temporary scrape marks. This "sexual" dimorphism is handy, but it has also led to the recent suggestion by Payne and E. Dorsey that callosities function as weap-

Francois Gohier

A spy-hopping southern right whale showing the dorsal side of its head.

ons for intraspecific aggression – males fighting over females. Besides this evidence of infighting, a female often makes things difficult for unwanted suitors by rolling belly-up and lying at the surface, and by sticking her tail high out of the water. *Note:* Some scientists consider the southern right whale to be the same species as the right whale (**8**). Arguments supporting *two* species include geographical separation and cranial differences between the two (in the arrangement and shape of the alisphenoid). In the field, the two species look alike, though Peter Best of South Africa has noted that the incidence of callosities along the top edge of the lower lips may be greater in the southern right whale.

Diet
Planktonic copepods; euphausiids (krill).

Reproduction
Gestation: about a year. Calves nurse for 1-2 years. Cows give birth every 3 years.

Status
Numbers estimated at about 3,000 for the entire southern ocean – more than for the (northern) right whale, yet still endangered.

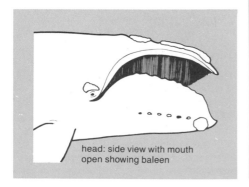

head: side view with mouth open showing baleen

One of the most endangered large whales, the bowhead spends its life at the edge of the Arctic pack ice, pushed south by advancing ice in the winter and following the retreating ice of summer.

Other names
Greenland right whale, Arctic right whale, Greenland whale, kiralick (Alaska Eskimo).

Distinguishing features
All black (no callosities or barnacles) except for large, irregular white chin patch and sometimes white on belly. Indentation or dip behind blowhole.

Description
Length: about 57 feet, up to about 65 feet.
Baleen: 230-360 dark gray plates on each side; fringes slightly lighter. Plates are the longest of any whale – up to 14 feet long.
Color: all black except for white chin patch and sometimes belly patch plus grayish stripe around tail stock. On the white chin patch are gray or black spots.
Body: thickset with huge head, about 1/3 of total length. Broad, spatulate flippers. No dorsal fin. Indentation behind blowhole most pronounced on older animals.
Calves: about 13-15 feet at birth.

Range and habitat
Along the pack ice of the Arctic, mostly around Alaska.

Habits
Travels alone or in pairs or trios, but seen in loose groups of several dozen on feeding grounds. Bowheads make distinctive calls that they repeat many times and which may be used to communicate.

Diet
Copepods, euphausiids, amphipods.

Reproduction
Gestation: about 13 months. Calves are born from March to Aug., with a peak in May, and nurse for about 12 months.

Status
Once abundant, bowheads were hunted to very low levels in the eastern Arctic as early as the 18th Century. They are still hunted by Natives off Alaska where the latest population estimates (4-year average 1978-82) range from 2500 to 3800.

Donald K. Ljungblad

The white chins of these bowhead whales off Alaska are easily visible from the air. The bowhead spends its life at the edge of the ice pack.

Pygmy Right Whale *Caperea marginata*

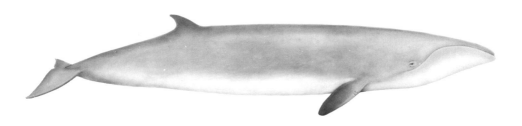

Found only in the cooler temperate waters of the southern hemisphere, the pygmy right whale is the smallest and least known of the baleen whales.

Other names
Kosemi kujira (Japan), gladkii kit (Russia).

Distinguishing features
Positive identification difficult even at close range, and whalers have probably included some pygmy rights in their minke whale counts. If a white band can be seen on the flippers, it's definitely a minke whale. Some southern hemisphere minkes, however, don't have it. Pygmy rights have the arched jaw characteristic of right whales, a rounded rostrum and (only visible on stranded animals) longer baleen than minkes.

Description
Length: about 15 feet, up to 21 feet for largest females.
Baleen: about 230 pale yellowish-white plates on each side with brown fringe; up to 27 inches long.
Color: dark gray or black dorsal surface; ventral surface paler gray. Some pale streaks on back and dark streaks from flipper to eye.
Body: slim compared to right whales but not as slim as a rorqual. Small falcate dorsal fin. Rostrum tapers to rounded point. Flippers narrow and rounded at tips. No callosities.

Range and habitat
Cooler temperate waters of southern ocean. Limited observations indicate inshore shallow waters and protected bays plus pelagic waters.

Habits
Little "surface active" behavior (breaching, lobtailing) compared to other right whales. Slow swimmer. Known only from stranded specimens until the 1960s when live pygmy rights were found in a South African bay. In 1967 pygmy rights were filmed briefly underwater in Plettenberg Bay, South Africa.

Diet
Copepods (from limited information).

Reproduction
Gestation: probably 10-11 months.

Status
Unknown. Rare, though perhaps not as rare as originally believed because of confusion with minke whale and the relatively remote range.

Tony Dicks / courtesy F. Hayes and G.J.B. Ross

The rarely seen pygmy right whale, photographed underwater in Plettenberg Bay, South Africa.

In recent Indian Ocean expeditions off Sri Lanka, researchers kept track of sperm whale groups by monitoring their incessant clicks as the whales dove deep for food, staying down for an hour at a time.

Other names
Cachalot (France), kashalot (Russia), hunshval (Norway), makkō kujira (Japan), cachalote (Spain), ballena esperma (Latin America).

Distinguishing features
Large squarish head; low hump-like or triangular dorsal fin; bushy blow, angled forward and to the left (because of off-center S-shaped blowhole). Prune-like skin texture.

Description
Length: males up to almost 60 feet, but usually about 50 feet. Females rarely exceed 37 feet.
Weight: up to 58 tons.
Teeth: about 25 teeth on each side of lower jaw; tooth sockets in upper jaw (rudimentary teeth present but unerupted).

Color: dark brown to dark gray. Belly, area around corners of mouth, and front of head often light gray to white. Undersides of flukes and flippers vary from brown to gray.
Body: massive with a large head that comprises 1/4 to 1/3 of total length. Low dorsal hump or fin that varies considerably. Bumps or crenulations from dorsal fin to tail flukes. Short, stubby flippers. Flukes shaped like adjoining right angle triangles, slightly rounded at tips, and deeply notched.
Calves: 11 1/2-15 feet and light tannish gray at birth, darkening gradually in the first months.

Range and habitat
World ocean from the equator to the edges of the polar ice; pelagic.

Habits
Complex social structure. Large groups of up to 50 whales are usually either bachelor bulls ("bachelor schools") or females with calves and juveniles ("mixed or nursery schools"). During the seasonal breeding, large males are

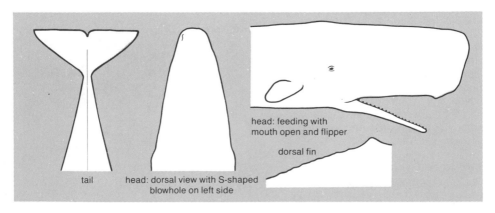

tail
head: dorsal view with S-shaped blowhole on left side
head: feeding with mouth open and flipper
dorsal fin

A large group of female and immature male sperm whales off Sri Lanka. Note S-shaped blowhole on left side of the head and the prune-like texture of the skin.

Hal Whitehead / WWF

Sperm whale flukes.

Margo Rice / WWF

believed to battle other males (evidence of tooth marks on skin) over "harems" of about 10 females. Other groups include large old bulls without harems swimming alone or in small groups. Pursuing squid in the deep canyons of the world ocean, sperm whales routinely dive more than 1,500 feet below the surface where they may stay down for more than an hour. Corpses tangled in submarine cable indicate they dive to 3,720 feet; they may reach more than 10,000 feet on occasion. Upon reaching the surface, they may blow more than 50 times before deep-diving again. Sperm whale calves, unable to stay down for long periods, remain near the surface and are sometimes "tended" by other members of the group when mother is down for the count.

Diet
Squid; octopus; variety of fishes.

Reproduction
Gestation: 15 months. Calves nurse for about 2 years. Cows bear one calf every 4-5 years.

Roger Payne / WWF

A sperm whale breaches in the Indian Ocean.

Status
Numbers estimated at 732,000 in the world ocean, 410,000 in the southern hemisphere. The mainstay of the whaling industry, sperms have been hunted for centuries and though their numbers have been reduced, they are not endangered.

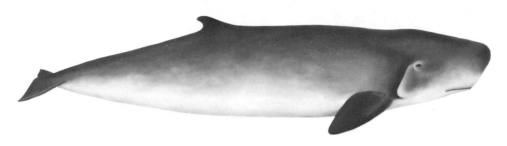

Small groups of pygmy sperm whales have been seen apparently sleeping at the surface with their tails hanging down and their conical heads exposed.

Other names
Komakkō kujira (Japan), cachalote pig-méo (Latin America), cachalot pigmée (France).

Distinguishing features
The conical snub-nosed head and small size (smaller than some dolphins) establishes a pygmy or dwarf sperm whale, but to distinguish between the two is difficult at sea. The dwarf sperm whale (**14**) is slightly smaller with a much larger dolphin-like dorsal fin located in the middle of the back. The pygmy sperm's dorsal fin is smaller, sickle-shaped and set farther back.

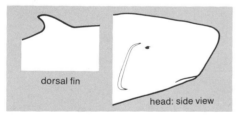

dorsal fin

head: side view

Description
Length: 9-11 feet, up to 12 feet.
Weight: 900 pounds.
Teeth: 12-16 (rarely 10-11) in each lower jaw; none in upper jaw.
Color: dark gray, occasionally bluish gray on dorsal side; lighter gray on ventral. White or pale gray crescent "bracket mark" known as "false gill".
Body: robust with conical snub-nosed head. Underslung lower jaw (plus "false

gill") give this little whale a shark-like appearance. Small falcate dorsal fin. Short, broad flippers. Notched flukes.
Calves: about 3½ feet at birth.

Range and habitat
Tropical and warm temperate world ocean; pelagic.

Habits
From few observations: travels slowly in groups of 1-7 individuals. Lethargic; often basks at the surface.

Diet
Mostly squid and cuttlefish; crabs, shrimps, fish.

Reproduction
Pregnant cows with still nursing calves have been found: they may give birth as often as once a year.

Status
Unknown. Rarely seen at sea, yet one of the most frequently stranded cetaceans on the U.S. east coast. May be more common than formerly believed.

J.P. Sylvestre

Foetus of the rare pygmy sperm whale. This specimen is kept in la Rochelle Museum in France.

Dwarf Sperm Whale *Kogia simus*

Like the two other sperm whales, the dwarf sperm is a deep diver with teeth (mainly) in the lower jaw used to catch squid, but its tall dorsal fin makes the surfacing dwarf sperm look like a dolphin.

Other names
Ogawa komakkō kujira (Japan).

Distinguishing features
See pygmy sperm whale (**13**).

Description
Length: 7-9 feet.
Weight: 300-600 pounds.
Teeth: 7-12 (rarely 13) in each lower jaw; sometimes up to 3 in each upper jaw.
Color: dark bluish gray on dorsal surface fading to lighter gray on flanks and dull white on belly.
Body: robust, with conical snub-nosed

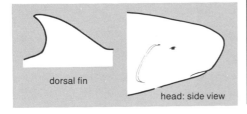

dorsal fin

head: side view

asymmetrical head. Underslung lower jaw and "false gill", as with pygmy sperm whale, make the dwarf sperm look somewhat like a shark. Tall, falcate dorsal fin situated near the middle of the back. Short, broad flippers. Notched flukes.
Calves: probably about 3 feet at birth.

Range and habitat
From limited information: tropical and warm temperate world ocean; pelagic.

Habits
Limited observations.

Diet
Squid; also assortment of deepwater fishes and crustaceans.

Reproduction
High percentage of stranded females with suckling calves are pregnant; thus may give birth as often as once a year.

Status
Unknown. Limited number of records, probably due to past confusion with pygmy sperm whale.

One of the few beaked whales occasionally sighted in the world ocean, Cuvier's beaked whale is called the "baby-faced whale", akabō kujira, by the Japanese whalers who sometimes catch them.

Other names
Goosebeak whale, goosebeaked whale, ziphius, akabō kujira (Japan), ziphius de Cuvier (France), ballena de Cuvier or zifios (Latin America).

Distinguishing features
Field identification is difficult. Larger than most other beaked whale species, the mature male Cuvier's has a white head and 2 small teeth visible on lower jaw even when mouth is closed. Compared to bottlenose whales (**18**) and (**19**), Cuvier's has a gently sloping forehead and a short beak.

Description
Length: 19-23 feet for adult females, 18-22 feet for adult males.
Teeth: 1 on each side of lower jaw, 2 total; usually erupt from gums of mature males only.

Color: tan or light brown body, often heavily scarred, can appear reddish in sunlight. White head in mature males and lighter head in older females.
Body: very robust, with small head and a beak shorter than other beaked whales. Upturned mouth-line. Head in profile looks somewhat like goosebeak. Dorsal fin, set far back on body, can be falcate or triangular, up to 15 inches high.
Calves: 6½-10 feet at birth.

Range and habitat
Tropical and temperate pelagic waters of the world ocean.

Habits
Little known. Seen in groups of up to 10, usually with at least 1 adult male.

Diet
Squid; deepwater fishes.

Reproduction
Unknown.

Status
Unknown.

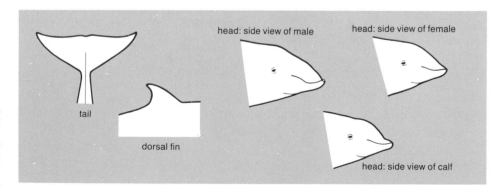

head: side view of male

head: side view of female

tail

dorsal fin

head: side view of calf

In the Antarctic summer of 1956-7, a single Arnoux's (pronounced Ar-news) beaked whale was closely observed when it became trapped in an ice pool along with 120 minke whales and 60 killer whales.

Other names
Southern giant bottlenose whale, New Zealand beaked whale, southern four-toothed whale, southern beaked whale, southern porpoise whale.

Distinguishing features
Identification at sea is difficult but possible. Somewhat bulbous forehead, but not as pronounced as southern bottlenose whale (**19**) (also longer beak). 2 teeth near tip of protruding lower jaw are visible on most mature males and females.

Description
Length: up to about 30 feet, females larger than males.

Teeth: 1-2 on each side at tip of lower jaw in males and females.
Color: dark back; blue-gray mottled flanks; gray or light gray belly; white scratches and scars.
Body: long round torso with triangular dorsal fin set far back on body.

Range and habitat
Probably circumpolar cooler offshore waters of southern hemisphere.

Habits
Unknown.

Diet
Squid.

Reproduction
Unknown.

Status
Numbers unknown; probably rare.

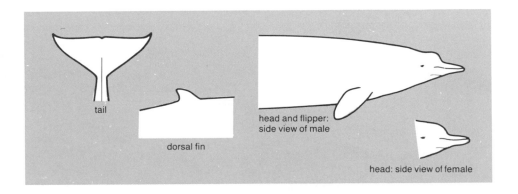

tail

dorsal fin

head and flipper: side view of male

head: side view of female

Baird's Beaked Whale *Berardius bairdii*

In studies associated with a small but regular fishery for these the largest of beaked whales, Japanese biologists have estimated that the gestation period is 17 months – the longest yet found for any cetacean.

Other names
North Pacific giant bottlenose whale, giant bottlenose whale, tsuchi kujira or tsuchimbo (Japan).

Distinguishing features
Field identification is difficult, but possible. Bulbous forehead, long beak that appears white-tipped from 2 protruding teeth. Long round torso, usually slate gray with many white scratches. Small, triangular dorsal fin, set far back on body, appears after blowhole submerged.

Description
Length: up to 42 feet, females larger than males.
Teeth: 1-2 on each side at tip of lower jaw in males and females. When mouth is closed, 2 teeth protrude.
Calves: about 15 feet at birth.

Range and habitat
Offshore temperate waters of the North Pacific.

Habits
Groups of 2-20, sometimes up to 30 animals which travel and blow cohesively. Segregation of sexes suggested by whaling records. Reportedly difficult to approach. On deep dives may disappear for 45 minutes or more, making tracking at sea difficult.

Diet
Squid, octopus, fishes (deep-sea), crustaceans.

Reproduction
Gestation: up to 17 months. Cows probably give birth about every 3 years.

Status
No estimates. Whaling may have reduced their numbers in certain areas.

Surfacing Baird's beaked whale off Oregon.

T.R. Wahl/ courtesy Stephen Leatherwood

The fearless northern bottlenose whale often approaches ships, a "fatal flaw" that Norwegian and other North Atlantic whalers have long exploited.

Other names
Bottlehead, grand souffleur à bec d'oie (France), bottlenosen (Norway), andhvaler (Iceland).

Distinguishing features
Bulbous forehead with dolphin-like beak. Long round torso usually brown or gray, fading in older males to white or yellow, especially around the head. Scratches and scars, particularly on males. Small curved dorsal fin. Much larger than other beaked whales in its range. They also have much larger foreheads, especially older males.

Description
Length: up to 32 feet for males; about 26 feet for females.
Teeth: 1 on each side near tip of lower jaw, erupting only in males.

Range and habitat
Deep Arctic and cooler temperate waters of the North Atlantic.

Habits
Travels in groups of 5-15 with some (at least seasonal) segregation by sex. May dive for an hour or more. Reported to be curious and will approach boats, including stationary ships with generators running. A young male and female stranded alive at Beverly Farms, Massachusetts, in the 1920s, made deep groaning and sobbing sounds that reportedly were heard a ½ mile away. Normally they live in deep water and can be seen at sea from the Gully off Sable Island, Nova Scotia, and at the edge of the continental shelf off Newfoundland and Labrador.

Diet
Squid, mainly. Also, herring, sea stars and other bottom invertebrates.

Reproduction
Gestation: about 12 months.

Status
Numbers unknown, but apparently reduced substantially by intense whaling prior to the early 1970s.

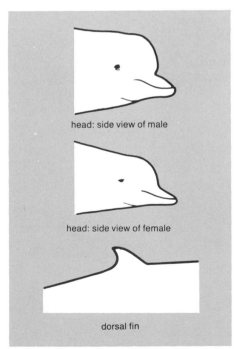

head: side view of male

head: side view of female

dorsal fin

Known mostly from a few southern hemisphere strandings, the southern bottlenose whale is apparently shy, not sharing the "curiosity" toward ships exhibited by its northern relative, the northern bottlenose whale (**18**).

Other names
Flathead bottlenose whale, ballena nariz de botella or gran calderon (Latin America).

Distinguishing features
Identification at sea is difficult. Steep, very bulbous forehead, especially in older males, and short, distinct beak may be enough to distinguish from other beaked whales of the southern hemisphere.

Description
Length: probably up to about 30 feet for males; about 24 feet for females.
Teeth: 1 on each side near tip of lower jaw, erupting only in males.

Color: brown or grayish with lighter head and scratches and scars, at least on large animals.
Body: long round torso (though perhaps not as long as the northern bottlenose whale) with small curved dorsal fin.

Range and habitat
Cooler offshore waters of southern hemisphere.

Habits
Unknown.

Diet
Squid; fish.

Reproduction
Unknown.

Status
Numbers unknown, but probably rare.

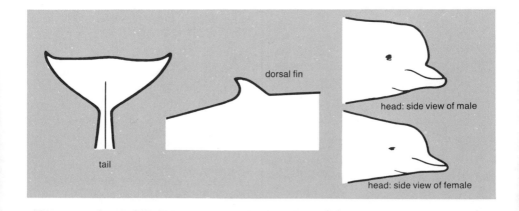

tail

dorsal fin

head: side view of male

head: side view of female

The Tasman beaked whale is the only beaked whale with a full set of upper and lower teeth as well as the characteristic large pair of teeth in the lower jaw.

Other names
Shepherd's beaked whale.

Distinguishing features
Positive identification at sea is probably impossible, but a longer, more pointed rostrum, and a steeper forehead than other beaked whales are subtle distinctions that have been noted after carefully studying stranded specimens. There is also the full complement of teeth in both sexes.

Description
Length: about 20-23 feet.
Teeth: 17-21 on each side of upper jaw, 18-30 on each side of lower jaw, including 1 on each side at tip of lower jaw in males.

Color: dark back, light belly and flanks (from few specimens).
Body: robust, with small dorsal fin.

Range and habitat
From strandings around New Zealand and, recently, Chile and Argentina, the range may be the cooler offshore waters of the southern temperate zone.

Habits
Unknown.

Diet
From one specimen: squid, fish, crab.

Reproduction
Unknown.

Status
Numbers unknown, but certainly rare.

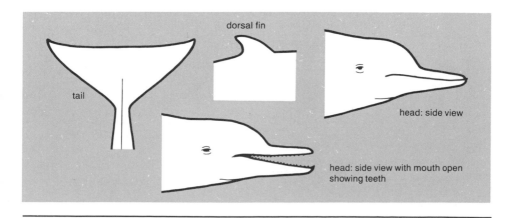

dorsal fin

tail

head: side view

head: side view with mouth open showing teeth

In 1804 English watercolor artist James Sowerby described this beaked whale, the first to be written about, from a specimen stranded along Moray Firth in Scotland. It has since become one of the most commonly stranded of the genus *Mesoplodon*.

Other names
North Sea beaked whale, dauphin du Havre or dauphin de Dale (France), spidshvalen (Norway), spitsdolfijn (Netherlands).

Distinguishing features
Positive field identification at sea is probably impossible. Unlike other beaked whales within its range, it has a small tooth (males only) on either side of the lower jaw about midway along its length.

Description
Length: about 15-17 feet, males larger.
Teeth: 1 on each side of lower jaw, erupted only in males.

Color: dark bluish gray, somewhat mottled.
Body: robust, with small curved dorsal fin and slight bulge to forehead.
Calves: about 6-7 feet long at birth.

Range and habitat
Mainly offshore cooler waters of the North Atlantic, especially the eastern North Atlantic.

Habits
Unknown.

Diet
Squid; deepwater fish.

Reproduction
Gestation: about a year. Births may occur in late winter or spring. Calves nurse for about a year.

Status
Unknown.

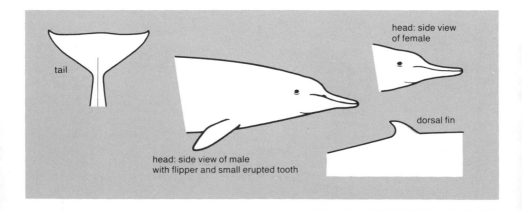

tail

head: side view of female

head: side view of male with flipper and small erupted tooth

dorsal fin

American Roy Chapman Andrews, beginning to make his mark as a naturalist in 1908, researched and identified the first skeleton of the rare austral species that now bears his name.

Other names
Bowdoin's beaked whale, deep-crested whale.

Distinguishing features
Positive field identification at sea is probably impossible. The male of this species – the southern "version" of Hubbs' beaked whale (**23**) – has 1 large tooth on either side of the lower jaw, about midway along its length.

Description
Length: up to about 14 feet.

Range and habitat
From a few strandings: cool temperate offshore waters of the central Indo-Pacific (around Australia and New Zealand).

Habits
Unknown.

Diet
Unknown.

Reproduction
Unknown.

Status
Numbers unknown, but certainly rare.

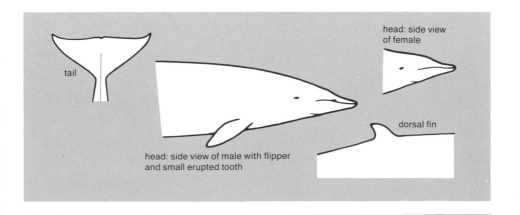

tail

head: side view of male with flipper and small erupted tooth

head: side view of female

dorsal fin

Carl Hubbs, the icthyologist who pioneered watching gray whales, found the first complete specimen of this beaked whale on the beach at La Jolla, California, in 1945.

Other names
Archbeak whale, ballena de Hubbs (Latin America), Hubbs' oogiha kujira (Japan).

Distinguishing features
Slightly bulbous white cap, immediately forward of the blowhole, is mainly evident in mature males of the species and should be enough to distinguish it from other beaked whales in the North Pacific. Forward half of beak is also white. The rest of body and head is dark gray to black with many scratches and scars.

Description
Length: up to 17½ feet.
Weight: 3300 pounds

Teeth: 1 on each side of lower jaw set on raised area midway along jaw (erupted only in males).
Body: robust, with small curved dorsal fin and slight bulge to forehead.
Calves: probably close to 8 feet.

Range and habitat
Probably offshore temperate waters of the North Pacific.

Habits
Unknown.

Diet
Squid; deepwater fish.

Reproduction
Unknown.

Status
Numbers unknown, but probably rare.

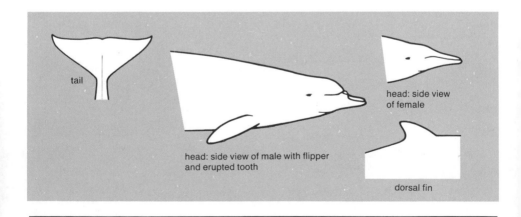

tail

head: side view of male with flipper and erupted tooth

head: side view of female

dorsal fin

The 2 teeth of the adult male Blainville's beaked whale, perched on the raised lower jaws, protrude as high or higher than the forehead – almost like a pair of horns.

Other names

Densebeak whale, dense-beaked whale, tropical beaked whale, ballena de Blainville (Latin America), kobuha kujira (Japan).

Distinguishing features

The large, protruding, often barnacle-covered teeth that tilt forward from the prominent lower jaws near the corners of the mouth, plus the flattened forehead, are the male characteristics that should enable identification, provided one or more mature males are present. The rest of the body is dark gray, often blotchy, with light areas toward the belly. There is also a depression on the head between the two raised areas of the jaw.

Description

Length: up to about 15 feet long.
Teeth: 1 large tooth on each side of raised lower jaw. The 2 teeth are 6-8 inches long, almost 3 inches wide and almost 2 inches thick. Only the tip of the tooth protrudes from the jaw.
Body: robust, with small curved dorsal fin and flat forehead.

Range and habitat

Offshore tropical to cooler temperate waters of the world ocean.

Habits

A few observations around Hawaii of groups of 5-12. These surfaced, rostrum pointing almost skyward, smashing their chins against the surface and did not raise their flukes as they dove. Diving times were 20-45 minutes or more.

Diet

Squid.

Reproduction

Unknown.

Status

Numbers unknown. Though known mainly from stranded specimens, it may not be as rare as other beaked whales.

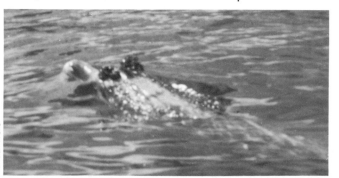

A male Blainville's beaked whale: note the dark barnacles growing on its teeth.

Randall Wells

Like most beaked whales, Gervais' beaked whale has 2 large teeth in the lower jaw which only erupt in mature males, and is probably a deep-diving pelagic squid-eater rarely, if ever, seen in the wild. Gervais' beaked whales are known from a few strandings along beaches touched by the Gulf Stream.

Other names
Antillean beaked whale, European beaked whale, Gulfstream beaked whale.

Distinguishing features
Gervais' beaked whale has a relatively small head, a gently sloping forehead and a tiny tooth on each side, set close to the tip of the lower jaw in males. Positive identification at sea is near-impossible.

Description
Length: up to about 16½ feet long.
Teeth: 1 on each side near tip of lower jaw in males.
Color: dark gray above, pale gray below, sometimes white at tip of upper and lower jaws.
Body: robust, with small dorsal fin and slight bulge to forehead.
Calves: about 6½ feet at birth.

Range and habitat
From strandings: warm offshore temperate and tropical waters of the western North Atlantic. Range may extend north and east along the Gulf Stream since a specimen was collected in the English Channel.

Habits
Unknown.

Diet
Unknown.

Reproduction
Unknown.

Status
Numbers unknown.

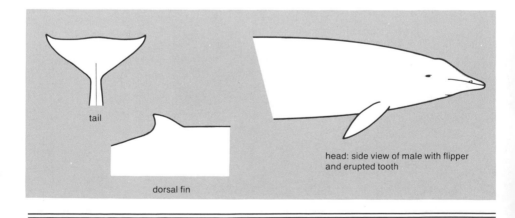

tail

dorsal fin

head: side view of male with flipper and erupted tooth

The ginkgo-toothed beaked whale, discovered by Japanese scientists Nishiwaki and Kamiya in 1957, gets its name from the shape of its protruding teeth which resemble the fan-shaped leaves of the ginkgo tree.

Other names

Japanese beaked whale, ichōha kujira (Japan).

Distinguishing features

Distinguishing between beaked whales at sea is very difficult, often impossible. A close look at the head of a male might reveal the tips of the 2 teeth on either side of the lower jaw in males (the teeth are smaller than those of Blainville's (**24**) and Stejneger's (**31**) beaked whales). The forehead should be dark like the body, not white as in Hubbs' beaked whale (**23**).

A female ginkgo-toothed beaked whale stranded at Del Mar, California.

Description

Length: at least 16½ feet.
Weight: about 3,300 pounds.
Teeth: 1 flattened tooth on each side midway along the raised part of lower jaw (mature males only).
Body: robust, with small curved dorsal fin and slightly bulbous forehead.

Range and habitat

Probably warm temperate and tropical North Pacific and Indian oceans, especially western North Pacific.

Habits

Unknown.

Diet

Unknown.

Reproduction

Unknown.

Status

Unknown, probably rare.

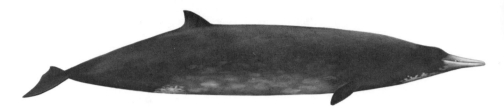

In the southern ocean biologist Dale W. Rice has seen Gray's beaked whales in their characteristic surfacing posture, sticking their pointed white snouts out of the water as they breathe.

Other names
Scamperdown whale, southern beaked whale.

Distinguishing features
The long, slender beak and straight mouthline of this relatively small beaked whale should be diagnostic for any beaked whale sightings in the southern hemisphere, though identification at sea is difficult.

Description
Length: up to about 18 feet for males, 16 feet for females.
Teeth: 1 small tooth on each side, near front of lower jaw (males only). Sometimes 17-19 pairs of vestigial teeth erupt near upper corners of mouth.
Color: back is dark brownish gray, flanks pale or mottled, white below.

Body: robust, with triangular dorsal fin, long beak and almost no bulge to the forehead.

Range and habitat
From limited information: the offshore cooler temperate waters of the southern hemisphere, though there is a single stranding from the northern hemisphere in the Netherlands.

Habits
One mass stranding of 28 and several possible identifications at sea suggest a highly social species.

Diet
Unknown.

Reproduction
Unknown.

Status
Numbers unknown. Perhaps not as rare as some beaked whales.

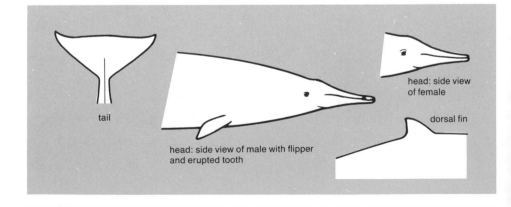

tail

head: side view of male with flipper and erupted tooth

head: side view of female

dorsal fin

Hector's beaked whale had been known only from a few skulls in the southern hemisphere until a mother, calf and mature male were stranded along the southern California coast in the late1970s.

Other names
New Zealand beaked whale, ballena de Hector (Latin America).

Distinguishing features
Positive identification at sea is very difficult. The 2 triangular-shaped teeth near the tip of the lower jaw are only found in mature males. The teeth of most beaked whales within the range of Hector's beaked whale are different. The male Cuvier's beaked whale (**15**) has 2 smaller front teeth and a very distinctive white head.

Description
Length: up to at least 14 feet from very limited records.

Teeth: 1 small triangular tooth on each side near the tip of lower jaw in mature males.
Color: dark gray brown on back with pale gray on belly and lower jaw. Scratches and scars on adult males.

Range and habitat
From limited evidence: cooler temperate waters of southern ocean and eastern North Pacific.

Habits
Unknown.

Diet
Squid.

Reproduction
Unknown.

Status
Unknown, but probably rare.

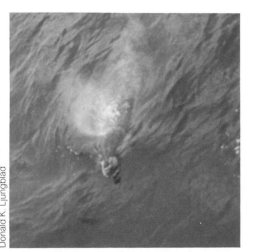

A rare encounter with a wild beaked whale off southern California- possibly a Hector's beaked whale.

Donald K. Ljungblad

This whale has been a puzzle for scientists: why do the teeth of the male straptoothed whale grow as he matures until they curve around the upper jaw, preventing the mouth from opening wide?

Other names
Straptooth beaked whale.

Distinguishing features
On males, the large "strap" teeth are unique.

Description
Length: 14-15 feet, up to 19 feet for males.
Teeth: 1 on each side of lower jaw of males; each tooth up to 13 inches long.
Color: bronze to dark purplish-brown on back, sometimes with light patches; white belly; gray flanks.

Body: robust, with small dorsal fin and relatively small head.

Range and habitat
From strandings: probably the cooler offshore temperate waters of the southern hemisphere.

Habits
Unknown.

Diet
Squid.

Reproduction
New Zealand strandings of pregnant females occurred in winter, so calving peak may be spring or early summer.

Status
Numbers unknown; perhaps not as rare as other beaked whales.

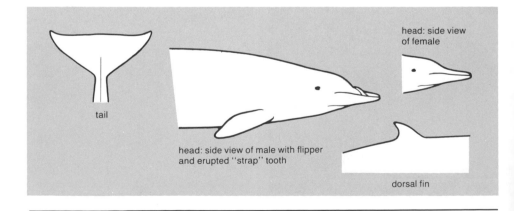

tail

head: side view of female

head: side view of male with flipper and erupted "strap" tooth

dorsal fin

Turn-of-the-century American biologist Frederick True found this rare whale stranded off North Carolina in 1912. He gave it the Latin name *mirus*, meaning wonderful. The name hints at his enthusiasm about the finding.

Other names
None.

Distinguishing features
Distinguishing this whale at sea from Cuvier's beaked whale (**15**) is very difficult. There are 2 small protruding teeth at the tip of the lower jaw in males of the species.

Description
Length: up to about 17 feet.
Teeth: 1 on each side at tip of lower jaw (males only).

Color: dark above and light below. Scratches on back, somewhat mottled below.
Body: very robust with bulging forehead.

Range and habitat
Offshore temperate waters of the North Atlantic; off South Africa (Indian Ocean).

Habits
Unknown.

Diet
Squid.

Reproduction
Unknown.

Status
Unknown, but probably rare.

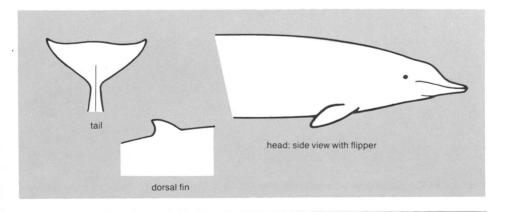

tail

dorsal fin

head: side view with flipper

In the North Pacific, Japanese fishermen have on a few occasions seen Stejneger's (pronounced *Sty*-ne-ger's) beaked whales chasing salmon near their boats.

Other names
Bering Sea beaked whale, sabertooth whale, ballena de Stejneger (Latin America), oogiha kujira (Japan).

Distinguishing features
The 2 protruding tusk-like teeth in the lower jaw of the male are unique. The forehead is dark – unlike the white-capped Hubbs' beaked whale (**23**). The long beak is unlike Cuvier's beaked whale (**15**). (The male Cuvier's also has the distinctive white head.) Distinguishing female or juvenile Stejneger's beaked whales, as with other beaked whales, is difficult if not impossible at sea.

Description
Length: up to about 17 feet.
Teeth: 1 large tooth on each side of lower jaw in mature males.
Color: grayish brown on back, lighter on belly with light pigmentation around neck and mouth. Males have scratches and adults have oval scars on flanks and around genital region.
Body: robust, with long beak.

The sabre-like teeth on this Stejneger's beaked whale erupt from the lower jaw in males only.

Range and habitat
Cooler waters of the North Pacific.

Habits
Unknown.

Diet
Unknown.

Reproduction
Unknown.

Status
Numbers unknown, but probably rare.

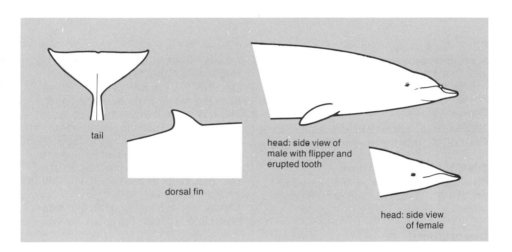

tail

dorsal fin

head: side view of male with flipper and erupted tooth

head: side view of female

32 Longman's Beaked Whale *Mesoplodon pacificus*

Longman's beaked whale is known from only 2 skulls: one from Australia in 1882, the other from Somalia in 1955. No one knows what it looks like, but from the skulls' size, it must be one of the larger beaked whales.

Other names
Indo-Pacific beaked whale.

Range and habitat
The 2 skulls came from the western tropical Pacific and the Indian Ocean.

Status
Unknown, but certainly rare.

Centuries ago, the male narwhal's tusk, sometimes recovered on northern isles, was thought to be the horn of the legendary unicorn.

Other names

Tugalik (Inuit), narval (Russia), narhvalus (Iceland), lighval or narwhal (Norway).

Distinguishing features

The male tusk which sometimes breaks the water; a darkly spotted or mottled back.

Description

Length: males up to about 16 feet, excluding the tusk; females slightly smaller.
Teeth: none in the mouth. 2 adult teeth are embedded in the upper jaw and, in the male, the left one erupts through the upper lip at about age 1. At maturity, it may reach 10 feet. Females, normally tuskless, are occasionally found with tusks. There are also a number of cases with males having 2 tusks; from the 19th Century there's a report of a 2-tusked female. Broken tusks are common, occurring in about 30-40% of adult males.
Body: cylindrical with smooth, finless back except for a few bumps along the mid-line ridge near the tail. Bellies are white in adult animals. Small, up-curled flippers, and flukes with rounded trailing edge (so pronounced in older males that flukes seem to be attached backwards).
Head: bulbous forehead with tiny mouth and hint of a beak.
Calves: about 5 feet at birth, and a dark blue blotchy gray.

Range and habitat

Enjoying the deep water of the high Arctic, narwhals spend much of their lives navigating through pack ice, right to the edge of the ice cap. In some areas they enter coastal waters during the spring break-up and stay until late summer.

Habits

Often segregated by sex, narwhals usually travel in groups of anywhere from a

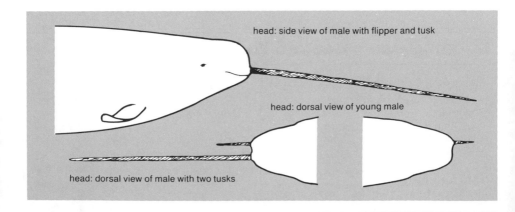

head: side view of male with flipper and tusk

head: dorsal view of young male

head: dorsal view of male with two tusks

Male narwhals swimming in eastern Arctic waters.

few individuals to about 20. When confined in ice, they sometimes open breathing holes by butting the fatty cushion of their foreheads or melons against ice up to 6 inches thick. Males are careful not to break their tusks, contrary to an earlier belief that the tusk might actually be the ice breaker. For more than a century scientists have enjoyed speculating on the function of the tusk, and the literature is filled with stories of dueling narwhals. Canadian zoologist Robin Best recently evaluated the various theories and found the best evidence supported the idea that the tusk is a secondary sexual characteristic. Like mountain sheep, narwhals may use the tusk to establish a dominance hierarchy in which physical or social advantage is gained by a longer tusk. Perhaps males with similar-sized tusks do engage in a little jousting. That would explain the scarring found on the head of many adult males.

Diet
Squid, polar cod, bottom fish like Greenland halibut, crabs and shrimps.

Reproduction
Gestation: about 14-15 months. Births mostly in summer.

Status
Total population is unknown. In the Canadian Arctic, where they are most abundant, they are thought to number about 10,000. The monetary value of the ivory tusks encourages Inuit hunters to pursue males, though they also kill both males and females for food.

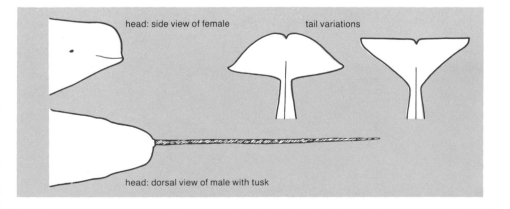

head: side view of female

tail variations

head: dorsal view of male with tusk

Early mariners called them "sea canaries" because of their astonishing variety of whistles, squeals and clicks, sometimes clearly audible above the surface.

Other names
White whale, beluga whale, belukha (Russia), hvidvisk (Norway).

Distinguishing features
The pure white color of adult belugas. Chubby body. No dorsal fin.

Description
Length: males up to about 15 feet; females somewhat smaller.
Teeth: up to 11 conical teeth in each side of upper and lower jaw, though often only 32 in all.
Body: chubby with creases and folds of fat. No dorsal fin. Flippers are broad and short and curl at the tips.
Head: small for the body size, but with an enlarged forehead or melon which changes in shape during sound production. Neck is clearly defined and flexible.

Up-curled flippers and flukes with slightly rounded trailing edge.
Calves: about 5 feet at birth and bluish gray, similar to narwhal calves. The darker colors gradually fade as they reach sexual maturity at about age 5 or 6.

Range and habitat
The shallow waters, rivers and estuaries of the Arctic are the beluga's usual home, though groups live year-round in the St. Lawrence River and in the North Pacific as far south as Cook Inlet and Yakutat Bay, Alaska.

Habits
Belugas travel in groups as small as 2 or 3, but in the summer they form herds of hundreds, even thousands, swimming far up many of the major northern rivers. In the Yukon River they have been spotted 600 miles inland and in the Amur River in Asia, 1,240 miles upstream. In 1966, a lost beluga swam right up the Rhine into the heart of Germany, creating a stir. Despite their long journeys and sometime

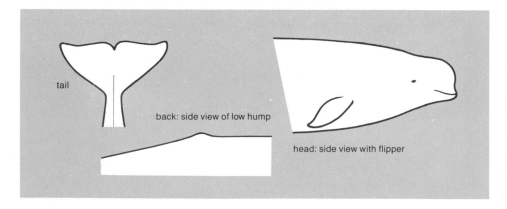

tail

back: side view of low hump

head: side view with flipper

wanderings, belugas are slow swimmers, typically moving at less than 5 to 6 mph, making them easy prey for killer whales (75). Polar bears also occasionally grab belugas, after waiting along narrow ice cracks for them to surface.

Diet
A wide variety of fish, crustaceans and cephalopods, including capelin, char, sand lance, pollock, several cod species, salmon, shrimps, and octopus.

Reproduction
Births occur mainly in summer after a gestation period of about 14 months. Calves nurse for about 20 months. The reproductive cycle is about 3 years.

Status
The total population is estimated at 62,000 to 88,000 animals. Belugas are taken for Native subsistence throughout most of the circumpolar range.

W. Hoek

J.P. Sylvestre

(Above) *Belugas converge on Cunningham Inlet, near Somerset Island in the Canadian Arctic.* (Below) *A beluga whale in captivity peers at curious visitors.*

Ganges River Dolphin (Susu) *Platanista gangetica*

As early as the first century, Pliny the Elder wrote about a certain "fish" in India's Ganges River with a beak like a dolphin.

Other names
Ganges susu, Gangetic dolphin, blind river dolphin.

Distinguishing features
Only found in the Ganges-Brahmaputra-Meghna river systems. Long, narrow beak. Broad flippers. Low ridge or hump instead of dorsal fin.

Description
Length: up to 8 feet.
Teeth: 27-33 each side, each jaw; sharp.
Color: gray to brownish-gray, darkening as the animal matures.

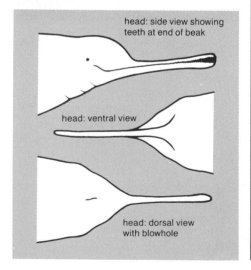

head: side view showing teeth at end of beak

head: ventral view

head: dorsal view with blowhole

Body: plump, with broad, large, rectangular-shaped flippers. Long beak; females have longer beak. Slight rise to dorsal ridge.
Calves: about 28 inches at birth.

Range and habitat
From tidal limits to the foothills of the Himalayas, including Ganges-Brahmaputra-Meghna river systems of India, Bangladesh and Nepal.

Habits
Usually sighted in pairs or alone, but scattered groups of 5-10 have been reported. With the Indus River dolphin, (**36**), it shares the distinction of being the only marine mammal having eyes with no lenses. Anatomical studies have shown that their eyes are capable of light reception but are almost blind. Like other river dolphins they use echolocation to hunt for fish. They feed in evening or at night, and are less active during the day. Normal swimming speed is 3-4 mph. Swims on side, like the Indus River dolphin. Occasionally leaps out of the water.

Diet
Fish and shrimp.

Reproduction
Gestation: about a year. Most births occur in April/May.

Status
Numbers 4000 to 5000 according to 1976 estimates. Some caught accidentally in fishing nets are often released. Habitat loss is increasing problem.

The Indus River dolphin was considered the same species as the Ganges River dolphin (**35**) until scientists Pilleri and Gihr identified slight anatomical differences between the two in 1971.

Other names
Indus susu.

Distinguishing features
Only found in the Indus River. Long, narrow beak. Broad flippers. Low ridge or hump instead of dorsal fin.

Description
Length: up to 8 feet.
Teeth: 27-33 each side, each jaw; sharp.
Color: gray to brownish-gray, darkening as the animal matures.
Body: plump, with broad, large, rectangular-shaped flippers. Long beak; females have longer beak. Slight rise to dorsal ridge.
Calves: about 28 inches at birth.

Range and habitat
From tidal limits to the foothills (at least historically) in the Indus River system of Pakistan and India.

Habits
Mother and calves seem to stay in shallower water where current is slower. See Ganges River dolphin (**35**).

Diet
Fish and shrimp.

Reproduction
Gestation: about a year. Most births in April.

Status
Numbers declining much more rapidly than Ganges River dolphin (**35**) because of dolphin hunters and construction of barrages that have divided the river, altering the dolphin's habitat and possibly migration patterns, and splitting the population. Close to extinction.

Steinhart Aquarium, San Francisco

Ventral view of an Indus River dolphin (Susu) in captivity.

In many of the brown to black tributaries of the Amazon River basin, this ungainly looking dolphin displays its pinkish body.

Other names
Pink porpoise, bouto (Brazil), bufeo (Latin America), inia (Guarayo).

Distinguishing features
The long beak, low dorsal ridge and coloring easily distinguish it from tucuxi (**47**), the only other dolphin in the Amazon.

Description
Length: 8-10 feet.
Teeth: 25-35 each side, each jaw.
Color: dark gray on back and top of head and tail, sides and ventral surface white to pinkish-gray to bright pink.
Body: heavy-set with rounded forehead and large wide flukes and flippers. Low dorsal ridge rather than dorsal fin.

Range and habitat
Amazon and Orinoco river basins of South America.

Habits
Often seen in pairs or single animals. Seen moving from river to lakes in early morning and late afternoon. Sometimes roll in shallow water. Some leaping observed, but no bow riding. Swimming speed 1-2 mph with short 7½-10 mph bursts.

Diet
Various fish (including catfish).

Reproduction
Gestation: a little more than 10 months.

Status
Numbers unknown, but still relatively common. Some have been captured for aquariums. There has been recent scientific debate over different forms of this dolphin, in various parts of the river, that may represent 2-3 species. Differences include: coloring, number of teeth, plus skeletal variation.

Steinhart Aquarium, San Francisco

Amazon River dolphins (Boutu) swim in a California aquarium.

Of all the dolphins, the little franciscana has the longest beak, relative to body size, and the most teeth (except for certain spinner dolphins) up to 240 of them.

Other names
La Plata dolphin, La Plata River dolphin.

Distinguishing features
The long beak, when seen; the prominent triangular dorsal fin, while unique among river dolphins, might be confused with other dolphins in its range.

Ricardo Praderi

A rare photograph of a young male franciscana, accidentally caught by shark fishermen off the coast of Uruguay.

Description
Length: males about 5 feet, females slightly larger.
Weight: up to 120 pounds.
Teeth: 50-60 small, sharp teeth on each side of each jaw, 200-240 in all.
Color: pale brownish or grayish, lighter on ventral surface.
Body: with true dorsal fin and no fleshy dorsal keel, unlike other river dolphins.
Calves: about 27½-29½ inches at birth.

Range and habitat
Coastal waters and estuaries of southeastern South America from southern Brazil to northern Argentina, especially the La Plata River estuary. Unlike other river dolphins, does not live *in* the rivers.

Habits
Little known; seems to travel in small groups of 1-5 animals. It has the best eyesight of any of the river dolphins.

Diet
Variety of fish, including croakers, toadfish and anchovies, plus squid, octopus and shrimp.

Reproduction
Gestation: about 10½ months. Calves nurse for 8-9 months.

Status
Unknown, but not numerous. Some are accidentally caught by shark fishermen every year off Uruguay.

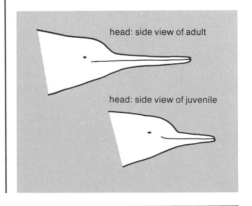

head: side view of adult

head: side view of juvenile

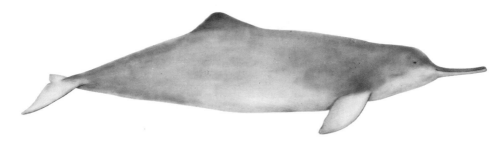

Long revered as the reincarnation of a drowned princess, the Chinese river dolphin has lived near humans for thousands of years.

Other names
White fin dolphin, white flag dolphin, pei c'hi (China).

Distinguishing features
Only found in the Yangtze River. Long beak and dorsal fin distinguish it from the finless porpoise (**44**).

Description
Length: about 7 feet.
Weight: 300 pounds.
Teeth: 31-34 in lower jaw, 32-34 upper.
Body: pale bluish gray above, white below. Long, upturned rostrum. Triangular-shaped dorsal fin. Short, rounded flippers.
Calves: about 2½ feet or more at birth.

Range and habitat
The Yangtze River and its tributaries, plus Lake Dongtinghu, though may have abandoned lake because of man-made changes (dikes and farms along the shore).

Habits
Little known. Group size varies from 3-4 to 10-12. A slow swimmer, it stays mainly in mid-channel, coming to shore only to feed. The species seems to travel widely to different regions of the river; surveys in the Hongho area of China have shown that the dolphins are there during late spring and early summer. The eyes are marginally functional and the species' bio-sonar ability may be highly developed.

Diet
Small fish, eel-like catfish.

Reproduction
Gestation: about 10 months. Births in March-April.

Status
Uncertain. Increased boat traffic and accidental take by fishermen are problems. In 1975, China awarded this dolphin full protection.

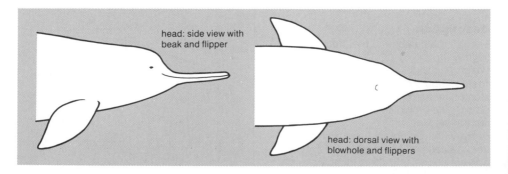

head: side view with beak and flipper

head: dorsal view with blowhole and flippers

The ancient Romans gave this little cetacean the name "porpoise" from the Latin "porcus piscus" meaning pigfish and even today they are called "puffing pigs" in eastern Canada.

Other names
Common porpoise (Britain), marsouin (France), nezumi iruka (Japan), morskaya svin'ya (Russia).

Distinguishing features
Smallest cetacean within its range, triangular dorsal fin, hint of beak.

Description
Length: about 5 feet, up to 6½ feet.
Weight: about 100-130 pounds.
Teeth: 19-28 on each side of both jaws.
Color: dark gray to black on dorsal surface, lighter below. Dark gray line from mouth to base of flipper.
Body: small and chunky with tiny flippers and small, triangular-shaped dorsal fin.
Head: beakless with slightly longer lower jaw.
Calves: 2.4-3 feet.

Range and habitat
Coastal waters including bays, estuaries and tidal channels in the temperate and ice-free boreal zone of the northern hemisphere.

Habits
Very active animals, they do not, however, ride the bow waves of ships like dolphins. They may travel up to about 14 mph when chased. Normal group size is less than 10 when feeding, though they are sometimes seen in groups of 50 or more. Work by David Gaskin in the Bay of Fundy suggests an alternately inshore/offshore movement, with movement offshore occurring during the winter months.

Diet
Variety of fish (small cods, herring, sole), squid, and crustaceans. Cooperative feeding has been observed.

Reproduction
Gestation: about 11 months with some evidence for 2-year birthing intervals. Calves nurse for about 8 months.

Status
World population is unknown, but numbers are declining, especially in European waters. Some suggest that nearshore activity and development is causing the decline. Some are accidentally caught and killed in fishermen's nets. High levels of PCB's have been measured in animals from the Bay of Fundy.

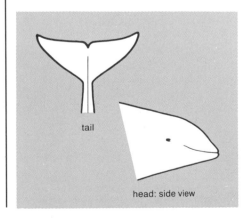

tail

head: side view

In 1950, scientist Ken Norris discovered an unusual porpoise skull on a Mexican beach in the northern Gulf of California. It turned out to be a new species, which he and William McFarland described in 1958.

Other names
Gulf of California porpoise, vaquita.

Distinguishing features
Similar to harbor porpoise (**40**) but within its range, the northern Gulf of California, it is the only porpoise. Bottlenose (**57**) and common dolphins (**50**) in the same area are much larger.

Description
Length: (from two mature females) 4.6 and 4.9 feet.
Teeth: 20-21 pairs in upper jaw, 18 pairs in lower jaw.
Calves: 2.4 feet at birth.

Range and habitat
Known from the shallower waters of the upper Gulf of California but may historically have occurred even further south along the Mexican mainland.

Habits
Unknown.

Diet
From one stomach: fish (grunt and Gulf croakers) and squid.

Reproduction
Unknown.

Status
Numbers unknown, but very low. Before 1975, gill netters in the upper Gulf of California accidentally caught an estimated 10 to perhaps hundreds a year; a few may still be caught in other fisheries. The damming of the Colorado River and heavy pesticide loads in the upper Gulf may preclude a possible comeback for this species.

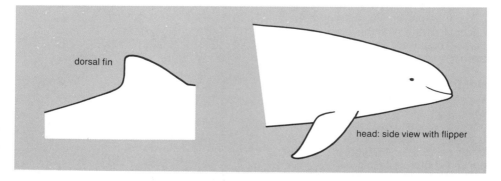

dorsal fin

head: side view with flipper

Natalie Goodall, who studies spectacled porpoises and other rare cetaceans from around Tierra del Fuego, is perhaps the only person to have seen and recognized this animal in the wild.

Other names
Marsopa de anteojos (Argentina).

Distinguishing features
The size and black back are similar to Burmeister's porpoise (**43**), but the white flanks, belly and flippers plus shape of dorsal fin are distinctive.

Description
Length: up to more than 7 feet.
Teeth: upper jaw, 18-23 each side; lower jaw, 16-19 each side.
Color: black dorsal, white ventral with white areas extending up the sides and usually including the flippers. Black lips and eye patches. White areas may expand with age.

Body: head is small and rounded. Large triangular dorsal fin and small flippers are rounded at tips.
Calves: about 2½ feet at birth.

Range and habitat
Known from western South Atlantic including offshore islands, from Uruguay to Tierra del Fuego, Argentina. A few records from mainly subantarctic islands in the Western Pacific and Indian oceans.

Habits
Unknown.

Diet
Fish and squid.

Reproduction
Unknown.

Status
Unknown.

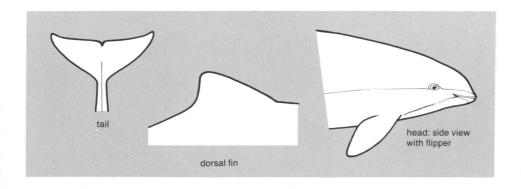

tail

dorsal fin

head: side view with flipper

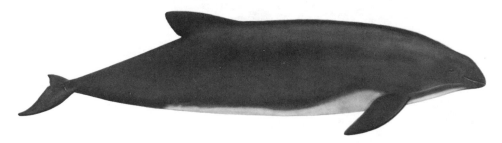

In the 1860s, the German entomologist and Buenos Aires museum director Herman Burmeister called this porpoise "spinipinnis" from the Latin meaning fin with spines, and referring to the spines or denticles found on the leading edge of the tiny backward-looking dorsal fin.

Other names
Black porpoise, marsopa espinosa (Latin America).

Distinguishing features
The spiny backward-looking dorsal fin.

Description
Length: up to about 6 feet.
Teeth: 14-19 on each side of each jaw.
Color: dark brown to black.
Body: chunky with narrower head and larger, more pointed flippers than other porpoises.

Range and habitat
Shallow coastal waters around southern South America from Uruguay to Peru.

Habits
Travels in groups of 2-8, according to Bernd and Melany Würsig who sometimes saw them while studying dusky dolphins (62) off Patagonia, Argentina. They found Burmeister's porpoises shy and unobtrusive like most porpoises and only once saw one jump.

Diet
Unknown.

Reproduction
Unknown.

Status
Numbers unknown, but may be abundant – especially on west coast of southern South America. Fishermen from Peru and Chile catch them and the meat is sold in the markets of Peru.

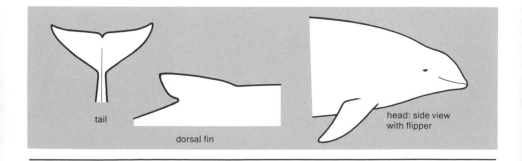

tail

dorsal fin

head: side view with flipper

The series of bumps or tubercles on the rear dorsal surface of the finless porpoise allows calves to ride on their mothers' back.

Other names

Black porpoise, sunameri (Japan), hai-chu (China), bhulga (India), tabi (Sindi of Pakistan).

Distinguishing features

No dorsal fin; small tubercles along slight dorsal ridge; globular head.

Description

Length: up to about 6 feet.
Weight: up to about 84 pounds.
Teeth: 13-22 on each side of each jaw with considerable individual variation.
Color: pale gray (may be bluish) with white areas on chin and throat.
Body: stocky with rounded head, no beak, distinct neck and large flippers.
Calves: about 2 feet at birth (15 pounds).

Range and habitat

Warmer coastal and inshore fresh waters, including rivers and lakes, of eastern Asia and Japan.

Habits

Travels in groups of 2-12. Swiss biologist Pilleri sometimes saw finless porpoises accompanying Chinese River dolphins (**39**) in the lakes and rivers of China.

M. Nakajima

A finless porpoise gets fed at Japan's Izu-Mito Sea Paradise.

Diet

Small fishes, squid, shrimp.

Reproduction

Gestation: about 11 months.

Status

Numbers unknown. Once caught extensively by fishermen around Japan, India, and China, but less often now.

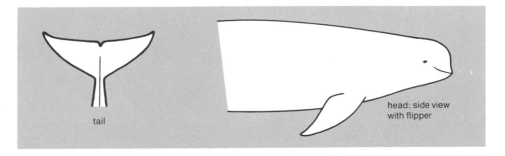

tail

head: side view with flipper

The speedy Dall's porpoise, when seen at the surface, is mostly a blur. It often throws up a splash called a "rooster tail", which is caused *not* by the tail but by the cone of water coming off the head as it breaks the surface.

Other names
Dall porpoise, True's porpoise, delfin de Dall (Latin America).

Distinguishing features
The short triangular dorsal fin trimmed in white, the large white flanks and the black, almost beakless head.

Description
Length: up to 7 feet.
Weight: up to about 480 pounds.
Teeth: 19-28 on each side of upper and lower jaw.

Color: black with striking white flanks, plus dorsal fin and flukes edged in white. Wide variation in dorsal fin, which can be all white or all black, and in flank.
Body: robust, with fairly small black head (some with white around lips) and protruding lower jaw. Triangular dorsal fin slightly falcate. Small flippers located near head. Thick peduncular keel (forward part of tail stock).
Calves: about 1 foot at birth.

Range and habitat
Mainly the immediate offshore waters of the North Pacific, from the southern Bering Sea south to Japan and California.

Habits
Travels in groups of 2-20, but several hundred have been seen in feeding areas. Occasional bow riders with high

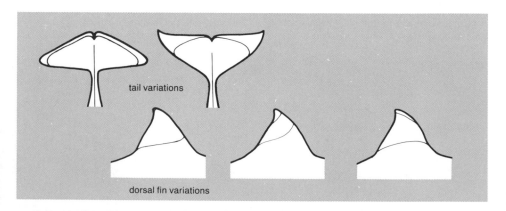

tail variations

dorsal fin variations

W. Rossiter

David Rugh / Nat'l. Mar. Mam. Lab., NMFS, NOAA

(Above) *A Dall's porpoise in Puget Sound displays a characteristic "rooster tail".* (Below) *A Dall's porpoise breaks the water in the southern Bering Sea.*

activity level, yet rarely leap. Killer whales (**75**) (and sharks) prey on Dall's porpoises (from observed feeding behavior and stomach studies), yet groups of killer whales and Dall's porpoises are often seen peacefully passing each other or sharing feeding areas.

Diet
Squid, schooling fish (capelin, mackerel, herring, anchovy); cephalopod molluscs.

Reproduction
Gestation: about 11 months, with most births July – Sept.

Status
Numbers about 920,000. Several thousand a year taken accidentally by Japanese high seas gill netters fishing for salmon.

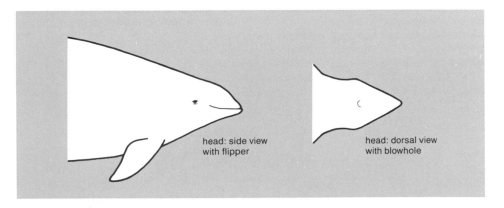

head: side view with flipper

head: dorsal view with blowhole

The characteristic light circular scars found on mature rough-toothed dolphins are believed to be caused by nibbling "cookie-cutter" sharks.

Other names
Dauphin à long bec (France), delfín de pico largo (Latin America).

Distinguishing features
Long, narrow rostrum with no separation between it and the rest of the head (smooth sloping forehead). White lips. Body has many small light patches.

Description
Length: up to 9 feet.
Teeth: 20-27 on each side of each jaw. The fine vertical wrinkles on the teeth give the species its name.
Color: charcoal gray or black, sometimes with purplish hue. Blotches are pinkish-white. White ventral surface sometimes pinkish. Tip of beak and either or both lips also pinkish-white.
Body: somewhat slim to stocky. Long dorsal fin and flippers are usually falcate. Large black eyes.

Range and habitat
Pelagic waters of the warm temperate and tropical zones.

Habits
Travels in groups of 10-20, up to 50 (from limited observations). Occasional bow riders. Seen travelling with herds of other tropical dolphins and pilot whales.

Diet
Pelagic fish and squid, molluscs.

Reproduction
Unknown.

Status
Numbers unknown. Some are killed in tuna purse seine fishery and a few have been captured for oceanaria. Formerly believed rare, more are being recognized at sea, especially around Hawaii.

A group of rough-toothed dolphins.

Bernd & Melany Würsig

Tucuxi is the "other" dolphin of the Amazon: smaller, duller in color, it travels in larger numbers, yet is sometimes more wary of river traffic than the Amazon River dolphin (**37**).

Other names
Tookashee (spelling variation of tucuxi) and pirayaguara (Tupi and Yagua Indian), buffeo negro (Brazil).

Distinguishing features
Very small; longer beak and smaller, less curved dorsal fin than the bottlenose dolphin (**57**) (which shares the coastal part of tucuxi's range), but darker coloring, a much shorter beak, and larger dorsal fin than the Amazon River dolphin (**37**). Much color variation that, along with geographical separation and size differences, may constitute several species. Definitive taxonomic studies yet to be done.

Description
Length: up to about 6 feet.
Weight: up to 100 pounds.
Teeth: 26-35 on each side of both jaws.
Color: varies widely, dark (brown, gray or black) above and pale below.
Body: moderately robust, with low sloping forehead.

Range and habitat
Rivers, lakes and coastal inshore waters of northeastern South America.

Habits
Travels in tight groups of 2-25. Active swimmer.

Diet
Fish, prawns, crabs.

Reproduction
Gestation: about 10 months.

Status
Numbers unknown, but relatively abundant.

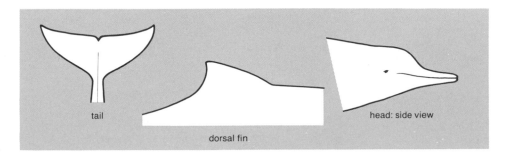

tail

dorsal fin

head: side view

This little-studied dolphin has 3 distinctive color variations: pure white, gray, and spotted. It may be 1 species – or 3.

Other names
Chinese white dolphin, Bornean white dolphin, speckled dolphin.

Distinguishing features
The dorsal hump or platform, with small dorsal fin mounted on top. Larger dorsal fin with no hump on dolphins living east of Indonesia. Long beak (much longer than bottlenose dolphins (**57**)).

Description
Length: 7-9 feet.
Weight: up to 630 pounds.
Teeth: 29-38 on each side of each jaw.
Color: varies widely by subspecies from white to gray to spotted.
Body: robust, with sloping forehead and long, slender beak.

Range and habitat
Coastal, inshore, and estuarine waters of the Indian Ocean from South Africa to southeast Asia plus eastern China and northern Australia.

Habits
Travel in small groups of 1-12. Acrobatic, but do not bow ride.

Diet
Unknown.

Reproduction
Unknown.

Status
Numbers unknown, but seems to be abundant in some areas of its range. Some are taken by fishermen.

A humpbacked dolphin swims close to the coast of South Africa.

The Atlantic humpbacked dolphin was at one time thought to be the only vegetarian dolphin, eating sea grass, leaves and mangrove seedlings. This early account, often repeated, somehow mismatched the skull of this dolphin with the stomach of a West African manatee. Unlike the manatee, the Atlantic humpbacked dolphin subsists on fish.

Other names
Cameroon dolphin.

Distinguishing features
The dorsal hump or platform, with small dorsal fin mounted on top.

Description
Length: up to about 8 feet.
Teeth: 26-31 on each side of each jaw.
Color: slate gray back and flanks, pale gray belly.

Body: robust, with sloping forehead and long, slender beak.

Range and habitat
Coastal tropical waters of West Africa.

Habits
Participates with bottlenose dolphins (**57**) and fishermen in the symbiotic herding of mullet off Mauritania. Fishermen hit the water with sticks to alert the dolphins who drive the fish inshore to their nets.

Diet
Fishes including mullet.

Reproduction
Unknown.

Status
Numbers unknown, but probably common locally.

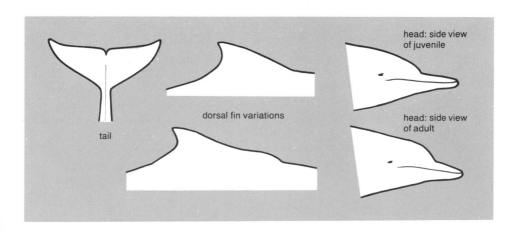

tail

dorsal fin variations

head: side view of juvenile

head: side view of adult

The species that inspired Aristotle and the ancient Greeks, and the first to be called "dolphin", the common dolphin still rides the bows of ships in the Mediterranean and throughout most of the temperate and tropical world ocean.

Other names
Saddleback, white-bellied porpoise, crisscross dolphin, delfin commun (Latin America), delfino (Italy), tobi iruka (Japan).

Distinguishing features
Crisscross pattern on the sides, with forward part tawny yellow or brown and rear part gray; black cape above pattern dips to a point on both flanks below dorsal fin and forms a V-shaped saddle.

Description
Length: up to about 8 feet.
Teeth: 40-55 small sharply-pointed teeth in each side of each jaw.

Body: slender, with well-defined beak and tall, curved dorsal fin.
Calves: 2½ feet at birth.

Range and habitat
Tropical and warm temperate waters of the world ocean, nearshore and pelagic.

Habits
Travels in groups of 40 to several thousand. The "original" bow riders, common dolphins are so eager that they may approach ships from long distances and ride for a long time. Some researchers suggest that ship bow riding may have originated from the practice of riding the bow waves of large baleen whales – something these and other dolphins still do.

Diet
Fish, anchovies, (smelt, lanternfish, sardine, herring) and squid.

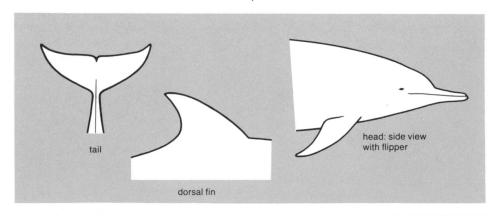

tail

dorsal fin

head: side view with flipper

Reproduction
Gestation: 10–11 months. Calves nurse for 4 months. Cows may give birth to 1 calf per year.

Status
Though world numbers unknown it is common. There is an eastern tropical Pacific estimate of 900,000 and a western North Atlantic estimate of 17,500. Many common dolphins are accidentally taken with other dolphins by purse-seine fishermen pursuing tuna in the eastern tropical Pacific. Soviet fisheries killed up to 120,000 a year in the Black Sea until severe depletion came in the mid-1960s.

Antonio M. Teixeira

Esteve Grau

Common dolphins off the coast of Portugal (above) and in the western Mediterranean (left). (Below) Common dolphins often travel in large herds such as this one off the coast of California near San Diego.

Stephen Leatherwood

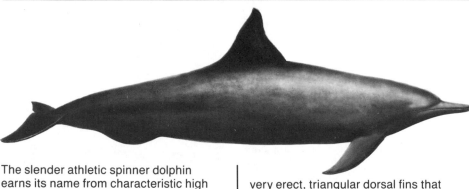

The slender athletic spinner dolphin earns its name from characteristic high spinning leaps.

Other names
Spinner, long-beaked dolphin, spinner porpoise, delfín tornillon or delfín churumbelo (Latin America), hashinaga iruka (Japan).

Distinguishing features
The erect triangular dorsal fin of mature males, black-tipped beak and lips, and spinning behavior are different from other small dolphins. In the Atlantic, the spinner has a longer beak, flippers and body than the clymene dolphin (**55**).

Description
Length: about 5-7 feet with males slightly larger.
Teeth: 45-65 on each side of each jaw.
Body: slender, with long, black-tipped beak, but much variation in body shape and color pattern. There are at least 4 geographical forms of the spinner in the eastern tropical Pacific. (1) The Costa Rican spinner is the longest; (2) the eastern spinner is the shortest. Both are dark gray with light areas on the throat, genital region, and behind the flipper, though the extent of the light areas is highly variable. The mature males of both forms have very erect, triangular dorsal fins that sometimes are curved forward with corresponding large ventral keels. (3) The northern and southern whitebelly spinners are especially variable in size and color pattern, but in general the whitebelly spinners and (4) the Hawaiian spinners are dark gray dorsally, with lighter gray flanks and white bellies. The Hawaiian form has the most falcate dorsal fin and almost no postanal hump.

Range and habitat
Tropical world ocean, mostly pelagic.

Habits
Groups of several hundred, often associating with spotted (**52**) and other oceanic dolphins. Spinner dolphins literally spin 2-7 times on the long axis of their body during a single leap.

Diet
Lanternfish and other fish; squid.

Reproduction
Gestation: about 10½ months.

Status
Probably numbers several hundred thousand in the eastern Pacific.

The spotted dolphin is the "porpoise" that more than any other has made whale watchers think twice before eating a tuna sandwich.

Other names
Spotter, spotted porpoise, delfín machado or delfín pintado (Latin America), arari iruka (Japan).

Distinguishing features
Extensive but varied spotting depending on age and geographical area. No strong pattern of stripes. Curved dorsal fin (rather than erect triangular dorsal fins of spinner dolphins). Demarcated white-tipped beak.

Description
Length: up to about 8 feet.
Teeth: 34-48 on each side of each jaw.
Color: slate gray back and pale belly with extensive spotting, but great variation depending on age and area.
Body: moderately robust, with long beak and curved dorsal fin. Variation in size and shape depending on form, several of which have been identified in various regions but have not been raised to the species level.
Calves: under 3 feet at birth, are unspotted. They go though several color phases, developing dark spots on the belly when they are about 5 feet, followed by light spots on the back. The ventral spots eventually lighten and "fuse" with the grayish belly.

Range and habitat
Tropical and warm temperate offshore and nearshore waters of the world ocean.

Habits
Coastal Central American form usually travels in groups of less than 100. Offshore forms aggregate in groups of more than 1,000 and often include spinner dolphins (**51**). Very surface-active with bow riding in some areas. Harassment by tuna fishermen may have decreased bow riding in fishing regions. William F. Perrin and others have studied these dolphins intensively to try to understand their often fatal association with yellowfin tuna. In the early 1970s, more than 100,000 spotted dolphins died each year. New release techniques and laws have cut the kill for all dolphins in the eastern tropical Pacific tuna fishery to about 20,000 a year – an improvement, but still too high a rate.

Diet
Fishes and squids.

Reproduction
Gestation: about 11½ months.

Status
Numbers estimated at more than 2 million in the eastern tropical Pacific. World numbers unknown.

Striped dolphins are not regular bow riders, but their acrobatic repertoire includes belly-up porpoising and reverse cartwheels as well as the usual dolphin breaches and assorted "tail work".

Other names
Streaker, streaker porpoise, whitebelly, euphrosyne dolphin, dauphin bleu-et-blanc (France), suji iruka (Japan), delfín listado (Latin America).

Distinguishing features
Pale blaze extending from the light flank up and back across the dark cape toward the dorsal fin. On each side, 2 black lines, *stripes*, run from the eye across the flank to the anus and from the eye to the flipper.

Description
Length: 6-7½ feet, up to 8¾ feet.

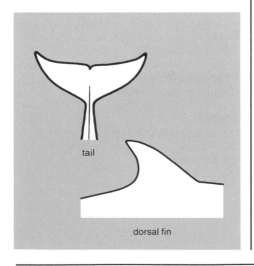

tail

dorsal fin

Teeth: 45-50 in each side of each jaw.
Color: dorsal side from beak to tail including flippers is dark gray to bluish gray. Ventral surface is white with pale gray flanks. Black patch around each eye and pattern of stripes along flanks are subject to some variation.
Body: slender, with well-defined beak and tall curved dorsal fin.
Calves: about 3 feet at birth, with adult color pattern.

Range and habitat
Tropical and warm temperate waters of the world ocean, mainly pelagic.

Habits
Travels in groups of several hundred. Off Japan, where they have been studied, there is a seasonal north-south migration and 3 mating seasons: Jan.-Feb., May-June, and Sept.-Oct. The population bands together in mating herds of about 225 and non-mating herds of about 750. There are also juvenile herds, though the calves stay with their mothers for 3 years in the mating herds.

Diet
Fishes, shrimp, squid.

Reproduction
Gestation: about 12 months. Calves nurse for about 1½ years.

Status
Numbers for the eastern tropical Pacific are estimated at more than 2 million. No world estimates. Striped dolphins are regularly taken in the yellowfin tuna fishery.

The Atlantic spotted dolphin regularly approaches divers in the Caribbean, swimming around them and with them, often for extended periods.

Other names
Spotter, spotted porpoise, Gulf Stream spotted dolphin.

Distinguishing features
Spots and white-tipped demarcated beak. Pale blaze extending up from flank. More robust and with a less distinct (paler) cape than the spotted dolphin (**52**), but distinguishing between the two difficult at sea.

Description
Length: up to 8 feet.
Teeth: about 28-37 on each side of both jaws.
Body: somewhat robust, with white-tipped demarcated beak and curved dorsal fin. *Calves*: born without spots, are gray above and white below.

Range and habitat
Tropical Atlantic.

Habits
Travels in groups of 20-50, up to several hundred at times.

Diet
Squids; fishes.

Reproduction
Unknown.

Status
Numbers unknown. A few have been taken for oceanaria.

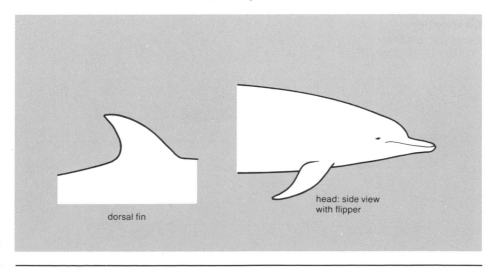

dorsal fin

head: side view with flipper

"Elevated" to a full-fledged species in 1977, the clymene (pronounced cly-*mee*-nee) is a small tropical dolphin similar to the spinner dolphin (**51**) but with a shorter beak, flippers and body, and a range restricted to the tropical Atlantic.

Other names
Short-snouted spinner dolphin.

Distinguishing features
Tall dorsal fin. Well-defined black-tipped beak is shorter than spinner dolphins. Dark-gray dorsal surface, pale gray flanks and white belly are similar to spinner except dark gray extends further down the flanks below the dorsal fin. Other subtle differences: the edges of the eye-to-flipper stripe on the clymene converge at the eye, whereas on the spinner they are parallel.

Description
Length: about 6 feet.

Teeth: 38-49 on each side of each jaw.
Body: slender, but shorter and broader than spinner dolphin. Dorsal fin about 6 inches high, slightly falcate.

Range and habitat
Tropical and subtropical Atlantic; pelagic.

Habits
Some spinning leaps have been observed, but not as high or extensive as those of the spinner dolphin.

Diet
Unknown.

Reproduction
Unknown.

Status
Unknown.

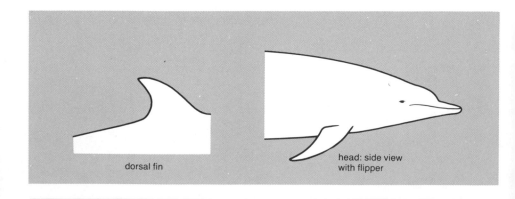

dorsal fin

head: side view with flipper

Fraser's dolphin was first seen alive in the early 1970s. Before then, the species was only known from a single carcass that had washed up on the beach in Sarawak (Malaysia) in 1895.

Other names
Sarawak dolphin, Sarawaku iruka (Japan).

Distinguishing features
Like the striped dolphin (**53**), Fraser's dolphin has stripes along its side and lives in offshore tropical seas. Fraser's dolphin, however, is more robust and has smaller flippers, dorsal fin and a very short beak.

Description
Length: up to 8.7 feet.
Teeth: 34-44 in each side of each jaw.
Color: complex pattern, including bluish-gray back, pinkish-white belly, and grayish-yellow stripe on side bordered above and below by whitish stripes.

Body: robust, with dorsal fin triangular to slightly falcate.

Range and habitat
Tropical and warm temperate waters of the world ocean.

Habits
Herds of 500 and more have been reported. They are fast swimmers and shy away from boats.

Diet
Fish, shrimp and squid indicate deep-diving habits.

Reproduction
Unknown.

Status
Unknown. Fishermen take a few in purse seines in the yellowfin tuna fishery.

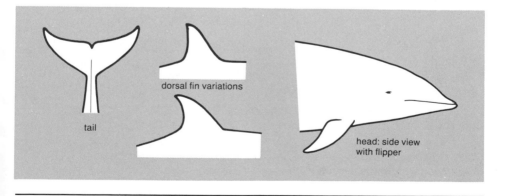

tail

dorsal fin variations

head: side view with flipper

Star of film, television and marine parks, the bottlenose dolphin in the wild is a curious bow rider – the cetacean who perhaps has most earned the epithet ''friend of man''.

Other names
Common porpoise, black porpoise (tuna fishermen), gray porpoise, delfín naríz de botella (Latin America), taiseiyo bandō iruka (Japan).

Distinguishing features
A relatively short beak, well-defined by crease at base; dorsal fin is high, falcate and broad at base; color varies, but usually medium gray above, pale gray below. These and other variations in several geographically isolated populations place the taxonomy in question.

Description
Length: 10-13 feet.
Teeth: 20-26 each side upper jaw and 18-24 each side lower jaw.

Body: robust. Grayish dorsal surface changes gradually to pale ventral surface, with many gradations in color. 2 dark lines extend from each eye to rostrum, plus a wider line or strip from blowhole to base of beak.
Calves: about 4 feet long at birth.

Range and habitat
Temperate waters of the world ocean. Distinct inshore and offshore populations; some migratory, others year-round residents.

Habits
Studies of individual identification through natural markings on dorsal fins have begun to illuminate group structure. Groups are divided by age and sex, though there is some intermingling. Sometimes group size varies by time of day, with small groups in the early morning and late evening and larger groups during the day. Group size sometimes increases with the depth of the water.

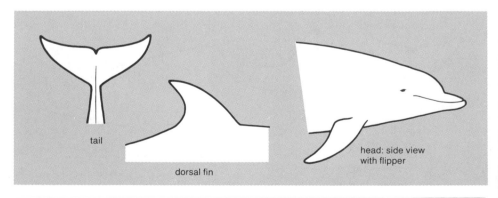

tail

dorsal fin

head: side view with flipper

Captive studies have shown good in-air vision, bio-sonar, and a wide range of sounds including a talent for mimicry. Current studies in Hawaii have focussed on teaching 2 captive dolphins language through acoustic and gestural techniques.

Diet

Very opportunistic: fish, squid, crustaceans, cephalopods. Sometimes feed on discards from fishing vessels, plus organisms brought to surface by vessel movement. Sometimes drive fish ashore, then come out of water on a muddy bank in pursuit, using their tails to get back in the water.

Susan Shane

Reproduction

Gestation: about 12 months. Calves nurse for 12-18 months.

Status

World population unknown, but not believed endangered.

Susan Shane

(Above and left) *Bottlenose dolphins off Port Aransas, Texas. Note dark eye region and demarcated beak.* (Below) *Bottlenose dolphins breaching in Sarasota Bay, Florida.*

Randall Wells / Earthwatch

Off New England and eastern Canada, Atlantic white-sided dolphins often feed side by side with fin (**5**) and humpback (**7**) whales. When the whales move on, the lags often follow, sometimes riding on the whales' bow waves.

Other names
Lag, jumper (Newfoundland), dauphin à flancs blancs (France/Québec), springhval (Norway).

Distinguishing features
Narrow white patch on the side connected to yellow or tan patch that runs toward dorsal ridge near tail flukes. Short black beak. Black back.

Description
Length: 6½-9 feet, males slightly larger.
Teeth: 30-40 small pointed teeth in each half of each jaw.
Color: black dorsal surface, including beak, tail, flippers. White ventral surface, including underside of beak. Gray flank with white and yellow or tan patches.

Body: somewhat robust, with short beak, sharply pointed dorsal fin and flippers.
Calves: about 4 feet at birth.

Range and habitat
Cooler temperate waters of the North Atlantic.

Habits
Usually travels in groups of about 50, but often up to 500. Fast swimming; frequent breaching.

Diet
Small pelagic fish; squid.

Reproduction
Gestation: 11 months. Calves, born in June-July, nurse about 18 months. Cows may bear calves about every 2 years.

Status
Total numbers unknown; estimated northwest Atlantic population is 24,000.

Jane M. Gibbs

Bruce M. Wellman

Atlantic white-sided dolphins breach in Stellwagen Bank waters off the coast of Massachusetts.

These acrobatic dolphins have been captured for many Pacific-rim oceanaria. Pacific white-sided dolphins sometimes surf on a ship's wake, rather than ride its bow.

Other names

Lag, hookfin porpoise, white-striped dolphin, kama iruka (Japan), delfín lagenorringo (Latin America).

Distinguishing features

Tall curved dorsal fin dark along forward side and light along trailing side. Short dark beak. White or light gray "suspenders" along upper flanks. Light gray area on forward flanks extends to rostrum.

Description

Length: up to about 7¹/₂ feet.
Teeth: 24-31 each side lower jaw and 23-32 each side upper jaw.
Color: black back with light gray sides and white belly.
Body: robust, with long flippers rounded at tips.

Calves: 2¹/₂-3 feet at birth.

Range and habitat

Temperate waters of the North Pacific, generally pelagic.

Reproduction

Travels in groups of 15-50 up to several thousand on occasion. Associates with northern right whale dolphins (**68**) and Risso's dolphins (**70**) on occasion. Sometimes smacks the water with its head or tail as it feeds.

Diet

Squid, herring, sardines, anchovies.

Reproduction

Gestation: about 10-12 months. Calves are usually born in the summer.

Status

Numbers for the eastern North Pacific are estimated at 30,000-50,000. No estimates for western North Pacific.

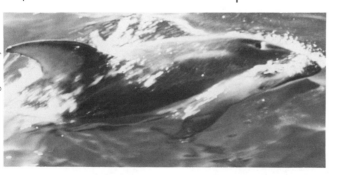

A Pacific white-sided dolphin off southern California.

The black-faced Peale's dolphin, though rarely seen by whale watchers, is common in the Strait of Magellan and the Beagle Channel near Tierra del Fuego, at the southern tip of South America.

Other names
Blackchin dolphin, delfín austral (Latin America).

Distinguishing features
Single white "spike" along each rear flank, unlike double spike of dusky dolphin (**62**); single-toned dorsal fin; all-black face. Only found off southern South America.

Description
Length: up to about 7 feet.
Teeth: 30 on each side of each jaw.
Color: dark back, flippers, flukes and head; light forward flanks, belly and rear spike (dorsal fin to fluke) on each side.
Body: robust.

Range and habitat
Cooler inshore waters around South America.

Habits
Travels in groups of 1-8. Bow rider.

Diet
Unknown.

Reproduction
Unknown.

Status
Numbers unknown, but reportedly common in parts of its range. A few caught by fishermen off Chile, sometimes for crab bait.

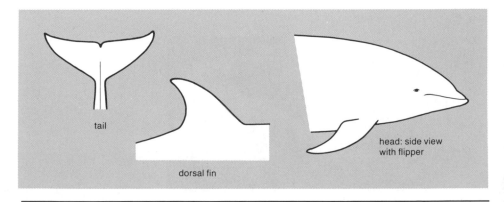

tail

dorsal fin

head: side view with flipper

The color pattern of this rarely encountered, southernmost lag resembles the intersecting parabolas of an hourglass.

Other names
Southern white-sided dolphin, delfín cruzado (Latin America).

Distinguishing features
White flank patches roughly hourglass-shaped; large dark area behind flippers unlike Peale's (**60**) and dusky dolphins' (**62**) light gray areas. Only found in Antarctic and subantarctic waters.

Description
Length: up to about 6 feet.
Teeth: about 28 on each side of each jaw.
Color: black back, flippers, flukes, and flanks with 2 large white areas on flanks and white belly.

Body: robust, with low, broad-based dorsal fin and flippers longer and more curved than other lags.

Range and habitat
Cold, offshore southern temperate and Antarctic waters.

Habits
Eager bow riders with occasional spinning behavior.

Diet
Squid.

Reproduction
Unknown.

Status
Numbers unknown.

Peter Beamish

Hourglass dolphins in Antarctic waters.

In the 1970s biologists Bernd and Melany Würsig lived with dusky dolphins at Península Valdés, Argentina, studying feeding strategies and social organization.

Other names
Fitzroy's dolphin.

Distinguishing features
Only lag within its range (large falcate dorsal fin, small beak) except around southern South America where Peale's dolphin (**60**) is encountered. The dusky dolphin's dorsal fin, however, is usually two-toned. Also, Peale's dolphin is the only lag with an all-black face.

Description
Length: up to 7 feet.
Weight: 300 pounds.

Bernd & Melany Würsig

A dusky dolphin breaches off the coast of Patagonia, Argentina.

Teeth: 24-36 on each side of both jaws.
Color: bluish-black back and snout. Dark strip from eye to flipper. Flippers and flukes dark. Dorsal fin usually two-toned. Some individual variation.
Body: very similar to Pacific white-sided dolphin (**59**), but dusky's rostrum is longer and its dorsal fin is larger, straighter and more subtly two-toned.

Range and habitat
Temperate waters of the southern hemisphere, often close to shore.

Habits
At Península Valdés, the Würsigs found that group sizes of non-feeding dolphins ranged from 6-15 but, when feeding, the groups grew to 300. They observed a general movement to deeper water and an increase in group size as the day went by – probably related to feeding. Speed, too, was related to feeding; mean speed when not feeding was 4 mph and when feeding almost 9½ mph. The dolphins seem to concentrate their prey near the surface, attracting many sea birds.

Diet
Southern anchovy; squid.

Reproduction
Gestation: about 11 months.

Status
Unknown, but probably not endangered.

Wary of ships, these largest of the lags are known around Newfoundland as "squid-hounds".

Other names
Lag, squid-hound (Newfoundland), dauphin à nez blanc (France/Québec), hvidnaese (Norway).

Distinguishing features
Short, usually white beak, but more visible is white patch on side extending up to back. Grayish saddle patch that looks white at a distance. Only found in northern North Atlantic.

Description
Length: up to about 10 feet.
Teeth: about 22-28 on each side of both jaws.
Color: black on dorsal side except for white beak and back (grayish saddle patch). White belly, beak and variegated patches of white, gray and black on flanks. Some geographical variations. *Body*: robust with tall, curved dorsal fin, and short beak. Sharp pointed flippers.

Range and habitat
Cooler temperate waters of the North Atlantic to the edge of the ice. Most northerly of the lags.

Habits
Usually travels in groups of up to 25, but groups of up to 1,500 have been seen off Newfoundland and in the Gulf of St. Lawrence.

Diet
Squid, cod, capelin, crustaceans.

Reproduction
Unknown.

Status
Numbers unknown, but probably not endangered.

Richard Sears / MICS

Breaching white-beaked dolphin.

On his voyage round the world in the mid-18th Century, Philibert Commerson encountered this dolphin in the Straits of Magellan, calling it "le Jacobin" because of its bold black and white coloring.

Other names
Piebald porpoise, Jacobite, jacobita or delfín de Magallanes (Latin America).

Distinguishing features
Bold coloring: black head and dorsal area from dorsal fin to tail; rest of body white, including white throat patch. Limited South Atlantic and southern Indian Ocean range.

Description
Length: up to about 5½ feet.
Teeth: 29-30, small and pointed on each side of both jaws.
Body: chunky, with rounded dorsal fin. Flippers rounded and somewhat oval shaped.

Range and habitat
Mostly inshore coastal waters of Atlantic coast of South America from Golfo San Matias to Tierra del Fuego, especially Strait of Magellan. Also, Falkland Islands; South Georgia; Kerguélen Island (southern Indian Ocean).

Habits
Usual groups are 2-4, up to 10. Synchronous breathing and diving patterns often observed.

Diet
Squids, euphausiids, various fish. In southern Argentina they are seen feeding in shallow water around harbors and beaches, and in kelp beds.

Reproduction
Newborn calves that were completely brown were observed in Jan. Young are black and gray with the gray turning white as they age.

Status
Numbers unknown, but apparently common in its range. Some taken for world oceanaria. Some accidentally netted every year by fishermen.

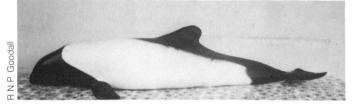

R.N.P. Goodall

A young female Commerson's dolphin, accidentally caught in fishing nets off Tierra del Fuego.

The rare black dolphin is "watched" only by the few fishermen working the coast of Chile who accidentally catch it in their nets.

Other names
Chilean dolphin, delfín negro or delfín chileno (Latin America).

Distinguishing features
Appears all black at sea—darker than Burmeister's porpoise (**43**)—with low rounded dorsal fin, compared to the spiny, triangular dorsal fin of Burmeister's.

Description
Length: about 4 feet, up to 5 feet and about 120 pounds.
Teeth: 28-31 on each side of each jaw.

Color: black above and on flanks, white belly.
Body: small and stocky.

Range and habitat
Cold inshore waters of Chile and Tierra del Fuego.

Habits
Travels in groups of up to about 14 animals. Shy and wary of boats.

Diet
Unknown.

Reproduction
Unknown.

Status
Numbers unknown, but rare.

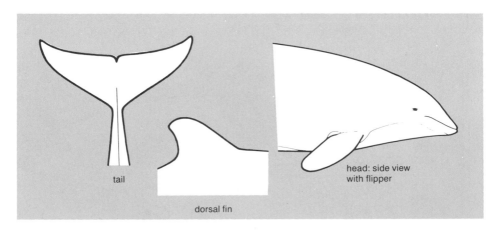

tail

dorsal fin

head: side view with flipper

Capt. Haviside (not Heaviside) brought the skull and skin of this rare South African dolphin back to England with him in 1827.

Other names
None.

Distinguishing features
Its small size and low, triangular dorsal fin are unique within its range.

Description
Length: 3.9 to 4.6 feet.
Teeth: 25-30 on each side of each jaw.
Color: black head and back; white pattern on belly extending in fingers up rear flanks and on both sides of flippers.
Body: small and stocky.

Range and habitat
Coastal waters from Cape of Good Hope to Cape Cross, South Africa.

Habits
In 1969, 3 Heaviside's dolphins were captured and recorded while still alive: they made no squeals or whistle-like sounds, only clicks and pulsed sounds.

Diet
From limited data: squid and bottom-dwelling fish.

Reproduction
Unknown.

Status
Numbers unknown, but certainly not numerous. Some are taken in purse-seine fisheries off South Africa.

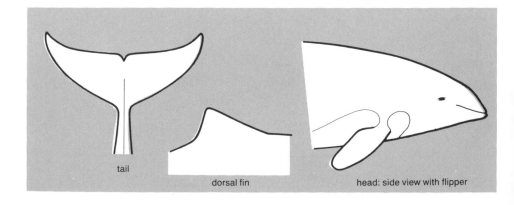

tail

dorsal fin

head: side view with flipper

The best known of the genus *Cephalorhynchus*, the New Zealand-native Hector's dolphin is a bow rider and sometime performer in oceanaria.

Other names
Little pied dolphin.

Distinguishing features
The pale gray or white disc on the forehead. Rounded dorsal fin. Only found around New Zealand.

Description
Length: 3.9-5 feet.
Teeth: 26-32 small teeth on each side of both jaws.
Color: complex arrangement of patterns with some variation. Sides of head, flippers, dorsal fin and tail all black. Tip of chin dark. Dorsal area pale gray with slight pink or brown tinge. Ventral surface white except between flippers where dark pigment extends across. White ventral area extends up the rear flanks in a long finger-like extension.
Body: short and stocky. Flippers rounded.

Range and habitat
Inshore coastal waters of New Zealand, often off estuaries and in deep inlets.

Habits
Travels in groups of 2-8, rarely 20 or more.

Diet
Horse mackerel, red cod, sand stargazer (bottom fish). Squid.

Reproduction
Calves pale colored, may be born mostly in early (austral) summer.

Status
Numbers unknown, but common within range. A few net entrapments reported every year.

Alan N. Baker

A Hector's dolphin flies through the water in Cloudy Bay, New Zealand.

These "smooth dolphins of the north wind", as their scientific name translates, speed along in groups of 15-200 all lined up and leaping clear of the water, re-entering about 20 feet away.

Other names
Kiti demi iruka (Japan), delfín de liso (Latin America).

Distinguishing features
The only dolphins in the North Pacific without a dorsal fin.

Description
Length: males up to 10 feet; females up to about 7½ feet.
Teeth: 37-49 sharply pointed teeth in each side, upper and lower.
Color: mostly black with variable white pattern on belly and white spot near tip of lower jaw.
Body: long and slender, tapering to narrow tail stock. No dorsal keel or fin. Short beak with no forehead or chin. Narrow flukes.
Calves: 32-40 inches at birth.

Range and habitat
Temperate waters of the North Pacific; pelagic.

Habits
Often travels in groups of more than 100 individuals. Often keeps company with Pacific white-sided dolphins (**59**). Fast swimmers: clocked at up to 25 mph. Occasionally bow-rides boats and other whales, especially fins (**5**) and grays (**1**).

Diet
Squid, lanternfish.

Reproduction
Calves probably born in early spring.

Status
Numbers unknown.

Kenneth C. Balcomb

A group of northern right whale dolphins breach off Santa Rosa Island, southern California.

Like their close relatives, the northern right whale dolphins (**68**), the southern right whale dolphins have no dorsal fin. Neither are related to right whales: these dolphins are lithe, fast, smooth-skinned, toothed cetaceans – quite the opposite of right whales.

Range and habitat
Delfín de liso (Latin America).

Distinguishing features
The only dolphins in the southern ocean without a dorsal fin.

Description
Length: 6-8 feet.
Teeth: 44-49 on each side of each jaw.
Color: black to purplish-brown above; white below and on flippers and underside of tail.
Body: slender. Narrow tail stock. No dorsal keel or fin. Short beak with no forehead or chin. Narrow flukes.

Range and habitat
Offshore southern temperate and subantarctic waters.

Habits
Travels in groups of 3 to 200-300, often in association with dusky dolphins (**62**) and pilot whales. Seems to be wary of ships. According to Cruickshank and Brown, who have observed the species off South Africa, the color differences on the flippers, head and body may permit individual identification studies.

Diet
Lanternfish; squid.

Reproduction
Unknown.

Status
Numbers unknown, but apparently common.

Southern right whale dolphins race through the off-shore waters of South Africa.

P. E. Malan / courtesy R. A. Cruickshank

"Pelorus Jack" was the nickname New Zealanders gave to a friendly Risso's dolphin who for 24 years around the turn of the century greeted and accompanied ships across Pelorus Sound—until he was found dead, a victim of gunshot wounds.

Other names

Grampus, gray grampus, delfín de Risso (Latin America), dauphin de Risso (France), hana gondō kujira (Japan).

Distinguishing features

Scarred white or gray skin; blunt head; tall curved dorsal fin.

Description

Length: about 10-13 feet.
Teeth: 7 or less on each side of lower jaw, none in upper.
Color: white to silver gray, except for dark dorsal fin, flukes and outside of flippers. Dark patch around eye. Scratch marks and oval scars from squid attacks.
Body: robust, with tall curved dorsal fin. Head is blunt with no beak. Long, pointed flippers. Broad flukes deeply notched.
Calves: about 5 feet at birth and uniformly light gray. As juveniles, skin changes to almost black before lightening.

Range and habitat

Tropical and warm temperate waters of the deep world ocean.

Habits

Travels in groups of a dozen or less up to several hundred. Acrobatic.

Diet

Squid; rarely fish.

Reproduction

Unknown.

Status

Unknown but probably numerous. Some are taken by shore-based whalers and for oceanaria, mainly in Japan.

M. Nakajima

Risso's dolphins perform at Japan's Izu-Mito Sea Paradise.

This light bluish-gray dolphin with the face of a beluga whale inhabits the rivers, lakes, and coastal waters from the Bay of Bengal to New Guinea and northern Australia.

Other names
Mahakam River dolphin or pesut maha-kam (Indonesia), lumba lumba (Malaysia).

Distinguishing features
Bulbous head, small rounded fin. Body looks gray, even white, as it breaks the surface of muddy river water. The finless porpoise (**44**), which frequents the same waters, is much smaller and has no dorsal fin.

Description
Length: about 6½-8 feet.
Teeth: 12-15 on each side of lower jaw; 12-19 on each side, upper.
Body: chunky, with small rounded dorsal fin and flippers. Blunt, beakless head with large melon.
Calves: 25 inches at birth.

Range and habitat
Fresh water rivers, lakes and shallow coastal waters of southeast Asia from the Bay of Bengal to northern Australia.

Habits
Travels in groups of 3-10. Often spits water from its mouth as it spy-hops. Reason for this behavior has not been explained, but in an Indonesian oceanarium several have been trained to reproduce it on command.

Diet
Fish.

Reproduction
Gestation: about a year.

Status
Numbers unknown, but apparently fairly common within its range.

Tas'an / Jaya Ancol Oceanarium

An Irrawaddy dolphin gives birth in an oceanarium, at Jakarta, Indonesia.

From captive and scant wild encounters, this rare dolphin is reported to be aggressive – like the pygmy killer whale (**73**) with which it is often confused.

Other names
Electra dolphin, Hawaiian blackfish, many-toothed blackfish, kazuha gondō kujira (Japan).

Distinguishing features
Much smaller than the false killer whale (**74**), but almost impossible to distinguish at sea from the pygmy killer whale. At very close range, it may be possible to notice the usually more pointed tips of the melon-headed whale's flippers and the presence of a ventral keel. The snout may also be a little more pointed.

Description
Length: 6-8 feet, up to 9 feet.
Teeth: small and numerous, 21-24 each side lower, 22-26 each side upper.
Color: black, whitish skin on lips. Lighter on belly, with white regions around genital and anal openings. Anchor-shaped gray patch on chest between flippers.
Body: slender, with rounded head tapering to blunt point with indistinct beak. Prominent, falcate dorsal fin.
Calves: 3.7 feet and 33 pounds (from male calf caught in a tuna net).

Range and habitat
Tropical and subtropical waters of the world ocean.

Habits
The few observations in the wild have been of large herds – up to 500. Most of what we know about them comes from mass strandings.

Diet
Fish; squid.

Reproduction
Unknown.

Status
Unknown. The species was only known from skeletons until a live specimen was caught in Japan in 1963. In 1965, a herd of about 500 swam into Suruga Bay, Honshu; about half of them were caught and eaten, but scientists had a good look and the new genus *Peponocephala* was established in 1966.

A rare melon-headed whale stranded on an Australian beach.

In captivity the ferocious pygmy killer has killed dolphins in its tank and may deserve the "killer" label far more than its larger and better known namesake, orca (**75**).

Other names
Blackfish, orca pigméo (Latin America), yume gondō kujira (Japan).

Distinguishing features
Much smaller than the false killer whale (**74**), but almost impossible to distinguish at sea from the melon-headed whale (**72**). At very close range, it may be possible to notice the usually more rounded tip of the pygmy killer's flippers and snout.

Description
Length: about 7½ feet, up to about 9 feet.
Teeth: 8-13 in each row above and below.
Color: black or dark gray, often with cape. White area on belly sometimes extends up the flanks. Mouth area is white, usually lips, sometimes chin too (looks like a white "goatee").
Body: slender, with rounded head and no beak. Prominent, falcate dorsal fin.

Range and habitat
The subtropical and especially tropical waters of the world ocean.

Habits
Groups of 5-10 up to 50, rarely more.

Diet
Unknown, but reports of preying on other dolphin species, especially the young.

Reproduction
Unknown.

Status
Unknown, but rarely seen.

Robert L. Pitman / Stephen Leatherwood

Pygmy killer whales ride the bow of a research vessel.

The false killer whale or "pseudorca" recently joined the killer whale (75) on the short list of whales which, at least sometimes, feed on other whales. False killers off Hawaii were recently seen attacking and killing a humpback whale calf.

Other names

Pseudorque (France), oki gondō kujira (Japan), orca falsa (Latin America).

Distinguishing features

All black except for faint anchor patch on chest. Tapered head. Unique long "bent" flippers with hump-like elbow at mid-point. Tall dorsal fin at mid-body.

Description

Length: up to 18 feet for males and 16 feet for females.
Weight: 3,000 pounds for males.
Teeth: 8-11 large teeth in each half of each jaw.
Color: all black with dark-gray anchor-shaped mark on chest.

Body: long and slim with gently tapering head. Variable dorsal fin but usually tall (up to 16 inches) and curved. Flukes pointed at tips.
Calves: 5-6 feet at birth, are lighter gray.

Range and habitat

Offshore tropical and warm temperate waters of the world ocean.

Habits

Highly gregarious in groups of 2-50, but 200 or more sometimes encountered. Potential size of groups is indicated by 1946 stranding of 800 false killer whales at La Plata, Argentina – the largest mass stranding of cetaceans ever recorded. Speed estimated at 14-16 mph. Often approaches ships and will bow ride. Bottlenose dolphins (57) are sometimes seen travelling with them.

Diet

Squid; pelagic fishes (mahi-mahi, yellowfin tuna, bonita); occasionally dolphins

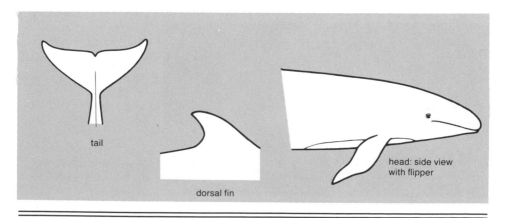

tail

dorsal fin

head: side view with flipper

and apparently sick or young humpback whales.

Reproduction
Calves may be born at any time of year.

Status
Numbers unknown. A few taken in small whale fisheries and by oceanaria.

(Above) *A false killer whale breaches in Hawaii's Sea Life Park.* (Below) *False killer whales race through waters of the eastern tropical Pacific.*

Eighteenth-century Spanish whalers called them "whale-killers" after watching them hunt in packs, subduing large baleen whales and feasting on the lips and tongues.

Other names

Orca, killer, blackfish, épaulard (Québec), spaekhogger (Norway), hahyrna (Iceland), kosatka (Russia), sakamata (Japan), orca (Latin America).

Distinguishing features

The tall dorsal fin – up to 6 feet high and erect on mature males; up to about 2 feet high and falcate on females and immature males. The white "eye patch" situated above and behind the eye, plus the white flank and belly, stand out against the glossy black body.

Description

Length: males average 23 feet, up to 32 feet; females are about 20 feet, up to 28 feet.
Weight: up to 8 tons.
Teeth: 10-13 conical teeth on each side of each jaw.
Body: robust, with conical head, sometimes with hint of beak. Dorsal fin tall, variable in shape. Large, paddle-shaped flippers (males 2-3 times larger than females).
Calves: about 7 feet long and 450 pounds at birth; have no saddle patch and, for the first months of life, are pinkish-orange or tan on their bellies and eye patches.

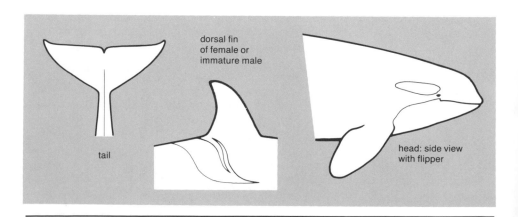

tail

dorsal fin of female or immature male

head: side view with flipper

Range and habitat
World ocean, especially cooler inshore waters, but also pelagic.

Habits
Travels in pods of 5-20 (up to 50) – permanent close-knit groups composed of males, females and young. Each pod has its own dialect or unique set of sounds. Pods often travel together for hours or days in superpods of more than 100 whales. Single pods average 3-4 knots, while superpods travel 5-6 knots. Top speed is estimated at 25 knots, close to 30 mph. To jump clear of the water, an orca must reach an exit speed of at least 11 yards per second or 22½ mph.

Diet
Fishes (salmon, cod, herring, etc.), marine mammals (seals, sea lions, at least 25 whale and dolphin species); squid; birds; leatherback sea turtle.

Reproduction
Gestation: about 14 months. Calves nurse for at least 1 year, maybe 2. In the Pacific Northwest, cows give birth on average once every 10 years (though some have given birth every 3 years).

Status
World population unknown, but apparently not endangered. Some whaling in small whale fisheries off Norway, Japan and in the Antarctic may have reduced local concentrations. Live-captures for oceanaria have occurred off British Columbia, Washington, Japan and Iceland.

Peter Thomas

(Above) *A killer whale spy-hops off northern Vancouver Island.* (Below) *Splashing with its tail, a killer whale plays on its side.*

Graeme Ellis / courtesy Michael A. Bigg

Travelling in herds of hundreds, even thousands, long-finned pilot whales seem to follow a leader or pilot.

Other names
Pothead, blackfish, chaudron (France), calderon or ballena piloto (Latin America).

Distinguishing features
Robust body with bulbous head. Black except for light anchor-shaped patch on belly. Dorsal fin low and broad-based, ahead of mid-body. Long, narrow flippers. Length of flippers may be used to distinguish long-finned pilot whales from short-finned pilot whales (**77**) in the North Atlantic: adult long-finned pilot whales have pectoral fins or flippers at least 1/5 of its body length; adult short-finned pilot whales have flippers up to 1/6 of body length. It is impossible to note these differences at sea; the overlapping range of the 2 species, however, is not extensive. (There is some overlap in these and other subtle "differences" – especially in the North Pacific – that creates confusion and constant argument even among taxonomists.)

Description
Length: about 13 feet on average, up to 20 feet, males larger than females.
Teeth: 7-12 on each side of each jaw.
Body: robust, with bulbous head (squarish in mature males) and low, thick dorsal fin.
Calves: 5 1/2 feet at birth.

Range and habitat
Cool temperate waters of the world ocean, nearshore and pelagic (some taxonomic controversy).

Habits
Canadian biologist David E. Sergeant researched summer groups of pilot whales off Newfoundland. He found the large herds contained twice as many cows as bulls, with one or more bulls "controlling" the harem. These bulls were often scarred from apparent battles over females.

Diet
Squid; fishes (if squid unavailable).

Reproduction
Gestation: 15-16 months. Calves nurse for about 20 months. Cows give birth on average once every 3 1/3 years.

Status
Numbers unknown. This species has been heavily whaled in the North Atlantic off Norway and Newfoundland.

Carola Sampera

Long-finned pilot whales in the western Mediterranean.

Short-finned pilot whales are very similar to their long-finned namesake, but are restricted to tropical and warm temperate waters of the world ocean. They too are social, though their groups are usually smaller than long-finned assemblies.

Other names
Pothead, blackfish, pilot whale, calderon or ballena piloto (Latin America), kobire gondō kujira (Japan).

Distinguishing features
Robust body with bulbous head. Black except for light anchor-shaped patch on belly. Dorsal fin low and broad-based, ahead of mid-body. Long, narrow flippers– but shorter than long-finned pilot whale (**76**).

Short-finned pilot whale breaches off Santa Catalina Island, California.

Description
Length: up to about 18 feet for males, 13 feet for females.
Teeth: 7-9 in each side of each jaw.
Body: robust, with bulbous head (squar-ish in mature males). Low, thick dorsal fin.
Calves: about 4½ feet at birth.

Range and habitat
Tropical and warm temperate waters of the world ocean, nearshore and pelagic.

Habits
Herds of a few to several hundred travel in tightly organized subgroups of adult males, cows and calves, and juveniles. They often spread out in long lines all abreast – probably a hunting maneuver. Squid abundance seems to determine movements for most groups, though regular inshore "residents" have been noted off southern California and in other areas. Herds susceptible to mass stranding.

Diet
Squid; variety of fish.

Reproduction
Gestation: probably 15-16 months. Calves nurse for 1-2 years. Cows may give birth every 3 years or more.

Status
Numbers unknown. A few are taken in small whale fisheries and for oceanaria.

A humpback whale blows alongside a whale watching vessel in Massachusetts Bay.

The Places
Guide to Subject Headings

Species
The number after each species refers to its listing in the species section and provides easy access to it. "Common" species can be seen from lookouts and available tours, ferries and cruises. Other species that are common to *offshore* waters of a given state or country but inaccessible may be listed as sporadic or rare, or not listed at all. On the other hand, for example, the rare right whales which can be reliably found in certain areas will be listed as "common" in those few areas. *Viewing access is the determining factor*. More specific information about time of year and exact locale is included under Lookouts and/or Tours.

Lookouts
Viewpoints from land accessible by car or hiking trail. Sightings from lookouts are rarely guaranteed, but patience and sometimes repeated visits will sooner or later reward. Binoculars are usually essential (for more suggestions, see Appendix 1), as are calm seas.

Tours
Ongoing commercial whale-watching tours, plus natural-history tours on which whales or dolphins are reliably seen and are at least part of the itinerary. Prices – in US dollars unless marked otherwise – are of course subject to change.

Ferries and Cruises
Regularly scheduled ferries and cruise ships on which whales and dolphins are regularly but incidentally seen. In most cases, ferries and cruises provide at best passing glimpses of cetaceans. Yet these opportunities are of interest in areas where few or no tours and lookouts exist.

Weather/Sea Notes
In general, calm water is better than rippled water and rippled water is better than choppy water. When waves start to whitecap, whale watching becomes very difficult. Sunny days are good for photography, but overcast days – minus the glare on the water – are often better for sightings.

Laws/Guidelines
Several states and countries have specific laws and guidelines for whale watching. For US and Canadian laws and guidelines see the section at the end of each country. See also General Guidelines for Whale Watching on page 116.

Oceanaria
Not exactly "whale watching". Yet the performing dolphins and killer whales in oceanaria do allow a close-up look at various species. Many whale watchers first become intrigued with cetaceans watching captive dolphins. Too, oceanaria are often good sources of information about local populations of whales and dolphins, and some even lead whale-watching tours of their own.

Museums

Most coastal cities have a whale display, a few whale or dolphin models, perhaps an articulated skeleton from an animal that stranded locally. The world's largest whale exhibit is in the British Museum in London: an entire exhibit hall is devoted to cetaceans. It's at least a step down to the whale exhibits of North America and the rest of the world. But then England, unlike North America in particular, has few *live* whales and dolphins, or at least few whale-watching opportunities, off its coast.

More information

Tourist bureaus are valuable sources of information: a few, like those in California, have current brochures on whale tours. Most have free road maps, brochures on state and provincial parks (where many whale lookouts are located), plus information on museums, oceanaria, hotels, camp grounds, restaurants. Most countries have tourism offices in New York, Toronto and London, and other large cities around the world. For the location of these offices, if not listed in this book, contact the nearest consulate or public library.

General Guidelines for Whale Watching

There is no doubt that whale watchers sometimes harass whales. Some of the harassment is ignorance: the excited boater pursuing closer and closer until almost on top of the whale, or driving in tight, high-speed circles around it. More often the harassment is inadvertent – for example when a boat cruises over a submerged whale, surprising it and the boat crew.

Some harassment is unavoidable if we are to watch whales at all. But how much can a whale take? Is harassment a serious problem or an inconsequential by-product of whale watching? To these questions there are few easy answers. The debate continues. Meantime, in the last decade, governments in some states and countries have begun to formulate laws, especially in the United States. (See United States: Laws/Guidelines page 155.)

The U.S. Marine Mammal Protection Act of 1972 was not devised to defend whales from whale watchers, but it does forbid the harassment of marine mammals. In the popular whale-watching areas of offshore Hawaii and California, the National Marine Fisheries Service, the federal agency charged with enforcing the Marine Mammal Protection Act, has attempted to define harassment, designing specific regulations. (See Hawaii and California: Laws/Guidelines page 154 and page 150.)

Drawing up general guidelines to cover all whale watching is difficult. An abiding concern for the animals is essential but not enough. Guidelines vary widely according to the situation. Whale watching from land, for example, would seem completely unobtrusive, yet noisy whale watchers can disturb whales resting or rubbing close to shore. Quiet is usually crucial for observing any animal. On the sea, however, many whale species seem to "prefer" the whale-watching boat with a steady engine over whale watchers in kayaks or sailboats who by accident or design suddenly "appear".

A conscientious whale watcher knows the species he is watching and the range of its behavior. He is in no hurry to draw close to a whale. He enjoys watching its undisturbed behavior from a distance, offering the whale the option to come to him. When he finds himself near a whale, which soon happens to all whale watchers, he doesn't panic. Calmly watching, he senses any sign of annoyance from the whale and respects the distance the animal wants to maintain. A conscientious whale watcher also understands the importance of good boat-handling skills and has local knowledge of the whale-watching area: tides, weather, currents, food distribution, water depths, etc. I do not recommend that prospective whale watchers rent a boat and go out alone looking for whales. There is no need to with the wide variety of tours available. Also, it's important, particularly in popular whale-watching areas, to keep boat traffic to a minimum.

If you're on a budget, watch them from land at one of the many "sure" spots, like the California coast during the gray whale migration. If you have your own boat and you know the area and there are no tours or satisfactory lookouts available – and if you have some prior experience with whales – then your own whale-watching cruise may be appropriate. Of course, if you're a salt-water fisherman or a diver in one of the areas covered in this guide, then you've probably encountered whales already. A good naturalist guide, however, is the quickest way to develop an eye and a sensibility for whale watching.

In addition to these guidelines and recommendations, don't neglect safety. The one time you forget the life jackets or survival suits may be the time you need them. Safety should be the province of the captain or tour operator. In these pages I have endeavored to include only reputable tour and charter companies. But be aware! If you have doubts about the operation, ask questions. With safety, it's better to err on the side of caution.

Are the whales themselves dangerous? In 1982, in Mexico's Scammon's Lagoon, a gray whale upset a small, local whale-watching boat. Two environmentalists died. These rare fatalities among hundreds of thousands of whale watchers are statistically insignificant, yet the mishap is tragic. It should serve as a reminder that whales are indeed huge animals and even a spy-hop, breach or casual flip of the tail can be "upsetting" for someone or some boat that is in the way. The sometimes violent courtship behavior of humpback whales points up the need to understand whale behavior before watching it. Before researchers off Maui caught the whales fighting, such courtship behavior was often termed "playful". Some play! Whales and dolphins are *wild* animals. In the interest of safety it's useful to review all the connotations that "civilized" humans have of the word "wild". Still, compared to other wild animals, whales are surprisingly gentle toward humans. And most extraordinary of all, as whale watchers know, some of them are even, apparently, *friendly*.

A humpback whale flips its tail as whale watchers sail for home off Massachusetts.

Herring gulls daringly try to snatch food from the mouth of a feeding humpback.

United States: Maine

Species

Common: fin whale (**5**), humpback whale (**7**), minke whale (**2**), harbor porpoise (**40**), right whale (**8**).
Sporadic: Atlantic white-sided dolphin (**58**), long-finned pilot whale (**76**).
Rare: sei whale (**3**), blue whale (**6**), white-beaked dolphin (**63**), beluga (**34**), killer whale (**75**), common dolphin (**50**).

Lookouts

1 One of the best whale-watching lookouts on the US east coast is also the most easterly point in the nation: Quoddy Head. From the cliffs of Quoddy Head State Park near Quoddy Head Light (candy-striped Coast Guard lighthouse), one can see fin whales, harbor porpoises, minke whales, humpback whales and right whales, in approximate order of likelihood. Best time: late July–late Sept. Access is from Maine's coastal Rt. 1. At Whiting, take Rt. 189 for about 10 miles. Proceed through West Lubec; before Lubec is a Texaco station and sign to Quoddy Head Light; turn right and 3 miles later take the left fork which leads to the park.

2 Another summer spot, good for harbor porpoises and the occasional minke whale, is on Mt. Desert Island, near the city of Bar Harbor. From Bar Harbor, take Rt. 233 to Somesville, turning left (south) on Rt. 102. Southwest Harbor is the next town. A mile past town, take 102A along the coast past Manset toward Bass Harbor. The cliffs and headlands along that 5-mile road and Bass Harbor Light near Bass Harbor, are all possible sites.

3 Another more remote spot is the tiny offshore island of Monhegan. It has harbor porpoises with occasional minke, humpback, and fin whales. It is also a great birding spot. Monhegan can be reached via passenger toll ferry from Port Clyde, about 15 miles south of Rockland (76 miles from Bangor). For ferry schedules and information on accommodations: Maine Publicity Bureau, 97 Winthrop St., Hallowell, ME 04347 (Tel. 207-289-2423).

Tours

The chance to see right whales lures many people to Machias, on the northeast coast of Maine, where Norm and Nona Famous offer naturalist-led programs to see whales, seals and seabirds. 3- to 5-day packages cost about $125 a day, including meals, lodging at a local inn and airport transportation from Bangor (2 hours away). Right-whale researcher Scott Kraus and his colleagues often guide the whale tours. Whale watchers spend 3–4 days on the water, depending on weather, and quarry includes right, fin, minke and humpback whales, and harbor porpoises. Season: early Aug.–early Oct. Contact: Seafarers, Box 428, RFD 1, Machias, ME 04654, (Tel. 207-255-8810).

The "Seafarers" program in Machias sails aboard the *M/V Seafarer* based in nearby Lubec, but skipper Butch Huntley also offers day trips to see whales from July–early Oct. The all-day tours visit the lower Bay of Fundy and Passamaquoddy Bay region and cost $35. Contact: Seafarers (above) or Butch Huntley, *M/V Seafarer*, 9 High St., Lubec, ME 04652 (Tel. 207-733-5584).

From Northeast Harbor on Mt. Desert

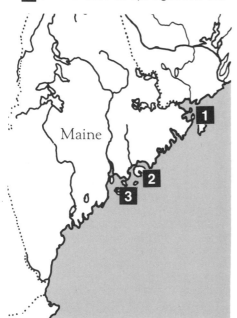

A right whale surfaces in the Bay of Fundy.

Island (near Bar Harbor), "Maine Whale-watch" has full-day naturalist-led whale and seabird cruises aboard the 42-foot *Island Queen*. The itinerary includes Mt. Desert Rock and Seal Island and views of humpbacks, fins, minkes, harbor porpoises, and sometimes right whales or Atlantic white-sided dolphins. Season is June–Sept., with day-trips July–Aug. and weekends only June and Sept. $20 per person. For reservations: Maine Whale-watch, c/o Beal and Bunker, Inc., Cranberry Isles, ME 04625 (Tel. 207-244-3575/7457). For more information: Capt. Bob Bowman, Box 78, Northeast Harbor, ME 04662 (Tel. 207-244-7429).

The Maine Audubon Society and Allied Whale (a non-profit research group affiliated with College of the Atlantic) both organize whale-watching cruises to Stellwagen Bank, Jeffreys Ledge and the lower Bay of Fundy. Chartering whale-watching boats based in Maine, New Hampshire and Massachusetts, both bring along their own naturalists. Programs are excellent. Allied Whale's day trips are on weekends in spring and autumn. Contact: (1) Allied Whale, c/o College of the Atlantic, Bar Harbor, ME 04609 (Tel. 207-288-5015); (2) Maine Audubon Society, Gilsland Farm, 118 US Rt. 1, Falmouth, ME 04105 (Tel. 207-781-2330).

7-day sailing and exploring cruises that include whale and dolphin watching along the Maine coast are offered in July on the 95-foot schooner *Harvey Gamage*. $440 from Rockland. Contact: Oceanic Society Expeditions, Fort Mason Center, Bldg. E, San Francisco, CA 94123 (Tel. 415-441-1106).

Ferries

The 2 car ferries between Maine and Yarmouth, Nova Scotia, often afford a passing look at various cetaceans.

(1) The better of the 2 is the *Bluenose* Bar Harbor, Maine, to Yarmouth, Nova Scotia, run with daily 6-hour sailings from June 19–Sept. 27. Reservations required. Contact: CN Marine, Terminal Supervisor, Bar Harbor, ME 04609 (Tel. 800-341-7981 in eastern US; 800-432-7344 in Maine) or CN Marine, Terminal Supervisor, Yarmouth, N.S. B5A 1K0 Canada (Tel. 902-742-3513). (2) The Portland, Maine to Yarmouth, Nova Scotia, ferry has daily service from early May–Oct. Crossing time is about 12 hours. Reservations required. Contact: Prince of Fundy Cruises, Box 4216, Station A, Portland, ME 04101 (Tel. 207-775-5616).

Weather/Sea Notes

Cold and often rough open sea conditions prevail; fog can be a factor even for watching from lookouts. Large tides.

Museums

Whale exhibit at Gulf of Maine Aquarium, Box 1489, Portland, ME 04104 (Tel. 207-772-2321).

There is a visitors' center with information about whale sightings at the West Quoddy Marine Research Station, Box 9, Lubec, ME 04652 (Tel. 207-733-8895).

More information

Maine Publicity Bureau, 97 Winthrop St., Hallowell, ME 04347 (Tel. 207-289-2423). *For more about whales in the lower Bay of Fundy, see Canada: New Brunswick, p. 162.*

United States: New Hampshire

Species

Common: fin whale (**5**), humpback whale (**7**), minke whale (**2**), Atlantic white-sided dolphin (**58**), harbor porpoise (**40**).
Sporadic: long-finned pilot whale (**76**), right whale (**8**).
Rare: white-beaked dolphin (**63**), common dolphin (**50**), bottlenose dolphin (**57**), killer whale (**75**), beluga (**34**), sei whale (**3**), sperm whale (**13**), Risso's dolphin (**70**).

Tours

Jeffreys Ledge at the north end of Stellwagen Bank is the usual destination of whale-watching boats leaving from New Hampshire and nearby ports in Massachusetts and Maine. From Hampton Beach, Smith and Gilmore offer 4- to 6-hour trips weekdays from May–Sept.

An Atlantic white-sided dolphin breaches off the Massachusetts coast. Note the narrow white patch on its flank.

Jane M. Gibbs

Minkes, fins, humpbacks and Atlantic white-sided dolphins are seen. The ship is the 75-foot *Seafarer*, with moderator on board. $10/person (4-hour cruises); $15 (6 hours). Contact: Smith and Gilmore Fishing Pier, Inc., 3A Ocean Blvd., Hampton Beach, NH 03842 (Tel. 603-926-3503).

From Viking Dock in Portsmouth, Viking of Yarmouth Cruises offers weekend-only tours early May–early June and mid-Sept.–mid-Oct. Naturalist Scott Mercer guides the all-day trips on the 110-foot *Viking Queen*. Adults $20; children $10. Contact: Viking of Yarmouth Cruises, Viking Dock, Market St., Portsmouth, NH 03801 (Tel. 603-431-5500).

Weather/Sea Notes
Windy and cool on the water even in mid-summer; can be cold in spring or fall.

More information
Office of Vacation Travel, Box 856, Concord, NH 03301 (Tel. 603-271-2665).

United States: Massachusetts

Species
Common: fin whale (**5**), humpback whale (**7**), minke whale (**2**), harbor porpoise (**40**), Atlantic white-sided dolphin (**58**).
Sporadic: right whale (**8**), long-finned pilot whale (**76**).
Rare: white-beaked dolphin (**63**), common dolphin (**50**), bottlenose dolphin (**57**), killer whale (**75**), sei whale (**3**), sperm whale (**13**), Risso's dolphin (**70**), beluga (**34**), striped dolphin (**53**).

Lookouts
The sandy dunes of Cape Cod, overlooking Cape Cod Bay, are good for watching families of fin whales from April–Oct., as they parade single-file into the bay looking for food. **1** One spot is 2 miles to the end of the road west of Wellfleet off US Rt. 6–from a high parking lot above the beach. **2** The best spot is usually Race Point, near Provincetown, at the tip of Cape Cod. Follow US Rt. 6 to Race Point Rd. The Cape Cod National Seashore Visitors' Center near the point has a high view, and researchers there should be up to date on whale sightings. Researchers from the Provincetown Center for Coastal Studies have logged a few sightings of the rare right whale in this area during winter and spring. For most species, summer is best, however. Besides fins and possibly rights, you may see humpbacks, minkes, harbor porpoises and Atlantic white-sided dolphins. Both the Race Point and Wellfleet sites are within the Cape Cod National Seashore. Contact: Cape Cod National Seashore, South Wellfleet, MA 02663 (Tel. 617-349-3785). To report whale sightings, contact the Provincetown Center for Coastal Studies (Tel. 617-487-3622).

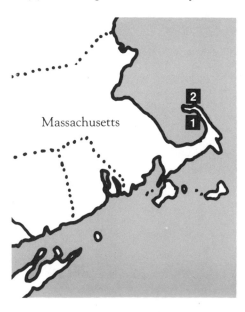

Massachusetts

Tours
The hub of east coast whale watching is Stellwagen Bank. Its popularity with whales and whale watchers has spawned a million-dollar industry in New England, and the research of biologists like Charles "Stormy" Mayo (Provincetown Center for Coastal Studies), Mason Weinrich (Cetacean Research Unit of Gloucester Fishermen's Museum) and others is an important by-product. A summer feeding area for cetaceans, Stellwagen Bank is an 18-mile-long narrow bank,

A humpback "stands" on its head.

the southern end of which is situated about 7 miles north of Provincetown. Stellwagen Bank is easily accessible from eastern Massachusetts' ports: Provincetown, Plymouth, Boston, Salem, Gloucester, and Newburyport.

From Provincetown: (1) On April 15, 1975, *Dolphin III* made the first organized whale-watching trip on the US east coast. Today *Dolphin IV* and *V*, captained by Al and Aaron Avellar, are the most popular whale-watching ships on the east coast. Stormy Mayo and his research group guide the cruises, show video tapes of whale behavior, and at the same time carry on research; besides sharing in the whale excitement, the public in effect participates in a scientific expedition. Based at MacMillan Pier, Provincetown, the Dolphin fleet sails 2–3 times daily from April–late Oct. Adults $12; Children $10. Contact: Capt. Al Avellar, The Dolphin Fleet,

MacMillan Pier, Provincetown, MA 02657 (Tel. 617-487-1900/off season: 255-3857). For schedule: The Dolphin Fleet, Box 162, Eastham, MA 02642. Dolphin fleet trips may also be booked through charter groups that organize excursions. Prices vary. Some are package trips that include lodging and bus fare from another city. Most are open to the public. Contact: (A) Greenpeace New England, 286 Congress St., Boston, MA 02210 (Tel. 617-542-8107); (B) The American Cetacean Society New York/New Jersey, Box 232, New Milford, N.J. 07646 (Tel. 201-335-1090); (C) Maine Audubon Society, Gilsland Farm, 118 US Rt. 1, Falmouth, ME 04105 (Tel. 207-781-2330); (D) Kay Money, Whale Research & Rescue Fund, Blue Sky Adventures, Box 126, Oak

Bill Byrne

Flukes of a sounding humpback whale, off Cape Ann, Massachusetts.

Ridge, NJ 07438 (Tel. 201-697-7233); (E) Connecticut Cetacean Society, Box 9145, Wethersfield, CT 06109; (F) Long Island Sound Taskforce of The Oceanic Society, Stamford Marine Center, Magee Avenue, Stamford CT 06902 (Tel. 203-327-9786); (G) Mystic Marinelife Aquarium, Coogan Blvd., Mystic, CT 06355 (Tel. 203-536-9631); (H) Nature Center for Environmental Activities, 10 Woodside Ave., Westport, CT 06880 (Tel. 203-227-7253); (I) Friends of the Museum of Comparative Zoology, Harvard University, Cambridge, MA 02138 (Tel. 617-495-2463); (J) New York Zoological Society, Zoological Park, Bronx, NY 10460 (Tel. 212-220-5100). (2) The *Ranger V* has 2 daily ½-day trips from MacMillan Pier, spring through autumn. Adults $10; children $8. Contact: Jerry Costa, *Ranger V*, MacMillan Pier, Provincetown, MA 02657 (Tel. 617-487-1582). New Jersey residents can take a package whale trip aboard the *Ranger IV*; contact: the Marine Mammal Stranding Center, 839 Massachusetts Ave., Atlantic City, NJ 08401 (Tel. 609-348-5018). (3) Princess Cruise Lines, based in Plymouth, also offers ½-day

trips (1 a day). The 94-foot *Cape Cod Princess* departs midday from Fishermen's Wharf Marina in Provincetown – May 1– Oct. 12. Adults $9.75. Contact: Princess Cruise Lines, Mayflower II State Pier, Box 192, Plymouth, MA 02361 (Tel. 617-747-2400/487-2274).

From Plymouth: (1) The *Capt. John & Son I* and *II* depart from Town Wharf at the harbor in Plymouth weekends April– Oct. 2 daily ½-day trips in July and Aug. Naturalists show films on board. Adults $13; children $10. Contact: Capt. John Boats, Inc. 117 Standish Ave., Plymouth, MA 02360 (Tel. 617-746-2643). (2) Spring and fall trips aboard *Capt. John & Son* may be booked through Greenpeace. Adults $20; Students $17. Contact: Greenpeace New England, 286 Congress St., Boston, MA 02210 (Tel. 617-542-8134). (3) Since 1977, the non-profit Web of Life Outdoor Education Center has conducted ½-day whale-watching trips aboard *Capt. John & Son* with slide shows and naturalist interpretation. Weekends only in May, June, Sept. and Oct. 2 daily ½-day trips. Adults $13; children $12.50. Contact: Web of Life Outdoor Education Center, Box 530, Carver, MA 02330 (Tel. 617-866-5353). (4) Princess Cruise Lines has day-trips, on the *Cape Cod Princess*, that stop at Province-

(Above) *A humpback displays open-mouth feeding behavior to whale watchers off Massachusetts.* (Below) *A mother and calf humpback dive in the waters off Stellwagen Bank.*

town *en route* to Stellwagen Bank to pick up more passengers. May 1–Oct. 12. Adults $13.50. Departure from Mayflower II State Pier. Contact: Princess Cruise Lines, Box 192, Plymouth, MA 02361 (Tel. 617-747-2400/487-2274).

From Boston: (1) J. Michael Williamson of Pelagic Systems Research has led whale-watching tours since 1978. May to early autumn trips last 8 hours, departing Boston Harbor aboard the 85-foot *Virginia C II*. Also special school trips out of Salem. Adults $18; children $12. Contact: J. Michael Williamson, Massachusetts Whale Watch, Box 213, Beverly Farms, MA 01915 (Tel. 617-468-7147). (2) Saturday-only full-day trips, May–Sept. aboard *Virginia C II*. Adults $18; children $12. Reservations: A.C. Cruise Line, 28 Northern Ave., Boston, MA 02110 (Tel. 617-426-8419). (3) The New England Aquarium offers daily 5-hour cruises that depart from the aquarium. Adults $20; children $16 (aquarium members get discount). Spring to early autumn. Contact: New England Aquarium, Central Wharf, Boston, MA 02110 (Tel. 617-742-8830).

From Salem: naturalists lead 1/2-day

trips aboard the 65-foot *New England Star*. Tuesday through Sunday from Memorial Day to Labor Day; weekends only in May and Sept. Adults $15; children $10. Departs from Pickering Wharf. Contact: Salem Whale Watch, Barnegat Transportation, Pickering Wharf, Salem, MA 01970 (Tel. 617-745-6070).

From Gloucester: (1) The Cetacean Research Unit of the Gloucester Fishermen's Museum organizes whale watches aboard *Daunty II* or *Miss Gloucester*. Mason Weinrich, Mark Cappellino, and other naturalists, provide scientific background. 1/2-day trips, twice daily from May–Sept. Adults $15; children $12. Contact: Gloucester Fishermen's Museum, Cetacean Research Unit, Rogers and Porter Sts., Box 159, Gloucester, MA 01930 (Tel. 617-283-1940). (2) *Daunty II* trips can also be booked through Gloucester Sightseeing Cruises, Inc., Cape Ann Whale Watch, 12 Clarendon St., Gloucester, MA 01930 (Tel. 617-283-5110). (3) *Miss Gloucester* trips can be booked through Capt. Bill's Whale Watch, 9 Traverse St., Gloucester, MA 01930 (Tel. 617-283-6995). (4) The Yankee fleet has guided twice-daily spring through autumn tours. Adults $15; children $10. Departures from Cape Ann Marina. Contact: The Yankee Fleet,

A fin whale passes a sail boat on Jeffreys Ledge, off Massachusetts.

Jane M. Gibbs

An Atlantic white-sided dolphin bow rides off Cape Cod.

W. Rossier

Gloucester Whalewatch, 75 Essex Ave., Route 133, Box 589, Gloucester, MA 01930 (Tel. 617-283-6089). (5) Whale watching out of Gloucester can also be arranged from Connecticut through a package tour company. Contact: New Britain Transportation Co., 257 Woodlawn Rd., Berlin, CT 06037 (Tel. 203-828-0511).

From Newburyport (near New Hampshire): naturalist Scott Mercer guides full-day excursions to northern Stellwagen Bank and Jeffreys Ledge aboard the 70-foot *Cetacea*. Daily except Monday, July 2–Labor Day; weekends only in May, June, Sept. and Oct. Cruises depart Hilton's Dock, a 1/2 mile east of Rt. 1, along the Merrimack River. Adults $20; children $15. Special sunset whale watches (4 hours) cost $15. Contact: New England Whale Watch, Inc., Box 825, Hampton, NH 03842 (Tel. 603-926-0952). These cruises can also be booked through Hilton & Strout, 54 Merrimac St., Newburyport, MA 01950 (Tel. 617-465-9885).

Educational whale-watching voyages to Stellwagen Bank include: (1) The Ocean Research and Education Society's sail and study programs for students who want to help research whales and earn college credit. Based in Gloucester, the non-profit "ORES" operates the 144-foot barkentine *Regina Maris* with frequent programs to study humpback and other whales on Stellwagen Bank. Tuition for a 12-week sail and study semester is $4,900 (includes living expenses for 6 weeks at sea but not for 6 weeks at shore-based classroom in Gloucester). Occasional non-credit expeditions cost $700 for 10 days–2 weeks. Excellent instructors like Ken Balcomb whose photo-ID work with humpback and killer whales is well known. Contact: The Ocean Research and Education Society, Inc., 19 Harbor Loop, Gloucester, MA 01930 (Tel. 617-283-1475). (2) The Sea Education Association's undergraduate program in oceanography includes research cruises aboard the 125-foot *Westward* to whale areas in the western North Atlantic. Contact: Sea Education Assoc., Inc., Box 6, Woods Hole, MA 02543 (Tel. 617-540-3954). (3) The Academy of the Atlantic has 2–3-week summer educational whale expeditions that feature visits to whaling museums, research centers and a week on Stellwagen Bank. For students aged 12–16. $1675. Paddington Marine

Enterprises, Box 108, Truro, MA 02666 (Tel. 617-487-2184). (4) The School for Field Studies in Cambridge offers month-long credit courses in marine mammal biology and cetacean behavioral ecology to undergraduates or advanced secondary students. Contact: School for Field Studies, 50 Western Ave., Cambridge, MA 02138 (Tel. 617-497-9000).

Weather/Sea Notes
Somewhat more benign than most open-ocean whale watching, but come prepared; can be cold and sometimes rough even during summer.

Oceanaria
Bottlenose dolphins at the New England Aquarium, Central Wharf, Boston, MA 02110 (Tel. 617-742-8830).

Museums
Whale skeletons exhibited in Victorian splendor at Museum of Comparative Zoology, Harvard University, Cambridge, MA 02138 (Tel. 617-495-1910).

Kendall Whaling Museum, 27 Everett St., Box 297, Sharon, MA 02067 (Tel. 617-784-5642).

Old Dartmouth Historical Society Whaling Museum, 18 Johnny Cake Hill, New Bedford, MA 02740 (Tel. 617-997-0046).

More information
Massachusetts Division of Marketing, 100 Cambridge St., Boston, MA 02202 (Tel. 617-727-3201).

For Provincetown: Cape Cod Chamber of Commerce, Hyannis, MA 02601 (Tel. 617-362-3225).

For Plymouth: Plymouth County Development Council, Box 1620, Pembroke, MA 02349 (Tel. 617-826-3136).

For Boston: Greater Boston Convention and Tourist Bureau, Inc., 15 State St., Boston, MA 02109 (Tel. 617-367-9275).

For Salem, Gloucester and Newburyport: North of Boston Tourist Council, Box 3031, Peabody, MA 01960 (Tel. 617-532-1449).

United States: New York

Species
Common: fin whale (**5**), minke whale (**2**). *Sporadic*: humpback whale (**7**), Atlantic white-sided dolphin (**58**), long-finned pilot whale (**76**), sei whale (**3**).

Tours
From the dock at Montauk, on Long Island, the 72-foot *Finback One* departs weekend mornings May–Sept. 6-hour cruises range up to 20 miles off Montauk, encountering mainly fin and minke whales. Naturalists aboard. Adults $25; children $15. Contact: Okeanos Ocean Research Foundation, Box 776, Hampton Bays, NY 11946 (Tel. 516-728-4522).

Weather/Sea Notes
Ranges from cool to cold at sea; can be rough.

Oceanaria
New York Aquarium, New York Zoological Society, Boardwalk at West 8th St., Seaside Park, Brooklyn, NY 11224 (Tel. 212-266-8500).

Museums
Full-size blue whale and dolphin models at American Museum of Natural History, Central Park West at 79th St., New York, NY 10024 (Tel. 212-873-4225).

More information
New York State Department of Commerce, Division of Tourism, 99 Washington Ave., Albany, NY 12245 (Tel. 518-474-4116).

United States: Maryland

Species
Common: fin whale (**5**), common dolphin (**50**), bottlenose dolphin (**57**), Risso's dolphin (**70**).
Sporadic: minke whale (**2**), sei whale (**3**), long-finned pilot whale (**76**), short-finned pilot whale (**77**), sperm whale (**12**), killer whale (**75**), Atlantic white-sided dolphin (**58**), Atlantic spotted dolphin (**54**), striped dolphin (**53**), right whale (**8**).

Tours
From Talbot Street Pier, 1 block south of the US Rt. 50 bridge in Ocean City, the 65-foot *Mariner* escorts whale and bird watchers to Baltimore Canyon, 60 miles out to sea along the 100 fathom line. *En route*, excellent naturalists led by Ron Naveen point out whales, sea birds, loggerhead sea turtles and 35-foot basking sharks. About 15 year-round day trips (most on Saturdays, with Sunday as an alternate), but best whale season is spring. Fin whales were seen on most April–June trips in 1982–83, and killer whales, sei whales and many dolphins were also recorded. From July–Sept., as the Gulf Stream and its eddies move closer to shore, tropical birds and dolphins (spotted and striped) are sometimes seen. 11- to 12-hour tour. $48/person. Contact: Ron Naveen, 2378 Rt. 97, Cooksville, MD 21723 (Tel. 301-854-6262).

Weather/Sea Notes
The open North Atlantic, if not choppy, is frequently rough. Cool to cold and sometimes wet.

Museums
Full-size blue whale model, dolphin casts, 40-foot basilosaur (fossil whale) at National Museum of Natural History, Smithsonian Institution, 10th St. and Constitution Ave. NW, Washington, DC 20560 (Tel. 202-357-1300).

More information
Office of Tourist Development, 1748 Forest Dr., Annapolis, MD 21401 (Tel. 301-269-3517).

United States: Virginia

Species
Common: bottlenose dolphin (**57**).

Susan Shane

Lookouts
1 From May–Nov., bottlenose dolphins are commonly seen from the shores of Virginia Beach in the southeastern corner of the state. At Seashore State Park there are good camping sites.

Weather/Sea Notes
"Resort weather", but could be windy and rather cool in late fall.

More information
Virginia State Travel Service, 6 N. Sixth St., Richmond, VA 23219 (Tel. 804-786-4484).

These bottlenose dolphins, off Port Aransas, Texas, were individually identified by the nicks and scratches mainly on their dorsal fins.

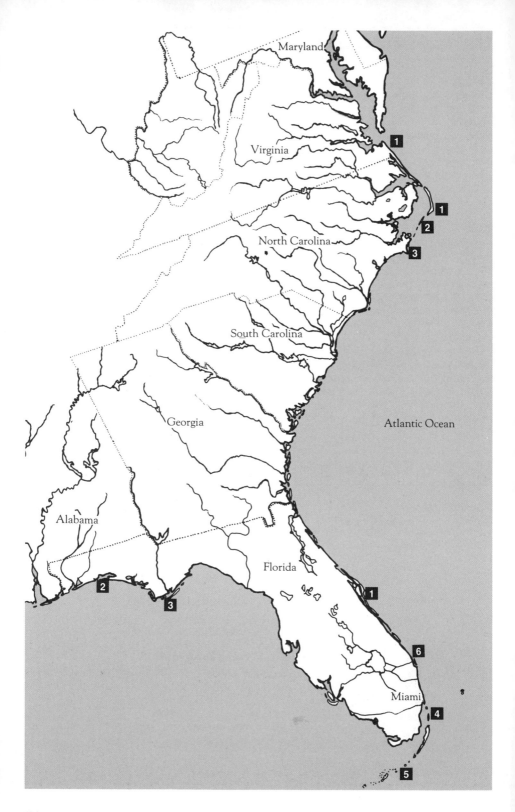

United States: North Carolina

Species
Common: bottlenose dolphin (**57**).

Lookouts
From late March–Nov., bottlenose dolphins range along the beach at **1** Cape Hatteras. During winter, the nearshore population may move south, perhaps to **2** Ocracoke Island where dolphins can be seen year-round from the beach. Even further south, there's more good dolphin watching along the sandy stretches of **3** Cape Lookout National Seashore.

Cape Hatteras National Seashore (which includes Ocracoke Island) is a 70-mile-long stretch of open beach on 3 islands connected to each other and to the mainland by ferries and bridges. Motels; summer camping. For maps and information, contact: Superintendent, Cape Hatteras National Seashore, Rt. 1, Box 675, Manteo, NC 27954.

Cape Lookout National Seashore to the south has no roads and is accessible only by boat. Camping is primitive and open all year. Write: Superintendent, Cape Lookout National Seashore, Box 690, Beaufort, NC 28516.

Weather/Sea Notes
Ranges from hot sunny days in summer to cool, windy winters. Check with park rangers for weather reports.

Museums
Shore-whaling history and skull from extinct Atlantic gray whale at Hampton Mariners Museum, Beaufort, NC 28516 (Tel. 919-728-7317).

More information
Travel and Tourism Division, Dept. of Commerce, 430 N. Salisbury St., Raleigh, NC 27611 (Tel. 919-733-4171).

United States: Florida

Species
Common: bottlenose dolphin (**57**).
Sporadic: Atlantic spotted dolphin (**54**), short-finned pilot whale (**77**).

Lookouts
The bottlenose dolphin – Florida's official salt water mammal – appears inshore year-round, peaking in some Atlantic areas in winter. Numerous possible lookouts from bridges and causeways crossing inland waterways and linking outer islands to mainland. A few of the better areas include: **1** Indian River (part of lagoon-like intracoastal waterway), between Titusville and Melbourne; **2** Choctawhatchee Bay, near Fort Walton Beach (2 state parks with campsites on Rt. 20 north of bay); **3** Apalachicola Bay, near Apalachicola (camping on St. Joseph Peninsula); **4** Biscayne Bay from Miami south including Biscayne National Park; **5** Florida Keys; and, from shore at **6** Jupiter Lighthouse, near Jupiter Inlet Colony, 20 miles north of West Palm Beach.

Tours
No specific whale-watching tours, but sightseeing tour boats regularly encounter bottlenose dolphins. Among boats reporting frequent sightings are: (1) Elliot Key Tour Boat across Biscayne Bay; inexpensive; best on winter mornings; contact: Biscayne National Park, Box 1369, Homestead, FL 33030 (Tel. 305-247-7275); (2) mainland to Shell Island; contact: Fish Hook Shell Island Tours, 4415 Thomas Dr., Panama City, FL 32407 (Tel. 904-234-5100); (3) mainland to Shell Island; contact: Tropic Star Shell Island Tours, 3605 S. Thomas Dr., Panama City, FL 32407 (Tel. 904-235-2809); (4) mainland to Dog Island across St. George Sound; contact: Dog Island Boat Service, Box 737, Carrabelle, FL 32322 (Tel. 904-697-3434); (5) Belle of St. Petersburg sightseeing tours; contact: Belle of St. Petersburg, 400 2nd Ave., St. Petersburg, FL 33701 (Tel. 813-866-3002); (6) 3½-hour Gulf tours; contact: Tin City Queen, 1200 5th Ave., S., Old Marine Marketplace, Naples, FL

Bottlenose dolphins in Florida waters (above) *and bow riding off the Texas coast* (below).

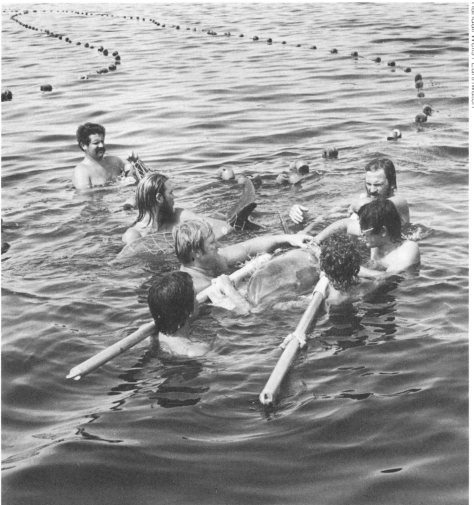

33940 (Tel. 813-261-4792).

A unique opportunity to assist in the research of wild bottlenose dolphins in Sarasota Bay with zoologist Randall Wells is offered by Earthwatch. Earthwatch programs are not tours but offer amateurs a chance to work as *paying* field assistants on research projects. The dolphin project is a several-year effort with 3 2-week research openings during summer. $1,290 plus air fare. Contact: Earthwatch, 10 Juniper Rd., Box 127, Belmont, MA 02178 (Tel. 617-489-3030).

Ferries and Cruises

Bottlenose dolphins are sometimes seen on ferry between mainland and Caladesi

Transferring a bottlenose dolphin from the net to a stretcher for measurement and marking, near Sarasota, Florida.

Island. Caladesi Island Ferry, 11 Palmwood Dr., Dunedin, FL 33528.

Weather/Sea Notes

Sometimes cool on inshore tour boats; lookouts warm to hot year-round. Large bays may be choppy.

Oceanaria

Bottlenose dolphins and killer whales at:
Miami Seaquarium, 4400 Rickenbacker Causeway, Miami, FL 33149 (Tel. 305-361-5705).
Sea World, 7007 Sea World Dr.,

Orlando, FL 32809 (Tel. 305-351-3600). Bottlenose dolphins only at:

Gulfarium, Fort Walton Beach, FL 32548 (Tel. 904-244-5169).

Gulf World, Box 14004, Panama City Beach, FL 32407 (Tel. 904-234-5271).

Marineland of Florida, Rt. 1, Box 122, St. Augustine, FL 32084 (Tel. 904-471-1111).

Ocean World, 1701 SE 17th St., Fort Lauderdale, FL 33316 (Tel. 305-525-6611).

Theater of the Sea, Inc., Box 407, Isla-morada, FL 33036 (Tel. 305-664-2431).

Flipper's Key West, 2407 N. Roosevelt Blvd., Key West, FL 33040 (Tel. 305-294-8827).

Busch Gardens/The Dark Continent, Box 9185, Tampa, FL 33674 (Tel. 813-988-5171).

More information

Florida Dept. of Commerce, Division of Tourism, 107 W. Gaines St., Tallahassee, FL 32304 (Tel. 904-488-7300).

United States: Alaska – Southeast

Species

Common: minke whale (2), humpback whale (7), gray whale (1), killer whale (75), Dall's porpoise (45), fin whale (5). *Sporadic*: harbor porpoise (40), sperm whale (12), Pacific white-sided dolphin (59), sei whale (3), blue whale (6). *Rare*: right whale (8), North Pacific giant bottlenose whale (17).

Tours

The Stephens Passage-Frederick Sound area, south of Juneau, is one of the main humpback summer-feeding grounds in southeast Alaska. Watching the humpbacks is the focus of 8- and 13-day natural-history cruises offered in late June, July and Aug. Extras are minke and killer whales, Dall's porpoises and other wildlife, including eagles. Also glaciers and abandoned whaling stations. About $150/day. Contact: (1) Oceanic Society Expeditions, Fort Mason Center, Bldg. E, San Francisco, CA 94123 (Tel. 415-441-1106). (2) Biological Journeys, 1876 Ocean Drive, McKinleyville, CA 95521 (Tel. 707-839-0178).

Nature Expeditions International offers 6 guided wildlife expeditions that include good humpback possibilities and certain sightings of Dall's porpoises and minke whales. The 16-day trips depart mid-June–mid-Aug. and time is divided between the 50-foot *M/V Chaik* and hiking excursions. 2 trips focus on Inland Passage; 4 include Mt. McKinley in central Alaska and Katmai National Park in southwestern Alaska. $2190–$2590 plus air fare. Contact: Nature Expeditions International, Box 11496, Eugene, OR 97440 (Tel. 503-484-6529).

Whales are part of the itinerary for the "Alaskan Odyssey" cruises aboard the 152-foot *Majestic Explorer*. 4 departures May–Sept. with best whale possibilities in early Sept. 13 days from about $2,500 plus air fare. Contact: Special Expeditions, Inc., 133 E. 55th St., New York, NY 10022 (Tel. 212-888-7980); or Exploration Cruise Lines, 1500 Metropolitan Park Bldg., Olive Way at Boren St., Seattle, WA 98101 (Tel. 206-624-8551).

Alaska Discovery, Inc., has naturalist-led 1-day to 2-week kayak and canoe tours that visit many of southeast Alaska's prime whale and porpoise inlets. Many summer departures at $100/day and up plus air fare. Contact: Alaska Discovery, Box 26, Gustavus, AK 99826 (Tel. 907-697-3431).

More southeast Alaska expeditions that include whale watching are offered by: (1) Wilderness Travel, 1760 Solano Ave., Berkeley, CA 94707 (Tel. 415-524-5111); (2) American Museum of Natural History, Central Park W. at 79th St., New York, NY 10024 (Tel. 212-873-1440); (3) Ecosummer Canada Expeditions Ltd., 1516 Duranleau St., Vancouver, B.C. V6H 3S4 Canada (Tel. 604-669-7741); (4) Ocean Voyages, Inc., 1709 Bridgeway, Sausalito, CA 94965 (Tel. 415-332-4681); (5) Glacier Bay Yacht/Seaplane Tours, Box 424, Juneau, AK 99802 (Tel. 907-586-6835).

Ferries and Cruises

Summer cruiseships, sailing from California, Seattle, and Vancouver through the Inside Passage to southeast Alaska often advertise the possibility of seeing whales and porpoises. July and Aug. are the best

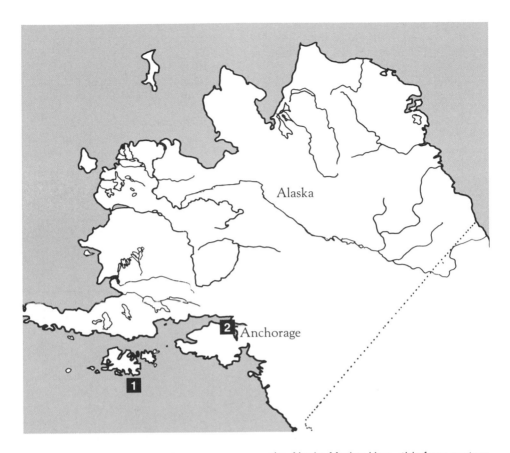

whale months. Contact: (1) Canadian Cruise Lines, Ltd., 401-1208 Wharf St., Victoria, B.C. V8W 3B9 Canada (Tel. 604-386-3844); (2) Cunard, Box 999, Farmingdale, NY 11737 (Tel. 212-661-7777); (3) Holland America Cruises, 2 Penn Pl., New York, NY 10121 (Tel. 212-947-8959); (4) Norwegian American Cruises, 3rd Flr., 29 Broadway, New York NY 10006 (Tel. 212-422-3905); (5) Paquet French Cruises, 1370 Ave. of the Americas, New York, NY 10019 (Tel. 212-757-9050); (6) Princess Cruises, 2029 Century Park E., Los Angeles, CA 90067 (Tel. 213-553-7000); (7) Royal Viking Line, 1 Embarcadero Ctr., San Francisco, CA 94111 (Tel. 800-227-4246); (8) Sitmar Cruises-Alaska, 1801 S. Hill St., Los Angeles, CA 90015; (9) Westours, 300 Elliot Ave. W., Seattle, WA 98119 (Tel. 206-281-1970); (10) World Explorer Cruises, 3 Embarcadero Ctr., San Francisco, CA 94111 (Tel. 415-391-9262). "Budget cruises" are offered by the State of Alaska's fleet of 9 ferryliners. Known as the Alaska Marine Hwy., this ferry system connects major ports in southeast Alaska with Prince Rupert, B.C., and Seattle, WA. Good whale-sighting opportunities are July–Aug. runs between Juneau and Petersburg, and between Petersburg and Sitka. Schedule: Traffic Mgr., Alaska Marine Hwy. System, Pouch R, Juneau, AK 99811. Reservations: (1) Seattle (Tel. 206-623-1970); (2) Anchorage (Tel. 907-272-4482); (3) Juneau (Tel. 907-465-3941).

Weather/Sea Notes
Summer temperatures average 50°F, but subject to extreme changes. Fog and rain often spoil whale watching. Can be rough in open waters.

Laws/Guidelines
Special regulations in effect for Glacier Bay National Monument. In the early 1970s, Glacier Bay became widely known as the summer home of about 25 humpbacks. Then, in mid-July 1978, the whales abruptly left and have returned only spo-

radically since. Was the steady traffic of private boats and large cruise ships to blame? Or did the whales simply find better food supplies elsewhere? The National Park Service is trying to minimize any disturbance to the whales by limiting boat traffic. From June 1–Aug. 31, special boat permits are required to enter Glacier Bay. For more information,

Photographed from the air, a gray whale feeds in the Bering Sea.

contact: Glacier Bay National Park, Gustavus, AK 99826 (Tel. 907-697-3522).

Museums
Alaska State Museum, Pouch FM, Juneau, AK 99801 (Tel. 907-586-9888).

More information
Alaska State Div. of Tourism, Pouch E-28, Juneau, AK 99811 (Tel. 907-465-2010).

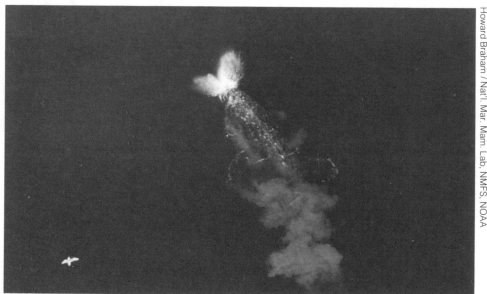

United States: Alaska–South Central Coast

Species
Common: minke whale (**2**), humpback whale (**7**), gray whale (**1**), killer whale (**75**), Dall's porpoise (**45**), harbor porpoise (**40**), fin whale (**5**), beluga (**34**).
Sporadic: sperm whale (**12**), Pacific white-sided dolphin (**59**), sei whale (**3**), blue whale (**6**).
Rare: right whale (**8**), Baird's beaked whale (**17**).

Lookouts
1 On Kodiak Island (access via jet from Anchorage or ferry from Homer or Seward), in Nov.–Dec. and April–May, the gray whale migration passes Narrow Cape, access via 1/2-hour trail from road 22 miles south of Kodiak. Kodiak Area

Chamber of Commerce, Box 1485, Kodiak, AK 99615 (Tel. 907-486-5557).
2 From the Seward Hwy. between Girdwood and Portage (about 35 miles south of Anchorage), belugas can be seen in Cook Inlet and Turnagain Arm during the spring eulachon runs (May–early June).

Tours
For the last decade, Jim and Nancy Lethcoe have shown guests the humpbacks and other whales of Prince William Sound. From June–Sept., they offer several 6-day "sailing and whale-watching" charters, guided by naturalists. The sailboats range from 22–44 feet. Not luxury cruises, these are quality wilderness

adventures. Prices start at $300/person per week, not including food. Special charters also available. Contact: Alaskan Wilderness Sailing Safaris, Box 701W, Whittier, AK 99693 (Tel. 907-338-2134).

Ferries and Cruises
The whales of Prince William Sound can be seen in summer aboard the *M/V Bartlett* which carries cars and passengers 5 days a week between Valdez and Whittier. Contact: Alaska Marine Highway,

Box 647, Valdez, AK 99686 (Tel. 907-835-4436).

Museums
Complete articulated skeletons of harbor porpoise and Bering Sea beaked whale at the Pratt Museum, Box 427, Homer, AK 99603 (Tel. 907-235-8635).

More information
Alaska State Div. of Tourism, Pouch E-28, Juneau, AK 99811 (Tel. 907-465-2010).

United States: Washington

Species
Common: killer whale (**75**), gray whale (**1**), Dall's porpoise (**45**), minke whale (**2**). *Sporadic*: harbor porpoise (**40**).

Lookouts
From June–Sept., San Juan Island is one of the best killer-whale-watching areas in the world. Access is via 1¹/₂-hour car ferry from Anacortes, Washington, or Sidney, British Columbia. Arriving in Friday Harbor, if on foot, one can rent a car or bicycle. The distances are fairly short: 7–8 miles to best viewing sites on west or south side of island. First stop in at the Whale Museum in Friday Harbor and check large posted map for recent whale sightings. Proceed to west side of San Juan Island, taking Bailer Hill Rd. which turns into West Side Rd. Best places on west side to pull off are **1** along West Side Rd., **2** in San Juan County Park, **3** near Deadman's Bay, just south of Lime Kiln Lighthouse (also good for harbor and Dall's porpoises). Also: **4** American Camp in San Juan Island National Historic Park, at island's southern tip. Minke whales are also possible here.

On the outer coast, gray whale migration lasts from late Oct.–Dec. and Feb.–May, but is best from March–May. Good lookouts, from north to south are: **5** Cape Flattery Viewpoint, access via Hwy. 112 from Neah Bay (66 miles west of Port Angeles) with ¹/₂-mile walk to Land's End (Makah Cultural & Resource Center has whaling displays); **6** Cape Alava and Sand Point, at end of 2 separate 3-mile trails from Ozette, 66 miles west of Port Angeles (well-maintained, part of Olympic

National Park; good in fall too); **7** the Kalaloch area (also part of Olympic National Park) along Hwy. 101 from Ruby Beach to southern boundary of the park (2 miles from Queets) has good views from road which runs above a series of beaches or from Kalaloch Lodge library; **8** Point Grenville, from Hwy. 109 on Quinalt Indian Reservation; **9** near Moclips and Pacific Beach on Hwy. 109; **10** in Westport, from new 50-foot viewing tower on the ocean; **11** Cape Disappointment, on hill beside lighthouse and from long jetty extending into the sea – access on road from Ilwaco (follow signs to Fort Canby) off Hwy. 101 in southwestern Washington. For trail maps, camping

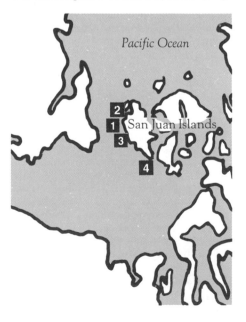

Graeme Ellis / courtesy Michael A. Bigg

(Above and below) Photographed in sequence, a killer whale breaches off Vancouver Island.

Graeme Ellis / courtesy Michael A. Bigg

and other information on lookouts #6 and #7, contact: Olympic National Park, 600 E. Park Ave., Port Angeles, WA 98362 (Tel. 206-452-4501).

Tours

From Westport, on the west coast, 1/2-day guided gray whale cruises are offered on weekends March–May. About $20. Also full-day charters. (1) Westport Whale Watch, Box 312, Westport, WA 98595 (Tel. 206-268-0430 or, in WA, 800-222-0430); (2) Northwest Educational Tours (Salmon Charters, Inc.), Box 545, Westport, WA 98595 (Tel. 206-268-9150 or, in WA, 800-222-0430); (3) Bran Lee Charters, Westhaven Dr., Westport, WA 98595 (Tel. 206-268-9177 or, in WA, 800-562-0163); (4) Cachalot Charters, Box 348, Westport, WA 98595 (Tel. 206-268-0323 or, in WA, 800-562-0141); (5) Coho Charters, Westport, WA 98595 (Tel. 206-268-0111 or, in WA, 800-562-0177); (6) Deep Sea Charters, Across from Float 6, Westport, WA 98595 (Tel. 206-268-9300 or, in WA, 800-562-0151); (7) Ed's Charters, Box 461, Westport, WA 98595 (Tel. 206-268-0047 or, in WA, 800-562-0107); (8) Gull Charters, Box 351, Westport, WA 98595 (Tel. 206-268-9186 or, in WA, 800-562-0175); (9) Harbor Charters, Box 312, Westport, WA 98595 (Tel. 206-268-0169 or, in WA, 800-562-0184); (10) Islander Charters, Westport, WA 98595 (Tel. 206-268-9166 or, in WA, 800-562-0147); (11) Neptune Charters, 2601 Westhaven Dr., Westport, WA 98595 (Tel. 206-268-0124 or, in WA, 800-562-0165); (12) Ocean Charters, Westport, WA 98595 (Tel. 206-268-9144 or, in WA, 800-562-0105); (13) Rainbow Charters, Westport, WA 98595 (Tel. 206-268-0124 or, in WA, 800-562-0165); (14) Rogers Sea Charters, Westport, WA 98595 (Tel. 206-268-0366); (15) Shamrock Charters, Box 466, Westport, WA 98595 (Tel. 206-268-0900 or, in WA, 800-562-0173); (16) Sunrise Charters, Box 592, Westport, WA 98595 (Tel. 206-268-0601 or, in WA, 800-562-0143); (17) Westport Charters, Westhaven Dr., Westport, WA 98595 (Tel. 206-268-9120 or, in WA, 800-562-0157).

From Neah Bay, gray whale watching is by charter only: (1) Morton's Resort, Box 136, Neah Bay, WA 98357 (Tel. 206-645-2250); (2) Makah Resort, Neah Bay, WA 98357 (Tel. 206-645-2366); (3) Big Salmon Resort, Neah Bay, WA 98357 (Tel. 206-645-2374).

From Sekiu (near Neah Bay), gray whale charters are offered by Coho Resort, Hwy. 112 W., Sekiu, WA 98381 (Tel. 206-963-2333).

From Ilwaco, gray whale charters are offered by E. Gilpin, Viking Charters, Star Route, Ilwaco, WA 98624 (Tel. 206-777-8236 or 642-2623).

1-day cruises to see killer whales (plus minke whales and Dall's porpoises) **in the San Juan Islands**, guided by naturalists, depart from Anacortes from late June–mid-Sept. (1) Greenpeace Northwest, 4649 Sunnyside Ave. N., Seattle, WA 98103 (Tel. 206-632-4326). 12 trips a season; $28, lunch extra. (2) Anchor Excursions, 4250 21st Ave. W., Seattle, WA 98199 (Tel. 206-282-8368). About 6 trips a season; $55 includes meals and stop at the Whale Museum in Friday Harbor. Also 2–3-day excursions to see killer whales for $285, including lodging and some meals.

A week-long cruise to see killer whales in the San Juan Islands, with visits to the Whale Museum and daily lectures and slide shows is offered in Sept. by Ronn Storro-Patterson. About $1,000 (from Friday Harbor). Contact: Biological Journeys, 1876 Ocean Dr., McKinleyville, CA 95521 (Tel. 707-839-0178).

Guided kayaking expeditions to see killer whales in the San Juan Islands last 2–8 days at about $50/day including all gear and 2 meals a day. (1) San Juan Kayak Expeditions, 3090 Roche Harbor Rd., Friday Harbor, WA 98250 (Tel. 206-378-4436); (2) Pacific Rim Expeditions, Box 2474, Bellingham, WA 98227 (Tel. 206-676-8550); (3) Tide Rip Tours, Box 4143, Bellingham, WA 98225 (Tel. 206-733-8077); (4) Northern Lights Expeditions, 8556 Sandpoint Way, NE, Seattle, WA 98115 (Tel. 206-524-1662).

"Whale School" and "Advanced Whale Workshop" are week-long summer field-study courses offered for university credit by Moclips Cetological Society in Friday Harbor. These excellent student programs focus on the natural history of local marine mammals. $600 includes meals and lodging. Contact: Moclips Cetological Society, Box 945, Friday Harbor, WA 98250 (Tel. 206-378-4710).

Ferries and Cruises

Occasional killer whale sightings (less often minke whales, Dall's and harbor porpoises) from Washington State Ferries, especially between Anacortes and Sidney, British Columbia, in Aug. and Sept. Many departures every day (with stops in Friday Harbor and on nearby islands). Contact: Washington State Ferries, Colman Dock, Seattle, WA 98104 (Tel. 206-464-6400 or, in WA, 800-542-0810/7052 or, in Victoria, B.C., 604-381-1551).

For Inside Passage cruises between Seattle and Alaska passing through killer whale and other whale areas, see Southeast Alaska.

Weather/Sea Notes

Gray whale season (winter-spring) usually rainy, cold and can be rough on the water. Summers are dry and warm but cold on boats. Waters around San Juan Islands relatively calm during summer, though excursions into Juan de Fuca Strait will encounter rough seas.

Museums

Killer whale and other cetacean skeletons, models, films, and excellent exhibits including an up-to-date map with local whale sightings at the Whale Museum. A public sighting network is run by the museum; report all cetacean sightings on the whale hotline 800-562-8832. The Whale Museum is on First St., a few blocks north of ferry terminal in Friday Harbor. Contact: Moclips Cetological Society, Box 945, Friday Harbor, WA 98250 (Tel. 206-378-4710).

More information

Washington State Dept. of Commerce & Economic Development, Gen. Admin. Bldg., Rm. G-3, Olympia, WA 98504 (Tel. 206-753-5630).

United States: Oregon

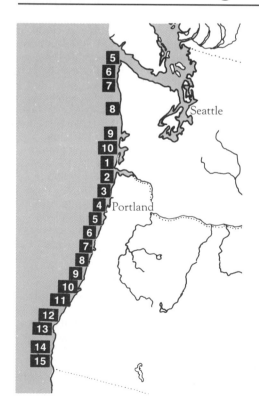

Species

Common: gray whale (**1**).
Sporadic: killer whale (**75**), harbor porpoise (**40**), Dall's porpoise (**45**).

Lookouts

Migrating gray whales pass from Dec.–May, with a mid-Feb. break between southern and northern migrations. The southern migration peaks the last week of Dec. and the first week of Jan. The northern migration peaks late March–April. Almost any headland or coastal wayside along Hwy. 101 will do.

Here are some of the better spots (from north to south): **1** Fort Stevens State Park, off County Rd. north of Warrenton, about 12 miles from Astoria; **2** Tillamook Head, access via good trail from Ecola State Park, north of Cannon Beach, off Hwy. 101; **3** Cape Falcon, via Oswald West State Park turnoff from Hwy. 101 and 2-mile trail; **4** Cape Meares beside lighthouse in Cape Meares State Park, access on road 10 miles west of Tillamook; **5** Cape Lookout, access via 3-mile trail from Cape Lookout State Park, 15 miles southwest of Tillamook; **6** Cascade Head, access via road then 3-mile nature trail, about 8 miles north of Lincoln City, off Hwy. 101; **7** Cape Foulweather, a high promontory near Rocky Creek Wayside, off Hwy. 101; **8** Yaquina Head, 50 yards beyond road to lighthouse off Hwy. 101, 3 miles north of Newport; **9** Cape Perpetua, promontory with parking at Yachats Ocean Road Wayside on Hwy. 101, 3 miles south of Yachats; **10** Heceta Head beside lighthouse, off Hwy. 101, about 15 miles south of Yachats; **11** Cape Arago, at Cape Arago State Park, access via road 14 miles west of Coos Bay off Hwy. 101; **12** Cape Blanco (Oregon's westernmost point), near lighthouse in Cape Blanco State Park, 6 miles by road off Hwy. 101, 10 miles (total) from Port Orford; **13** Cape Sebastian, access via Cape Sebastian State Park off Hwy. 101, short trail; **14** Samuel H. Boardman State Park, including Cape Ferrelo, several lookouts along Hwy. 101 between Pistol River and Brookings; **15** Sporthaven Park in Brookings, a beach and campground on south side of Chetco River mouth.

For free gray-whale-watching fact sheets, contact: Marine Science Center, Oregon State University, Marine Science Dr., Newport, OR 97365 (Tel. 503-867-3011).

For more information on some 70 coastal waysides situated in state parks, contact: State Parks & Recreation Division, 525 Trade St., SE, Salem, OR 97310 (Tel. 503-378-6305).

Tours

Gray whale watching in Oregon is mostly by charter, though charter companies sometimes schedule 1- to 3-hour trips in peak periods, particularly March–May.

From Garibaldi (on Tillamook Bay), scheduled tours guided by naturalists are offered by Trollers Charters, Vandecoevering Fisheries, Box 452, Garibaldi, OR 97141 (Tel. 503-322-3666/3796).

From Tillamook, whale charters can be arranged through Joe's Deep Sea Fishing, Mooring Basin Rd., Tillamook, OR 97141 (Tel. 503-322-3395).

In Depoe Bay, scheduled cruises and charters are offered by Tradewinds Ocean Sportfishing, Box 123, Depoe Bay, OR 97341 (Tel. 503-765-2345).

In Newport, scheduled spring 1/2-day trips are offered by the Oregon Museum of Science & Industry; others are mainly charter companies: (1) Oregon Museum

Whale watchers reach out to touch a friendly gray whale mother and calf in San Ignacio Lagoon, Mexico.

H & M Landing

of Science & Industry, 4015 SW Canyon Rd., Portland, OR 97221 (Tel. 503-222-1500); (2) Sea Gull Charters, 343 SW Bay Blvd., Newport, OR 97365 (Tel. 503-265-7441); (3) Newport Tradewinds, 653 SW Bay Blvd., Newport, OR 97365 (Tel. 503-265-2101); (4) Newport Sportfishing, 1000 SE Bay Blvd., Newport, OR 97365 (Tel. 503-265-7558).

From Winchester Bay, whale charters are available: Thompson Charters, Box 722, Winchester Bay, OR 97467 (Tel. 503-271-3133).

From Charleston, on Coos Bay: B & B Charters, Charleston Boat Basin, Charleston, OR 97420 (Tel. 503-888-4139).

In Harbor (across river from Brookings in SW Oregon) scheduled cruises are planned in 1984: Leo's Sporthaven Marina, Box 2215, Harbor, OR 97415 (Tel. 503-469-3301).

Weather/Sea Notes
Cold, often rainy and rough on the water from Dec.–May gray whale season. Best weather days are in spring. Calm water essential for short-based spotting, and overcast skies usually better than sun because there's no glare on the water.

Museums
Whaling artifacts and other materials at Tillamook County Pioneer Museum, 2016 2nd St., Tillamook, OR 97141 (Tel. 503-842-4553).

More information
Oregon Travel Information Section, 101 Transportation Bldg., Salem, OR 97310 (Tel. 503-378-6309).

United States: California – North & Central

Species
Common: gray whale (**1**), Pacific white-sided dolphin (**59**), humpback whale (**7**), blue whale (**6**), northern right whale dolphin (**68**), Dall's porpoise (**45**), harbor porpoise (**40**).
Sporadic: fin whale (**5**), minke whale (**2**), sei whale (**3**), killer whale (**75**), false killer whale (**74**), Risso's dolphin (**70**), short-finned pilot whale (**77**), common dolphin (**50**).

Lookouts
The gray whale is mostly migratory in California waters. Yet for an animal "just passing through", it receives an extraordinary welcome. Hundreds of thousands of Californians and visitors from around the world watch the whales pass every year – many from lookouts along the coast. The season is Dec.–May with a southward peak in early Jan. and a northward peak in March. Cows with calves return mostly in May. Certain sites are better on southward migration, others on northward.

From north to south, these are some of the accessible lookouts: **1** Point St. George, about 5 miles northwest of Crescent City near St. George Reef Light Station; **2** Crescent Beach Overlook, at Crescent Beach, 1/2 mile south of Crescent City; **3** Patrick's Point State Park on Hwy. 101 from the steep overlook around Rocky Point (camping; Tel. 707-677-3570); **4** Vista Point, 14 miles north of Eureka on Hwy. 101, across from Arcata Airport; **5** MacKerricher State Park, 3 miles north of Fort Bragg on Hwy. 1, especially from the grassy headlands on Laguna Point, 1/4 mile beyond parking lot at western terminus of Mill Creek Rd. (camping; ranger-guided whale programs on weekends; Mendocino Coast Whale Festival in March at Veterans Hall in Fort Bragg, with films, cruises, exhibits of whales, wine-tasting; Tel. 707-964-3153); **6** Mendocino Headlands State Park, outside town of Mendocino off Hwy. 1 at end of Little Lake Rd. (ranger-guided whale programs on weekends; also site of Mendocino Coast Whale Festival in March; Tel. 707-937-5804); **7** Manchester State Beach off Hwy. 1 near Manchester, 30 miles south of Mendocino (camping; Tel. 707-882-2463); **8** Point Arena near lighthouse off Hwy. 1 at end of Lighthouse Rd., 3 miles north of town of Point Arena; **9** Gualala Point at Gualala Point County Park, off Hwy. 1, a mile south of Gualala and about 110 miles north of San Francisco; **10** Salt

Point in Salt Point State Park, ¹/₂ mile from park entrance off Hwy. 1, 90 miles north of San Francisco (camping; best late Feb.–April; Tel. 707-847-3221); **11** Stillwater Cove County Park on Hwy. 1, 3 miles north of Fort Ross (camping; Tel. 707-847-3245); **12** Fort Ross State Historic Park, about 10 miles north of Jenner on Hwy. 1 (Tel. 707-865-2391); **13** Bodega Head, off Hwy. 1 to end of Westside Rd., west of Bodega Bay, south of Sonoma Coast State Beaches (parking; camping); **14** Point Reyes National Seashore, about 45 miles north of San Francisco off Hwy. 1, near western end of Sir Francis Drake Hwy., especially from old lighthouse (10 a.m.–4:30 p.m. Thurs.–Mon., best Jan. 1–15), from Chimney Rock area (best mid-March), from Tomales Point (best in May for cows and calves) and from Point Reyes Beach South (visitor center near lighthouse with whale materials; ranger-guided whale programs from Dec.–April; 1-day whale-watching seminars in Jan.; for more information, weather and whale activity reports, contact: Point Reyes National Seashore, Point Reyes, CA 94956; Tel. 415-669-1534/Seminars 663-1200); **15** Cliff House in San Francisco near Golden Gate Park at north end of Great Hwy. and Point Lobos Ave.; **16** Gray Whale Cove State Beach, on Hwy. 1, 10 miles south of San Francisco (parking); **17** Montara State Beach, 12 miles south of San Francisco off Hwy. 1, from cliffs above beach (parking; Feb.–April best; Tel. 415-726-9278); **18** Half Moon Bay State Beach in Half Moon Bay, access from Venice Blvd. or Young Ave., off Hwy. 1, especially from area between Venice Beach and Roosevelt Beach (parking; Tel. 415-726-9278); **19** San Gregorio State Beach, from cliffs north and south of parking area, off Hwy. 1, 11 miles south of Half Moon Bay; **20** Año Nuevo State Reserve, from cliffs off Hwy. 1 at New Year's Creek (reservations needed because of restricted access to nearby elephant seal breeding area; Tel. 415-879-0228); **21** Pebble Beach/Bean Hollow State Beach, 16 miles south of Half Moon Bay off Hwy. 1, from 2-mile footpath between the 2 beaches (parking; Tel. 415-726-9278); **22** Greyhound Rock, beach access off Hwy. 1, 32 miles south of Half Moon Bay; **23** Davenport, 37

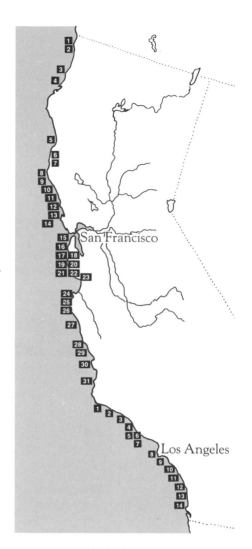

San Francisco

Los Angeles

miles south of Half Moon Bay on Hwy. 1, from the cliffs on hwy. across from Whaler tavern; **24** Point Piños on Ocean View Blvd. in Pacific Grove, near end of Lighthouse Ave. (westernmost landfall at south end of Monterey Bay); **25** Point Lobos State Reserve, south of Carmel on Hwy. 1, and on hwy. lookouts for 18 miles south to Point Sur (parking; Tel. 408-624-4909); **26** Garrapata Beach, 7 miles south of Carmel on Hwy. 1 (parking; ranger-guided whale programs on Saturdays); **27** Julia Pfeiffer Burns State Park, 37 miles south of Carmel on Hwy. 1 (camping; parking; ranger-guided whale programs on weekends in Jan.–Feb.); **28** San Simeon State Beach, 5 miles south of San Simeon off Hwy. 1 (camp-

Jim Darling / WCWRF

A gray whale shows its flukes as it dives off Vancouver Island.

ing; San Simeon "Whaling Days" in Nov.; Tel 805-927-3500); **29** Leffingwell Landing and Moonstone Beach Dr. Lookout in Cambria from north end of Moonstone Beach Dr. to ¼ mile south of intersection on Hwy. 1; **30** Montana de Oro State Park, 10 miles south of Morro Bay, access via Pecho Valley Rd., from Los Osos, especially at Point Buchon (occasional ranger-guided whale programs); **31** Point Sal at Point Sal State Beach, off Hwy. 1 at end of Brown and Pt. Sal roads, about 10 miles west of Guadeloupe in the Santa Maria area.

For more information on the some 270 state parks and beaches ($2 for complete California parks' guide), contact: Dept. of Parks and Recreation, Box 2390, Sacramento, CA 95811 (Tel. 916-445-6477). For more on interpretive whale programs, call individual park numbers above or Dept. of Parks and Recreation (Tel. 916-445-4624).

Tours

Most California ports have tours or charters to see the winter/spring gray whale migration. The trips vary from 2–8 hours at sea. From north to south, offerings include:

From Crescent City, charters to see gray whales through Crescent City Harbor District, 101 Citizens Dock, Crescent City, CA 95331 (Tel. 707-464-6174).

From Eureka, gray whale charters are offered by (1) The *Becky*, 1133 King Salmon, Eureka, CA 95501 (Tel. 707-442-8212); (2) King Salmon Charters, 1125 King Salmon, Eureka, CA 95501 (Tel. 707-442-FISH).

From Fort Bragg, gray whale watching is by charter only, except during the Mendocino Coast Whale Festival in March. (1) Anchor Charter Boats, 780 N. Harbor Dr., Box 0002, Fort Bragg, CA 95437 (Tel. 707-964-4889/4542); (2) Sportsman's Dock, 32100 N. Harbor Dr., Fort Bragg, CA 95437 (Tel. 707-964-2619/7671); (3) Jerry's Charters, 102 S. Main, Fort Bragg, CA 95437 (Tel. 707-964-2410); (4) Yacht Incredible, 510A Cypress St., Fort Bragg, CA 95437 (Tel. 707-964-0201); (5) Noyo Store, 32450 N. Harbor Dr., Fort Bragg, CA 95437 (Tel. 707-964-9138); (6) Lady Irma, Box 103, Fort Bragg, CA 95437 (Tel. 707-964-3854); (7) Helipad Aviation, Inc., Box 1563, Ukiah, CA 95482 (Tel. 707-468-5510; helicopter tours during Mendocino Coast Whale Festival).

San Francisco Bay area gray whale

Jim Darling / WCWRF
A gray whale calf sticks its head above water near Vancouver Island.

cruises depart from Sausalito or from Pillar Point, north of Half Moon Bay (south of San Francisco on Hwy. 1), except as noted below. Schedules go from late Dec.–end of April, mostly on weekends, though some have daily midweek tours or charters. Besides migrating grays, harbor and Dall's porpoises are sometimes seen. About $20 for naturalist-guided 2½-hour excursion (less for groups, children, senior citizens, members of environmental group or museum). First 3 listed below are the most popular, contact: (1) The Whale Center, 3929 Piedmont Ave., Oakland, CA 94611 (Tel. 415-654-6621); (2) Oceanic Society, Bldg. E, Fort Mason Center, San Francisco, CA 94123 (Tel. 415-474-3385); (3) Sierra Club, 6014 College Ave., Oakland, CA 94618 (Tel. 415-658-7470; 7-hour trips depart St. Francis Yacht Harbor); (4) Marine Mammal Fund, Bldg. E, Fort Mason Center, San Francisco, CA 94123 (Tel. 415-775-4636; trips depart Bodega Bay); (5) Captain John's, Box 155, Half Moon Bay, CA 94019 (Tel. 415-728-3377); (6) American Cetacean Society, 210 Garces St., San Francisco CA 94132 (Tel. 415-239-6011); (7) Marin Adventures, Marin Community College, Kentfield, CA 94904 (Tel. 415-485-9581); (8) Coyote Point Museum, San Mateo, CA 94401 (Tel. 415-342-7755); (9) YMCA Point Bonita Center, Bldg. 981, Fort Barry GGNRA, Sausalito, CA 94965 (Tel. 415-561-7656); (10) Biological Journeys, 1007 Leneve Pl., El Cerrito, CA 94580 (Tel. 415-527-9622).

From Santa Cruz harbor, gray whale migration tours last 3 hours and cost $12–$16. (1) Shearwater Journeys, Box 7440, Santa Cruz, CA 95061 (Tel. 408-425-8111; naturalist-guided; also has departures from Monterey); (2) Tom's Fisherman's Supply, Inc., 2210 E. Cliff Dr., Santa Cruz, CA 95062 (Tel. 408-476-2648). Santa Cruz charters offering gray whales include: (3) Stagnaro Charter Boats, Municipal Wharf, Santa Cruz, CA 95062 (Tel. 408-423-2020); (4) The Mariner Charters, 413 Lake Ave., Santa Cruz, CA 95062 (Tel. 408-475-5411; sailboats); (5) Witchcraft Charters, Box 2835, Santa Cruz, CA 95063 (Tel. 408-462-0844; sailboats).

From Monterey, gray whale tours last 1½–6 hours, most days from late Dec.–April (best month Jan.). Prices range from $8–$30 depending on length of tour, presence of naturalist, kind of boat. (1) Shearwater Journeys, Box 7440, Santa Cruz,

Humpbacks feeding together.

CA 95061 (Tel. 408-425-8111); (2) Green-peace, Bldg, E, Fort Mason Center, San Francisco, CA 94123 (Tel. 415-425-1446); (3) Nature Explorations, 2253 Park Blvd., Palo Alto, CA 94306 (Tel. 415-324-8737); (4) Princess Monterey Cruises, 39 Fisher-man's Wharf, Monterey, CA 93940 (Tel. 408-372-BOAT/372-2203); (5) Chris' Fish-ing Trips, 48 Fisherman's Wharf, Monte-rey, CA 93940 (Tel. 408-375-5951); (6) Randy's Fishing Trips, 66 Fisherman's Wharf, Monterey, CA 93940 (Tel. 408-372-7440); (7) Sam's Fishing Fleet, Inc., 84 Fisherman's Wharf, Monterey, CA 93940 (Tel. 408-372-0577); (8) Frank's Fishing Trips, 96 Fisherman's Wharf, Monterey, CA 93940 (Tel. 408-372-2203).

Morro Bay boat excursions catch migrating grays daily from Dec.–Feb. Adults $8; children $5. Virg's Fish'n, 1215 Embarcadero, Morro Bay, CA 93442 (Tel. 805-772-1222/2216).

Outside of gray whale season, several excursions visit the **Gulf of the Faral-lones**, west of San Francisco. Part of the Pt. Reyes-Farallon Islands National Marine Sanctuary, the Farallones and the surrounding waters support a large popu-lation of marine mammals and seabirds.

Cetacean possibilities include hump-backs, blues, minkes, seis, orcas, grays and various porpoises and dolphins. The full-day trips depart from various San Francisco area ports from late May–Oct., usually on weekends. All are naturalist-guided; about $40. (1) The Whale Center, 3929 Piedmont Ave., Oakland, CA 94611 (Tel. 415-654-6621); (2) Oceanic Society, Bldg. E, Fort Mason Center, San Fran-cisco, CA 94123 (Tel. 415-474-3385); (3) Natural Excursions, 4990 Shoreline Hwy., Stinson Beach, CA 94970 (Tel. 415-868-1221).

Shearwater Journeys of Santa Cruz has many whale, seal and seabird tours throughout the year to the **Monterey Sea-valley, Cordell Bank** (extraordinary vari-ety of marine mammals), and within **Monterey Bay**. Pacific white-sided dol-phins and Dall's porpoises are seen year-round; best time for humpback and blue whales is late July–early Sept. Other logged species include Risso's dolphins, northern right whale dolphins and the uncommon Baird's and Cuvier's beaked whale. Full-day trips range from $25–$36. Naturalist on board. Trips depart from Fisherman's Wharf in Monterey on 55- or 36-foot fishing boats. Contact: Shearwa-ter Journeys, Box 7440, Santa Cruz, CA 95061 (Tel. 408-425-8111).

Cordell Bank whale-watching trips from Bodega Bay in Sept.–Oct. are offered by Marine Mammal Fund, Bldg. E, Fort Mason Center, San Francisco, CA 94123 (Tel. 415-775-4636).

Weather/Sea Notes
Cold and often rough at sea during gray whale migration; tours usually don't operate in roughest weather. Rain and fog sometimes factors, especially off northern California and from lookouts. Mornings often best from lookouts, before winds cause whitecaps.

Laws/Guidelines
(See California – Southern.)

Oceanaria
Killer whales and bottlenose dolphins at Marine World Africa U.S.A., Marine World Pkwy., Redwood City, CA 94065 (Tel. 415-591-7676).

Pacific white-sided dolphins at Steinhart Aquarium, California Academy of Sciences, Golden Gate Park, San Francisco, CA 94118 (Tel. 415-221-5100).

Museums
Whale displays at California Academy of Sciences, Golden Gate Park, San Francisco, CA 94118 (Tel. 415-221-5100).

More information
Latest details on many whale-watching tours available by sending self-addressed, stamped envelope to California Office of Tourism, Dept. WW, Suite 200, 1030 13th St., Sacramento, CA 95814 (Tel. 916-322-1396).

For San Francisco to southern Oregon: Redwood Empire Assoc., 1 Market Pl., Spear St. Tower, Suite 1001, San Francisco, CA 94105 (Tel. 415-543-8334).

For the Mendocino coast: Fort Bragg-Mendocino Coast Chamber of Commerce, Box 1141, Fort Bragg, CA 95437 (Tel. 707-964-3153).

For San Francisco Bay area: San Francisco Convention & Visitors Bureau, 201 Third, Suite 900, San Francisco, CA 94103 (Tel. 415-974-6900).

For Santa Cruz: Santa Cruz County Convention & Visitors Bureau, Box 1476, Santa Cruz, CA 95061 (Tel. 408-423-6927).

For Monterey area: Monterey Peninsula Chamber of Commerce & Visitors & Convention Bureau, Box 1770, Monterey, CA 93940 (Tel. 408-649-3200).

United States: California – South

Species
Common: gray whale (**1**), Pacific white-sided dolphin (**59**), short-finned pilot whale (**77**), bottlenose dolphin (**57**). *Sporadic*: humpback whale (**7**), fin whale (**5**), minke whale (**2**), sei whale (**3**), blue whale (**6**), killer whale (**75**), false killer whale (**74**), northern right whale dolphin (**68**), Risso's dolphin (**70**), Dall's porpoise (**45**), common dolphin (**50**).

Lookouts
The modern era of whale watching from boat and lookout began in the San Diego area. In the late 1940s, Carl Hubbs and his students on the campus of Scripps Institution of Oceanography watched and counted migrating gray whales from La Jolla, and by the late 1950s naturalist-guided tours began on a regular basis, spreading throughout southern California and, eventually, to northern California and other coasts. Gray whale season is Jan.–April especially Jan.–Feb., except as noted.

From north to south, the lookouts are: **1** Gaviota State Beach, off Hwy. 101, 30 miles northwest of Santa Barbara (best Feb.–April; camping); **2** Arroyo Burro Beach County Park and Shoreline Park, off Hwy. 101 in Santa Barbara (best Feb.–April; parking on bluffs); **3** Pitas Point, 6 miles north of Ventura off Hwy. 101; **4** Ventura, from lookout tower in park beside Island Packers on Spinnaker Dr.; **5** Anacapa Island, access via ferry from Ventura to Channel Islands; **6** Point Mugu Rock and Point Mugu State Park, about 12 miles south of Ventura off Hwy. 1 (camping); **7** Point Dume, about 7 miles northwest of Malibu on Hwy. 1; **8** Palos Verdes including Point Vicente

County Park and Marineland of the Pacific, near Long Point, on Palos Verdes Dr. W. (viewing telescope; whale slide shows; also captive marine mammals; Tel. 213-377-1571); **9** Point Fermin Park, beside lighthouse at south end of Gaffey St. in San Pedro, metropolitan Los Angeles (land post operated since 1971 by Cabrillo Marine Museum; whale exhibits, film, and group lectures by reservation; Tel. 213-548-7562; cetacean center open early Jan.–late Mar.); **10** Corona Del Mar State Beach from bluffs on Ocean Blvd. off Hwy. 1, south of Newport Beach; **11** Blue Lantern Lookout Park in Dana Point at foot of Blue Lantern St., off Hwy. 1, 18 miles south of Newport Beach ("Festival of Whales" each weekend in Feb. with parades, films, exhibits and whale tours; Tel. 714-496-6677); **12** Torrey Pines State Beach and Reserve, west of N. Torrey Pines Rd., about 2 miles north of Scripps Institution of Oceanography campus in La Jolla; **13** Point La Jolla, from Coast Walk and viewpoints on La Jolla Blvd. in La Jolla (Dec.–Feb. best); **14** Point Loma, 10 miles west of San Diego city center on Catalina Blvd., at Cabrillo National Monument's glassed-

in observatory or at "Whale Overlook", 100 yards south of old lighthouse (ranger-naturalists answer questions; visitor center open 9 a.m.–5:15 p.m. daily; coin-operated telescopes; Cabrillo National Monument, Box 6670, San Diego, CA 92106; Tel. 619-293-5450).

For more information on state parks and beaches, contact: Dept. of Parks and Recreation, Box 2390, Sacramento, CA 95811 (Tel. 916-445-6477; special number for whale programs is 916-445-4624).

Tours

From Santa Barbara, the viewing season for gray whales lasts from late Jan.–early May. 2½-hour tours are mostly on weekends and prices start at $12.50 (children $8; school groups $5, per child). Most tours use the 88-foot *Condor*, and can be booked through: (1) Sea Landing, Breakwater, Santa Barbara, CA 93109 (Tel. 805-963-3564); (2) Santa Barbara Museum of Natural History, 2559 Puesta Del Sol Rd., Santa Barbara, CA 93105 (Tel. 805-682-4711/2212); (3) American Cetacean Society, Box 20204, Santa Barbara, CA 93120 (Tel. 805-687-3255).

From Ventura, half- and full-day trips to see migrating grays last from late Dec. through March. Some are scheduled daily. Cruises sometimes include pilot

A short-finned pilot whale breaches off Santa Catalina Island, California.

and other whale sightings and many dolphins. Contact: (1) Island Packers, 1867 Spinnaker Dr., Ventura, CA 93001 (Tel. 805-642-1393); (2) Fisherman's Quay Sportfishing, 1591 Spinnaker Dr., Ventura, CA 93001 (Tel. 805-644-3594); (3) Ventura Sportfishing Landing, 1500 Anchors Way, Ventura, CA 93001 (Tel. 805-644-7363); (4) Dave Willhite's Sportfishing Yacht Charters, 446 Alpine Ct., Ventura, CA 93004 (Tel. 805-647-3161).

From Oxnard (south of Ventura), migration excursions last 2–3 hours and cost about $10. Contact: Capt. Jack's Landing, 4151 S. Victoria Ave., Channel Islands Harbor, Oxnard, CA 93030 (Tel. 805-985-8511).

In the Los Angeles area, daily 2$\frac{1}{2}$-hour migration tours depart from San Pedro, Redondo Beach, Long Beach and Marina Del Rey. The season is Christmas–mid-April, and besides gray whales, boats sometimes encounter Pacific white-sided dolphins, fin, pilot and killer whales. (1) The Cabrillo Marine Museum and the American Cetacean Society co-sponsor most of the whale watching with 14 boats operating from 4 landings. They provide naturalists and have oriented their program toward school groups, taking up to 2,000 children a day to meet the whales. Price for school or other organized groups during the week is $4.25/person. Cabrillo Whalewatch, 3720 Stephen White Dr., San Pedro, CA 90731 (Tel. 213-832-4444 for information; 832-2476 for reservations). For individual or weekend reservations on Cabrillo Whalewatch-guided boats, contact tour listing (2) through (5) below; prices range from $4–$8; (2) Catalina Cruises, Berth 95-96, Box 948, San Pedro, CA 90733 (Tel. 213-547-0802/832-4521); (3) Ports O'Call Sportfishing, Berth 79, San Pedro, CA 90731 (Tel. 213-547-9916); (4) 22nd Street Skipper's Landing, 141-22nd St., San Pedro, CA 90731 (Tel. 213-832-8304); (5) Redondo Sportfishing, 233 N. Harbor Dr., Redondo Beach, CA 90277 (Tel. 213-372-2111); (6) Queen's Wharf Sportfishing, Berth 55, Long Beach, CA 90802 (Tel. 213-432-8993); (7) Fisherman's Village, 13763 Fiji Way, Marina Del Rey, CA 90291 (Tel. 213-827-5097).

From Newport Beach, south of Los Angeles, gray whale migration tours depart from Balboa Pavilion and extend from Dec. 26–early April. The daily 2$\frac{1}{2}$-hour cruises sometimes include other cetaceans, especially Pacific white-sided and bottlenose dolphins and pilot whales. Weekday: Adult $7; children $5. Weekend: Adult $8; children $5. (1) The Orange County chapter of the American Cetacean Society sponsors whale watching and provides guides for boats operated by tours (2) and (3) below. They also present illustrated whale lectures to schools and other groups, and have developed a special program to educate boat owners about whale harassment. Contact: Whalewatch/Orange County, 400 Main St., Balboa, CA 92661 (Tel. 714-675-9881); (2) the 77-foot *Western Pride* is operated by Davey's Locker Sportfishing, 400 Main St., Balboa, CA 92661 (Tel. 714-673-1434); (3) the 115-foot *Catalina Holiday* is run by Catalina Passenger Service, 400 Main St., Balboa, CA 92661 (Tel. 714-673-5245); (4) whale charters from Burns Charters, 2602 Newport Blvd., Newport Beach, CA 92663 (Tel. 714-675-2867).

From Dana Point, daily whale-watching tours from Jan.–March last 2–3 hours or longer by charter. Contact: Dana Wharf Sportfishing, 34675 Golden Lantern, Dana Point, CA 92629 (Tel. 714-496-5794).

In Oceanside (midway between Los Angeles and San Diego), daily 2-hour tours extend from Dec. 26–March 15. Contact: Helgren's Oceanside Sportfishing Trips, Inc., 315 Harbor Dr. S., Oceanside, CA 92054 (Tel. 619-722-2133).

In San Diego, gray whale watching lasts from Christmas–March, with peak in Jan. Cruises are 2–3 hours, or longer by charter. Some full-day cruises visit the Coronado Islands on north migration. Adult prices for regularly scheduled tours start at $7. (1) Gray whale-watching pioneer Raymond Gilmore, who has been guiding tours since 1959, still leads them for the San Diego Natural History Museum. Dec. 26–Jan. 22 only, mostly on weekends. Contact: San Diego Natural History Museum, El Prado in Balboa Park, Box 1390, San Diego, CA 92112 (Tel. 619-232-3821); (2) H & M Landing, 2803 Emerson St., San Diego, CA 92106 (Tel. 619-222-1144 or, in Los Angeles,

Santa Barbara

CALIFORNIA

San Miguel   Santa Cruz   **5**
Santa Rosa   Anacapa Island   Los Angeles

CHANNEL ISLANDS

Pacific Ocean   Catalina Island

213-626-8005); (3) Fisherman's Landing, 2838 Garrison St., San Diego, CA 92106 (Tel. 619-222-0391); (4) Seaforth Sportfishing, 1717 Quivira Rd., San Diego, CA 92109 (Tel. 619-224-3383); (5) Point Loma Sportfishing, 1403 Scott St., San Diego, CA 92106 (Tel. 619-223-1627); (6) Islandia Sportfishing, 1551 W. Mission Bay Dr., San Diego, CA 92109 (Tel. 619-222-1164); (7) Fish 'n Cruise, 4215 Narragansett, San Diego, CA 92107 (Tel. 619-222-2464); (8) Baja Frontier Tours, 3863 Cactusview Dr., San Diego, CA 92105 (Tel. 619-262-2003).

Longer whale excursions (4–12 days) visit California's **Channel Islands** and nearby islands off Mexico's northern Baja peninsula. Prices range from $80–$140/day, departing from San Diego or Ventura. All trips guided by naturalists. (1) For 4-day gray whale migration tours to San Martin and other offshore Baja islands, contact Pacific Sea-Fari Tours, 530 Broadway, Suite 1224, San Diego, CA 92101 (Tel. 619-226-8224); (2) 7-day sailing expeditions to the Channel Islands in Feb. and March to view gray whale migration plus other marine and land mammals. Contact: Oceanic Society Expeditions, Fort Mason Center, Bldg. E, San Francisco, CA 94123 (Tel. 415-441-1106); (3) 8-day natural-history expeditions to the Channel Islands that include gray and other whales and dolphins from: Nature Expeditions International, Box 11496, Eugene, OR 97440 (Tel. 503-484-6529); (4) 7- to 12-day sailing expeditions to Santa Catalina and the Channel Islands include whale watching from late Dec.–March. Ocean Voyages, 1709 Bridgeway, Sausalito, CA 94965 (Tel. 415-332-4681).

(For 1- to 2-week excursions departing San Diego for the gray whale mating and calving lagoons of Baja California, see Mexico: The Lagoons of Baja California).

Weather/Sea Notes

Cool and occasionally rough at sea during gray whale migration. Warm to hot at lookouts.

Laws/Guidelines

The National Marine Fisheries Service, the Federal agency charged with protecting whales, has drawn up specific guidelines for gray whale watching off the coast of California. Aircraft should not fly lower than 1,000 feet while within a horizontal distance of 100 yards from a gray whale. There are five directives for boaters. Vessels (1) should not be operated at speeds faster than a gray whale while paralleling and within 100 yards of a whale; (2) should not be operated at speeds faster than the slowest whales while paralleling or between groups of whales and within 100 yards of them; (3) should be operated at a constant speed while paralleling or following a gray whale and within 100 yards of the whale; (4) should not be used to separate a whale from a calf; (5) should not be used to herd or drive whales.

NMFS guidelines conclude with an attempt to define harassment as any action that "substantially disrupt[s] the normal behavioral pattern of a gray whale." Such disruptions might be manifested by "a rapid change in direction or speed; escape tactics such as prolonged diving, underwater course changes, underwater exhalation; or evasive swimming patterns such as swimming away rapidly at the surface; attempts by a female to shield a calf from a vessel or a human observer by tail swishing or by other movements to protect her calf."

For more information on NMFS guidelines, which are subject to change, contact: National Marine Fisheries Service, Southwest Region, 300 S. Ferry St., Terminal Island, CA 90731 (Tel. 213-548-2518).

Oceanaria

Killer whales, a pilot whale, and several Pacific white-sided and bottlenose dolphins at Marineland of the Pacific, Box

A close encounter with a "friendly" gray whale in San Ignacio Lagoon, Mexico.

937, Rancho Palos Verdes, CA 90274 (Tel. 213-377-1571).

Killer whales and bottlenose dolphins at Sea World, 1720 South Shores Rd., San Diego, CA 92109 (Tel. 619-234-3153).

Museums
Whale display and regular whale-oriented programs at Cabrillo Marine Museum, 3720 Stephen White Dr., San Pedro, CA 90731 (Tel. 213-548-7562).

Whale displays at San Diego Natural History Museum, El Prado in Balboa Park, Box 1390, San Diego, CA 92112 (Tel. 619-232-3821).

More information
For San Diego: San Diego Convention & Visitors Bureau, 1200 3rd Ave., Suite 824, San Diego, CA 92101 (Tel. 619-232-3101).

For Los Angeles: Greater Los Angeles Visitors & Convention Bureau, 505 S. Flower St., Level B, Los Angeles, CA 90071 (Tel. 213-488-9100).

For Ventura: Ventura Visitors & Convention Bureau, 785 S. Seaward Ave., Ventura, CA 93001 (Tel. 805-648-2075).

For Santa Barbara: Santa Barbara Conference & Visitors Bureau, Box 299, Santa Barbara, CA 93102 (Tel. 805-965-3023).

United States: Hawaiian Islands

Species
Common: humpback whale (**7**), bottle-nose dolphin (**57**), spinner dolphin (**51**), spotted dolphin (**52**), false killer whale (**74**), short-finned pilot whale (**77**).
Sporadic: sperm whale (**12**), rough-toothed dolphin (**46**).
Rare: Bryde's whale (**4**), fin whale (**5**), pygmy sperm whale (**13**), melon-headed whale (**72**), pygmy killer whale (**73**), Cuvier's beaked whale (**15**), Blainville's beaked whale (**24**).

Lookouts
Whale watching in the Hawaiian Islands revolves around the humpback whales that come every year to mate and raise their calves. Season is Dec.–April, with peak in Feb./March. Other cetaceans – especially bottlenose and spinner dol-

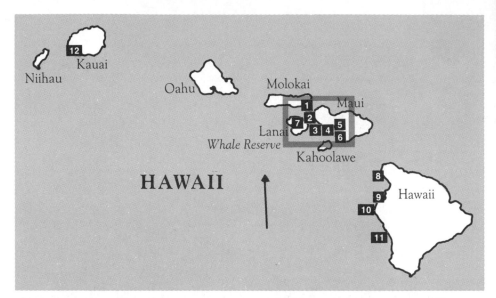

HAWAII

phins – occur most of the year.

On Maui, almost any west side spot has good whale possibilities. North to south along Hwy. 30: **1** at Kaanapali Beach Resort, north of Lahaina, from 4–12th floors of ocean front rooms in 8 luxury hotels or from beach front spots like the Sheraton Bar or Rusty Harpoon Restaurant in Whalers' Village shopping center; **2** in Lahaina, on Front St., from the Lahaina Shores Hotel, Kimo's Restaurant, and Lahaina Civic Center parking lot; **3** in Olawalu, from bluffs behind general store (take dirt road off Hwy. 30 to top); **4** at Papawai Point lookout, a pull-off on Hwy. 30, 2 miles west of Maalaea Harbor. Continuing south on Hwy. 31 along Maui's Kihei Coast: **5** Kalama Park, across from Kihei Town Center; **6** in Wailea, from the Westin Wailea Hotel and Hotel Inter-Continental Maui, including the latter's Makani Coffee Shop and Lanai Terrace Dining Room.

On Lanai, there's good humpback watching on the northeast coast, especially from **7** Shipwreck Beach and east, access via Hwy. 440, 17 miles from the airport on the other side of the island.

On Hawaii (the big island), humpback whales can sometimes be seen in season **8** along Hwy. 270 on the northern lee coast from Lapakahi State Historical Park (north of Kawaihae) to Upolu Pt. This and the following locales (continuing south along the lee coast) may also allow year-round views of spinner and bottlenose dolphins, and less often pygmy killer whales and short-finned pilot whales: **9** Kiholo Bay, **10** Keahole Pt., and **11** Kealakekua Bay, near Capt. Cook's Monument.

On Kauai, there are fair humpback and dolphin lookouts along the island's southwest coast, especially **12** from Hwy. 50 between Kekaha and Hanapepe.

Tours

As early as the 1950s, the Wailupe Whale Watchers got together on Oahu to share the excitement of returning humpback whales. Although the many tour boats that leave Kewalo Basin on Oahu sometimes encounter spinner and bottlenose dolphins and (occasionally during winter) humpback whales, the center for whale watching in the last decade has been west Maui, especially **Lahaina**. There, one can "go shopping" for a whale-watching tour. From late Dec. to late April, boats are lined up along Wharf St. in Lahaina, across from the Pioneer Inn. Each has a sign with daily tour times, prices, plus reservation clerk. In 1983, prices ranged from $15–$30 for a 2–3 hour cruise. Contact: (1) Aloha Activity Center (70-foot *Kaulana*), Bldg. C, 2435 Kaanapali Pkwy., Lahaina, HI 96761 (Tel. 808-667-9564); (2) Greenpeace, Front St., Lahaina, HI 96761 (Tel. 808-667-2059); (3) *Lin Wa* Cruises, Berth #3, Wharf St., Lahaina, HI 96761 (Tel. 808-661-3392/ 667-9266); (4) Hawaiian Reef Divers, 129

(Above) *A humpback tail lash off Hawaii.* (Below) *As this Hawaiian humpback dives the killer whale teeth marks on its flukes provide a means for individual identification.*

Lahainaluna Rd., Lahaina, HI 96761 (Tel. 808-667-7647); (5) Seabird Cruises, 120 Dickenson St., Lahaina, HI 96761 (Tel. 808-661-3643); (6) *Mareva* (38-foot sloop), Slip 63, Wharf St., Lahaina, HI (Tel. 808-667-7013); (7) Pacific Whale Foundation (*Aikane II*), Azeka Place, Suite 302, Kihei, HI 96753 (Tel. 808-879-6530).

At Kihei, south of Lahaina on west Maui, daily whale-watching tours during humpback season include: (1) Ocean Activities Center, Box 1082, Kihei, HI 96753 (Tel. 808-879-4485); (2) Unicorn Tours, Azeka Place, Suite 301, Kihei, HI 96753 (Tel. 808-879-6333); (3) Kihei Sea Sports (50-foot *Sea Sport*), Kihei, HI 96753 (Tel. 808-879-1919).

The **island of Hawaii** has no whale-watching tours, but sailing and sightseeing tours on the lee (Kona) coast often encounter whales and dolphins. Contact: Kona Activities Center, Box 1035, Kailua-Kona, HI 96740 (Tel. 808-329-3171).

Longer expeditions (Jan.–April) to see Hawaii's humpbacks for $100/day and up include: (1) 7-day sails aboard the 35-foot *Stacked Deck* offered by Oceanic Society Expeditions, Fort Mason Center, Bldg. E, San Francisco, CA 94123 (Tel. 415-441-1106); (2) 14-day tours of Hawaii with 1–2 days of whale watching from Nature Expeditions International, Box 11496, Eugene, OR 97440 (Tel. 503-484-6529); (3) 8-day sails with Ronn Storro-Patterson and Ron LeValley concentrating on humpbacks from Biological Journeys, 1876 Ocean Dr., McKinleyville, CA 95521 (Tel. 707-839-0178).

Chris Newbert is leading week-long free-diving trips in June to take underwater photos of dolphins and pilot whales along Hawaii's Kona Coast. Contact: Oceanic Society Expeditions, Fort Mason Center, Bldg. E, San Francisco, CA 94123 (Tel. 415-441-1106).

Weather/Sea Notes
Tropical; sun intense even on the water and protection (hats; cover-up; sunscreen) is essential. Rough seas will preclude even land whale watching, but most whale watching is done in protected bays and channels.

Laws/Guidelines
The following actions *violate* the Marine Mammal Protection Act as it is interpreted in Hawaii to protect humpback whales:

(1) Vessels, swimmers and divers
– approaching within 300 yards of a humpback whale in the designated calving and breeding area off Lanai and Maui. (See map.)
– approaching within 100 yards of a humpback in all other areas within 200 miles off the Hawaiian Islands.
– travelling faster than a whale or repeatedly changing vessel speed while between 100–300 yards.
– herding or driving whales; separating a whale from a calf.
(2) Aircraft flying lower than 1000 feet while within a horizontal distance of 300 yards from a whale, including hovering, circling or buzzing whales.
(3) General: Any other act or omission that substantially disrupts the normal behavior of a whale resulting in, for example, the whale abruptly changing direction or speed; diving for prolonged periods; interrupting breeding or nursing; tail swishing to protect a calf from a vessel or human observer; and/or abandoning a previously frequented area.

A copy of the detailed regulations (subject to change) are available from Western Pacific Program Office, National Marine Fisheries Service, Box 3830, Honolulu, HI 96812 (Tel. 808-946-2181).

Oceanaria
Bottlenose and spinner dolphins at Sea Life Park, Makapuu Point, Waimanalo, Oahu, HI 96795.

Museums
See humpback whale films, whaling artifacts, and check latest whale sightings at the *Carthaginian II* (Whaling Museum), a fully rigged 19th-Century bark replica permanently moored in Lahaina Harbor on Wharf St., opposite the Pioneer Inn. Daily 9–4:30. The Lahaina Restoration Foundation, Box 338, Lahaina, HI 96761 (Tel. 808-661-8527).

Sperm whale skeleton and more whaling artifacts at Whalers' Village and Museum in Kaanapali, an outdoor display at a shopping center near Lahaina.

More information
Hawaii Visitors Bureau, 801-2270 Kalakana Ave., Honolulu, HI 96815 (Tel. 808-923-1811).

United States: Laws/Guidelines

The Marine Mammal Protection Act of 1972 is a federal law that prohibits persons under US jurisdiction (or US citizens abroad) from taking marine mammals. Taking is defined as "harassing, hunting, capturing, killing, or attempting to harass, hunt, capture, or kill." Taking is permitted for subsistence by Eskimos, Aleuts, and Indians of the North Pacific and Arctic Ocean as long as stocks can support a harvest. Taking may also be authorized by special permit for scientific research, public display (oceanaria), and incidentally in commercial fishing operations. The National Marine Fisheries Service (NMFS) is the federal agency that enforces the act, issues permits, and publishes rules and regulations for managing marine mammals. Among these rules and regulations are specific directives for whale watching in Hawaii and California. See the Laws/Guidelines listing under these states. For whale watching in other areas, detailed "definitions" of harassment have not been developed. For more information on the Marine Mammal Protection Act of 1972, including current interpretations, status of species, and news of research and management, consult the MMPA Annual Report, available from the Office of Protected Species and Habitat Conservation, NMFS, Washington, DC 20235 USA.

Species

Common: humpback whale (**7**), fin whale (**5**), long-finned pilot whale (**76**), minke whale (**2**), harbor porpoise (**40**), Atlantic white-sided dolphin (**58**), white-beaked dolphin (**63**).
Sporadic: sei whale (**3**), blue whale (**6**), killer whale (**75**), sperm whale (**12**).
Rare: right whale (**8**), beluga (**34**), northern bottlenose whale (**18**).

Lookouts

Sooner or later, the serious whale watcher finds himself in Newfoundland. Steep cliffs along a 5,500-mile-long coastline (6½ times the length of California's) provide good views of whales. Season for small cetaceans – harbor porpoises, white-beaked dolphins and Atlantic white-sided dolphins – is spring–fall. Humpback, fin and minke whales are common April–Oct. Presence and exact location of whales depends on food abundance. Humpbacks, minkes and fins eat capelin, a small silvery fish related to smelt. Pilot whales (called potheads) eat squid. Ask any Newfoundland fisherman about capelin and squid. He knows where they are. Detecting whale watchers, he may talk about his fishing problems when a humpback or minke gets caught in his net. Newfoundland whale research has revolved around these tangled animals as researchers try to rescue the whale without ruining the net. Sometimes the whale drowns, but the researchers learn a lot. Besides fishermen, the Whale Research Group at Memorial University of Newfoundland in St. John's (Tel. 709-753-5495) and Ceta Research Inc. in Trinity (Tel. 709-464-3269) will advise of current whale abundance around Newfoundland.

One of the best places to watch humpbacks feeding is **1** near St. Vincent's in St. Mary's Bay. From St. John's, take the Trans-Canada Hwy. (Hwy. 1) to Hwy. 90. Follow 90 south to St. Vincent's. After Holyrood Pond comes a long sandy beach – about 2 hours total driving from

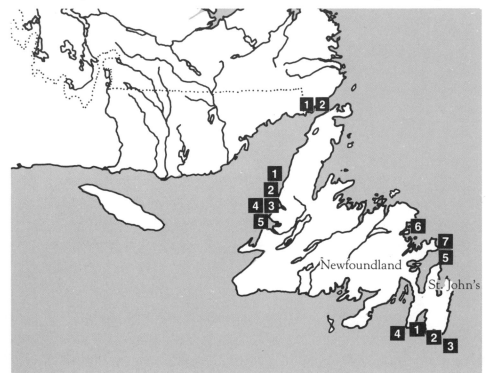

A humpback whale pokes its head above water as it is caught in a net off Newfoundland.

St. John's. When the capelin spawn (mid-June–mid-July) humpbacks feed as close as 20 yards from shore.

Closer to St. John's (about 30 minutes drive) is **2** Holyrood Arm, good for squid during summer and potheads, too. Take the Trans-Canada Hwy. from St. John's to Hwy. 62, turn right and follow the signs to town of Holyrood, turning left at Hwy. 60. Beyond Holyrood is Holyrood Arm, the southernmost inlet of Conception Bay. If you don't see the potheads, inquire at Holyrood or nearby Lakeview about the squid. Squid concentration changes from year to year.

More summer sites on the Avalon Peninsula for inshore potheads, humpbacks, minke whales and various dolphins: **3** Cape Race at the village of Cape Race, 82 miles south of St. John's on winding Hwy. 10 to the village of Portugal Cove South, then from the turnoff another 12 miles to Cape Race; **4** Cape St. Mary's, at the sea bird sanctuary (2nd largest gannetry in North America) on the southwestern tip of the Avalon Peninsula, about 125 miles from St. John's; **5** Bay

de Verde at the north end of Conception Bay, off Hwy. 70, about 115 miles from St. John's.

Good summer whale sites around eastern central Newfoundland include **6** outside the old village of Salvage at the eastern end of Hwy. 310 off Trans-Canada Hwy., 55 miles east of Gander; **7** around Cape Bonavista in the villages of Newman's Cove and Elliston, a few miles off Hwy. 230 and about 175 miles east of Gander.

Tours

Peter Beamish is a whale researcher who, in the late 1970s, turned to whale tourism. Since then, Beamish's Ocean Contact has escorted people from around the world to meet Newfoundland's whales. Beamish and his wife Chris run the Village Inn, visiting whale-watcher's headquarters in the fishing outport of **Trinity** on Trinity Bay. Whale watchers

157

enjoy hikes around the bay, family-style meals, evening whale movies and plenty of whales. Day trips on a 32-foot sailing yawl or larger power and sail boats that tow rubber Zodiac inflatables (for close encounters). Also, kayaks with windows in the hulls for underwater whale watching. Week-long packages from St. John's at $885 to $1,085 [Can] depending on time of year. Full-day or 1/2-day charters are also available. Whale season is June–late Sept. Contact: Ocean Contact Ltd., Box 10, Trinity, Trinity Bay, Nfld. A0C 2S0 Canada (Tel. 709-464-3269).

Near Terra Nova National Park, in Eastport on Bonavista Bay, are daily guided charters to see whales, sea birds and other sights. About $4 [Can]/person/hour. Contact: Brent Marsh, Ocean Recreation Ltd., Box 3, Site 24, R.R. #1, Eastport, Nfld. A0G 1Z0 Canada (Tel. 709-677-2620).

In St. John's, Harbour Charters has 1/2-day whale-watching and sightseeing tours for $18 [Can]. Contact: Capt. C. E. Anonsen, Harbour Charters, 22 Pilot's Hill, St. John's, Nfld. A1C 3M2 Canada (Tel. 709-754-1672).

At the village of **Southern Harbour**, 85 miles west of St. John's, Lady Carla Charters offers several day and overnight summer excursions to the islands of Placentia Bay that include whale watching. About $30 [Can]/hour, for up to 6 people. Contact: Lady Carla Charters, Box 77, Southern Harbour, Placentia Bay, Nfld. A0B 3H0 Canada (Tel. 709-463-8589).

The Pelley Inn, in **Springdale**, about 2 hours drive from Gander, offers daily boat and plane charters, weekend tours, and week-long holidays in Notre Dame Bay and White Bay. Whales are often sighted. Contact: Pelley Inn, Springdale, Nfld. A0J 1T0 (Tel. 709-673-3931).

For longer expedition-style tours led by naturalists, contact (1) Canadian Nature Tours, FON Conservation Centre, 355 Lesmill Road, Don Mills, Ont. M3B 2W8 Canada (Tel. 416-444-8419); (2) Biological Journeys, 1876 Ocean Dr., McKinleyville, CA 95521 USA (Tel. 707-839-0178).

Unique sail and study programs for students who want to partake in whale research and earn college credit are offered by The Ocean Research and Education Society. Based in Gloucester, Massachusetts, this non-profit educational society operates a 144-foot, 3-masted barkentine called *Regina Maris* that periodically comes to Newfoundland to study humpback and other whales. Tuition for a 12-week sail and study semester is $4,900 [US] and includes living expenses for 6 weeks at sea; the other 6 weeks are spent at a shore-based classroom in Gloucester. Sometimes there are special non-credit expeditions at $700 [US] for 10 days – 2 weeks. Excellent instructors and programs that contribute to scientific work on whales. Contact: The Ocean Research and Education Society, Inc., 19 Harbor Loop, Gloucester, MA 01930 USA (Tel. 617-283-1475).

Ferries and Cruises

Most of Newfoundland's cetaceans can be seen from inexpensive CN Marine ferries linking North Sydney, Nova Scotia, and Argentia, 80 miles west of St. John's (18-hour sail; 3 times a week in summer), and between Argentia and Channel-Port-aux-Basques, Nfld. Along the remote southern coast, a less frequent, longer ferry stops in many villages. Contact: CN Marine Reservations Bureau, Box 250, North Sydney, N.S. B2A 3M3 Canada (Tel. 902-742-3513 or, in Maine, 800-432-7344; continental US, 800-341-7981).

More short ferry runs logging whale sightings include (1) Ramea-Burgeo-Grey River Ferry with continuous service on the south coast (Tel. 709-625-2241); (2) St. Brendan's Ferry with 2 trips daily during summer from Burnside near Terra Nova National Park (Tel. 709-884-5964); (3) the Fogo Island Ferry across Hamilton Sound 5 times weekly during summer (Tel. 709-266-2407).

Weather/Sea Notes

Often wet and cold from the water during summer. Fog also a problem.

Museums

Whale displays at Newfoundland Museum, 285 Duckworth St., St. John's, Nfld. A1C 1G9 Canada (Tel. 709-737-2460).

Abandoned whaling factory at Dildo, Trinity Bay.

More information

Department of Development, Tourism Branch, Box 2016, St. John's, Nfld. A1C 5R8 Canada.

Canada: Newfoundland – Western

Species
Common: fin whale (**5**), long-finned pilot whale (**76**), minke whale (**2**), harbor porpoise (**40**), Atlantic white-sided dolphin (**58**), white-beaked dolphin (**63**).
Sporadic: humpback whale (**7**), blue whale (**6**).
Rare: killer whale (**75**), sei whale (**3**), sperm whale (**12**), right whale (**8**), beluga (**34**).

Lookouts
At Gros Morne National Park, 2 hours drive from Stephenville airport or about 4 hours drive from the ferry at Channel-Port-aux-Basques, are several fair whale and dolphin lookouts, especially June–early Aug. when whales pursue prey into near-shore waters: **1** Cow Head, a 2-mile walk west from the village of Cow Head, off Hwy. 430; **2** Green Point and **3** Lobster Cove Head off Hwy. 430; **4** Salmon Point, a mile hike off Hwy. 430 between Rocky Harbour and Bonne Bay; and **5** Green Garden, a 2-mile hike from Hwy. 431 along marked trails. Contact: Gros Morne National Park, Box 130, Rocky Harbour, Nfld. A0K 4N0 Canada (Tel. 709-458-2417).

Tours
Summer sightseeing tours that sometimes include whales are offered in Gros Morne National Park. 2-hour tour $15 [Can]/person. Contact: Reg Williams, Bontours, Norris Point, Nfld. A0K 3V0 Canada (Tel. 709-458-2730).

Whale charters can be arranged for $25/hour or $250 [Can]/day during summer. Contact: (1) Scott Shears, Gros Morne Boat Charters, Rocky Harbour, Nfld. A0K 4N0 Canada (Tel. 709-458-2425); (2) Leslie Hiscock, Norris Point, Nfld. A0K 3V0 Canada (Tel. 709-458-2733).

Ferries and Cruises
The frequent Bonne Bay Ferry between Norris Point and Woody Point in Gros Morne National Park is sometimes good for whale and dolphin spotting (Tel. 709-458-2414).

The CN Marine ferry between North Sydney, Nova Scotia and Channel-Port-aux-Basques is another possibility. Contact: CN Marine Reservations Bureau, Box 250, North Sydney, N.S. B2A 3M3 Canada (Tel. 902-742-3513 or, in Maine, 800-432-7344; continental US, 800-341-7981).

Museums
Whale display at River of Ponds Provincial Park, on Hwy. 430 north of Gros Morne National Park.

Canada: Newfoundland – Labrador

Species
Common: humpback whale (**7**), fin whale (**5**), long-finned pilot whale (**76**), minke whale (**2**), harbor porpoise (**40**), Atlantic white-sided dolphin (**58**), white-beaked dolphin (**63**).
Sporadic: beluga (**34**), narwhal (**33**), sei whale (**3**), blue whale (**6**), killer whale (**75**), sperm whale (**12**), northern bottlenose whale (**18**).

Lookouts
During summer, with a peak in June–July, large whales funnel through the 11-mile-wide Strait of Belle Isle that separates Newfoundland from Labrador and eastern Québec. Access via car ferry at St. Barbe on the northern peninsula of Newfoundland. The ferry lands at Blanc-Sablon, Québec, where the gravel 50-mile-long Labrador Hwy. (Hwy. 510) begins. Driving east into Labrador, find a spot along the road with an unobstructed view of the strait, perhaps at **1** L'Anse-au-Clair, a mile from ferry, or **2** Amour Point about 8 miles away on the road that veers right after Forteau Bay. A small provincial park at Pinware River might serve as a base camp.

Ferries and Cruises
The seasonal Strait of Belle Isle ferry

between St. Barbe, Newfoundland, and Blanc-Sablon, Québec, is good for large whales, especially June–July. It's an 80-minute crossing.

CN Marine has 2 ferries between Lewisporte (35 miles NW of Gander) and Goose Bay, Labrador. Budget cruises, they traverse prime whale areas. Even northern bottlenose whales, belugas and narwhals are possibilities. More likely are humpbacks, fins, minkes, and plenty of dolphins – plus icebergs during summer, some great coast, and probably rough weather. The *Sir Robert Bond* leaves twice a week during summer and takes 30–36 hours. $38.75 [Can] 1-way, more for cabin. The other, smaller ferry stops at 20–25 remote ports along the way and takes 5 1/2 days. $65 [Can] 1-way, plus $10/day for a berth (residents get first choice). Optional return via air from Goose Bay. Contact: CN Marine Reservations Bureau, Box 250, North Sydney, N.S. B2A 3M3 Canada (Tel. 902-742-3513 or, in Maine, 800-432-7344; continental US, 800-341-7981).

Canada: Nova Scotia

Species

Common: fin whale (**5**), humpback whale (**7**), long-finned pilot whale (**76**), minke whale (**2**), harbor porpoise (**40**), Atlantic white-sided dolphin (**58**).

Lookouts

The Digby Neck area of southwestern Nova Scotia is a frequent late-summer feeding ground for humpback and fin whales. Possible lookouts include: **1** "Northern Light" (local name) at northern tip of Brier Island about a mile north of Westport; **2** on the Bay of Fundy coast, a 1/2-mile west of Freeport at southwestern end of Long Point (opposite Northern Light on Brier Island); **3** lighthouse at southwestern tip of Brier Island. The first spot is best; first 2 are also good for harbor porpoises.

To see long-finned pilot whales, stake a lookout at the other end of the province on Cape Breton Island. On the Gulf of St. Lawrence side of Cape Breton Highlands National Park are 2 possibilities. Follow the Cabot Trail (hwy.) north to the national park. At **4** French Mountain Lookoff (before French Mountain) and **5** Skyline Trail, best times for pilot whales are July–Aug. depending on the squid. Fin whales are a possibility. Contact: Cape Breton Highlands National Park, Ingonish Beach, Cape Breton, N.S. B0C 1L0 Canada (Tel. 902-285-2270).

Tours

During July–Aug., Capt. Bill Crawford offers 3 whale cruises a day on the 40-foot *Bonnie Maureen III*. Pilot (and sometimes fin) whales are seen on 75% of the days. In June, Sept. and Oct., the cruises run less often, and tours focus on cormorants, guillemots, gannets – and the sea caves of **Cape Breton Highlands National Park**. The 3-hour cruises depart from Government Wharf at Cheticamp Harbour opposite the church. $15 [Can]/person. Contact: Cheticamp Boat Tours, Box 10, Grand Etang, Cape Breton, N.S. B0E 1L0 Canada (Tel. 902-224-3376).

There's often good whale watching on a birding tour to Nova Scotia (and New Brunswick) usually offered in Sept. by Wings, Inc. Departing from Bangor, Maine, the 12-day tour visits **Brier Island** in the Digby Neck area and takes a boat offshore to Moore Ledge. Red phalaropes, puffins and Wilson's storm-petrels know their way around here – and so do fins and humpbacks. Costs about $1,030 [US], plus air fare. Contact: Wings, Inc., Box 974, Northeast Harbor, ME 04662 USA (Tel. 207-276-5077).

The humpbacks off the **south coast of Nova Scotia** are part of the summer curriculum of The Ocean Research and Education Society. Based in Gloucester, Massachusetts, this non-profit educational society offers 12-week sail and study programs for college credit – 6 weeks are spent in a classroom and 6 weeks at sea, photographing and assisting with research into humpbacks and other whales. Tuition of $4,900 [US] includes all living expenses at sea. Contact: The Ocean Research and Education Society, Inc. 19 Harbor Loop, Gloucester, MA 01930 USA (Tel. 617-283-1475).

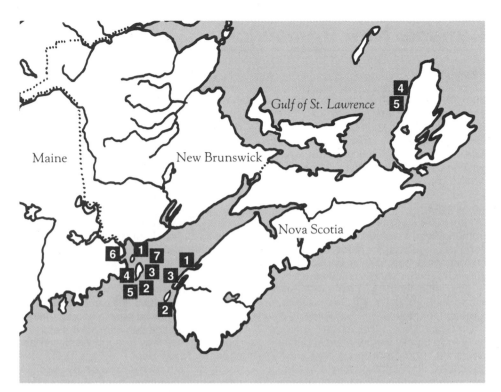

Ferries and Cruises

4 major ferry routes to and from Nova Scotia are inexpensive whale-watching opportunities. The best are part of the Canadian National Marine system; all require reservations. (1) The Portland, Maine, to Yarmouth, Nova Scotia, ferry features daily service on the 12-hour run from early May–Oct. Contact: Prince of Fundy Cruises, Box 4216, Station A, Portland, ME 04101 USA (Tel. 207-775-5616). (2) The Bar Harbor, Maine to Yarmouth, Nova Scotia, *Bluenose* has daily 6-hour crossings from June 19–Sept. 27. Contact: CN Marine, Terminal Supervisor, Bar Harbor, ME 04609 USA (Tel. 800-341-7981 in eastern US; 800-432-7344 in Maine) or CN Marine, Terminal Supervisor, Yarmouth, N.S. B5A 1K0 Canada (Tel. 902-742-3513). (3) North Sydney, Nova Scotia, to Argentia, Newfoundland, and (4) North Sydney, Nova Scotia, to Channel-Port-aux-Basques, Newfound-land, are frequent ferries connecting Newfoundland to the mainland. Contact: CN Marine Reservations Bureau, Box 250, North Sydney, N.S. B2A 3M3 Canada (Tel. 902-742-3513 or, in Maine, 800-432-7344; continental US, 800-341-7981).

Weather/Sea Notes

During the summer whale-watching season, days are warm, rarely hot or humid, but cold on the water. Fog and rain, too, are factors.

Museums

Whale display at Nova Scotia Museum, 1747 Summer St., Halifax, N.S. Canada B3H 3A6 (Tel. 902-429-4610).

More information

Nova Scotia Tourism, Box 456, Halifax, N.S. B3J 2R5 Canada (Tel. 902-424-5000 or, in Maine, 800-492-0643; continental US, 800-341-6096).

Canada: New Brunswick

Species

Common: right whale (**8**), fin whale (**5**), humpback whale (**7**), minke whale (**2**), harbor porpoise (**40**).
Sporadic: Atlantic white-sided dolphin (**58**), long-finned pilot whale (**76**).
Rare: sei whale (**3**), blue whale (**6**), white-beaked dolphin (**63**), beluga (**34**), killer whale (**75**).

Lookouts

On the lower Bay of Fundy, an hour drive from the nearest large airport at Saint John, is a good harbor porpoise spot with fin and minke possibilities, especially July–Oct. Take Hwy. 1 to St. George, turning left at junction of Hwy. 772. Follow road past Back Bay to **1** Green's Point (Letete) Lighthouse.

On Grand Manan Island, a 1½-hour toll ferry from Blacks Harbour and about 3 hours total from Saint John, there are 4 good lookouts for fin and minke whales, and harbor porpoises from late July–late

Sept.: **2** Swallowtail Head and **3** Northern Head, both visible from ferry and a short walk or drive after landing at North Head; researchers led by University of Guelph Professor David E. Gaskin have studied harbor porpoises from these points and have identified the area as one of the species' strongholds in the world; **4** Dark Harbour, 5 miles from North Head on the only road to island's west side has fin whales later in fall than other areas; **5** Southern Head, about 15 miles drive to island's southern tip is foggier than other areas.

On Deer Island (access via short ferry from Eastport, Maine, or free ferry from Letete, New Brunswick), follow road to island's southern tip, **6** Deer Island Point. Campground here is good vantage for porpoises and sometimes whales threading their way through Western Passage from July–Sept.

Any of the above lookouts may yield right whale sightings, but probably best (though still slim) opportunity is from **7** East Quoddy Light at north tip of Campobello Island. Easy access from Maine but from Canadian mainland, 2 ferries are

Long-finned pilot whales swim through the lower Bay of Fundy.

Nona Famous / Seafarers

A right whale surfaces near Grand Manan Island in the Bay of Fundy.

necessary: first to Deer Island, then to Campobello Island. 5 miles north on Hwy. 774 leads to East Quoddy Light. Look east from the light toward the distant island group called The Wolves. Besides the occasional right whale, a minke often works the area between these islands from July–Sept. Also sometimes fin whales and harbor porpoises.

Tours

The rediscovery of a summer concentration of the rare right whale in the lower Bay of Fundy in the last decade sent whale-sized ripples through the North American whale-watching community. Full-day trips to see them (plus fins, minkes and harbor porpoises) aboard a 45-foot fish boat are $99 [Can]. Zoologist David E. Gaskin and his research associates lead the trips. 3-, 4-, or 7-day packages at $399, $549, and $989 [Can], respectively, include daily expeditions, plus home-cooked meals, comfortable accommodation at century-old Marathon Inn on Grand Manan Island, and pick-up and drop-off at Saint John airport. The Marathon Inn is open from May 1 to Canadian Thanksgiving, but best whale watching occurs from Aug. 1–Sept. 15. Contact: James Leslie, Ocean Search, Marathon Inn, Box 129, North Head, Grand Manan Island, N.B. E0G 2M0 Canada (Tel. 506-662-8144).

Ferries and Cruises

Harbor porpoises, fin and minke whales are seen from July–Oct. aboard the *M/V Grand Manan* or *Lady Manan* car ferry between mainland New Brunswick at Black's Harbour and North Head, Grand Manan Island.

Occasional whale sightings on summer car ferries linking Deer Island and Eastport, Maine; Deer Island and Campobello Island; and free car ferry between Deer Island and Letete on mainland New Brunswick.

Weather/Sea Notes

A hazard to navigation, fog may also cancel lookout whale watching, though sometimes confined to local patches, and lifting by midday. Sept. and Oct. are most fog free. Occasional summer rain and rough seas may also reduce visibility. Cold on the water. Large tides.

More information

Tourism New Brunswick, Box 12345, Fredericton, N.B. E3B 5C3 Canada (Tel. 800-561-0123 in Canada; 800-322-7004 in Maine; 800-343-0812 in rest of US). *For more about whales in the lower Bay of Fundy, see United States: Maine, p. 119.*

Canada: Québec – St. Lawrence River (Fleuve Saint-Laurent)

Species

Common: beluga (**34**), minke whale (**2**), fin whale (**5**), blue whale (**6**), harbor porpoise (**40**).
Sporadic: Atlantic white-sided dolphin (**58**), long-finned pilot whale (**76**), killer whale (**75**), humpback whale (**7**).

Lookouts

The food-rich mouth of the cold, deep Saguenay River and the adjacent shores of the massive St. Lawrence estuary lure large numbers of whales every summer. Among them are belugas, uncommon at this latitude, and blue whales – uncommon at any latitude. With patience, they can be seen from lookouts on the north side of the St. Lawrence – lookouts where scientists from the Arctic Biological Station study them. For belugas (present year-round but best viewed June–Nov.), minke and fin whales (summer–fall), plus harbor porpoises: **1** Pointe Noire on Hwy. 138 about 125 miles east of Québec City, near Baie-Sainte-Catherine, overlooking the mouth of the Saguenay Fjord (Pointe Noire Marine Centre, open early summer–mid-Oct., has beluga exhibits and films; trail from center to whale lookout; Tel. 418-237-4383; for more on cen-

Researchers use unique pigmentation patterns to distinguish blue whales in the Gulf of St. Lawrence.

ter, local lodging and whale cruises, contact: Société Linnéenne Saint-Laurent, C.P. 9880, Ste-Foy, P.Q. G1V 4C5 Canada); **2** Tadoussac, a 5-minute ferry across the Saguenay from Pointe Noire, beside the ferry dock.

The best blue whale lookouts are downstream on the north side of the St. Lawrence (also harbor porpoises, fin and minke whales and, sometimes, belugas and the odd humpback): **3** at Cap-de-Bon-Désir, an old lighthouse on the river, 12 miles from the Tadoussac ferry and 1 mile off Hwy. 138 at the village of Grandes-Bergeronnes. If lost, ask in Grandes-Bergeronnes: "Où sont les baleines bleues?" The last few years, a week-long Festival de la Baleine Bleue, with pageants, crafts, whale items and thousands of visitors, has been staged in Aug. (For next year's dates, call 418-235-4491); **4** At Les Escoumins, 10 miles past Grandes-Bergeronnes, near the wharf and pilot station (place where ferry pilots are exchanged).

On the south side of the St. Lawrence River, belugas pass in late summer near the wharf at **5** Rivière-du-Loup, access via 2 1¼-hour ferries from north side or on Hwy. 20 (Autoroute Transcanadienne).

Tours

Commercial whale watching in Canada

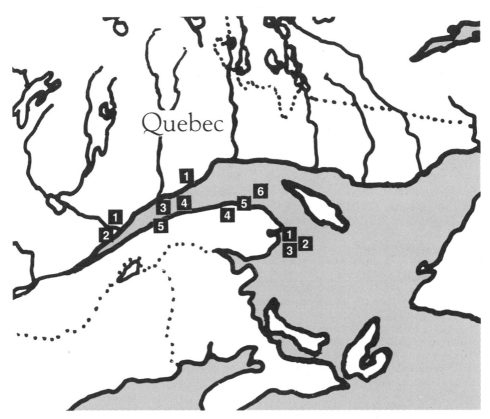

began in the St. Lawrence River in 1971. The first trips were organized by the Zoological Society of Montréal. They are still offering weekend trips, 4–5 of them during Aug.–Sept. The 3-day/2-night trips out of Montréal cost $225 [Can] (plus a $15 contribution to the society for non-members) and include: transport from Montréal, a 10-hour river cruise, 2 meals on the boat, and 2 nights hotel. The ship is the 110-foot *M/V St-Barnabe*, an ex-US Navy minesweeper. Naturalists give presentations in English. Contact: The Zoological Society of Montréal, Mezzanine Floor, 2055 rue Peel, Montréal, P.Q. H3A 1V4 Canada (Tel. 514-845-8317).

Since 1979, the non-profit Société Linnéenne (Linnean Society) in Québec City has developed French Canadian interest in whale watching, and is today the main tour organizer in Québec. The naturalist interpretation is given in French and English. There are several types of tours: (1) "Whales in the St. Lawrence" Option A is a 9-hour cruise aboard the 180-foot *Gobelet d'Argent*. From late July–early Oct., it departs several times a week from Trois Pistoles, about 160 miles from Québec City, $75 [Can]. (2) "Whales in the St. Lawrence" Option B includes Option A plus a night's hotel and round-trip bus from Montréal, $171 [Can] and up–a 2-day/1-night excursion. (3) "The Saguenay Fjord" includes a 3-hour cruise of the St. Lawrence on one day and a 6-hour cruise on the Saguenay the next, both aboard the *Jos Lachance II*. Hotel in Tadoussac plus bus from Montréal, $164 [Can] and up. Late June–early Oct. Belugas are part of an in-depth exploration of the Saguenay fjord. (4) "St. Lawrence Cruises" are 3-hour cruises aboard the *Jos Lachance II* departing from the pier at Tadoussac or Baie-Ste-Catherine 1–3 times daily from Aug. 1–mid-Sept. Adults $19, children $15 [Can]. For schedule and reservations, contact: Société Linnéenne Saint-Laurent, C.P. 9880, Ste-Foy, P.Q. G1V 4C5 Canada (Tel. 418-237-4383).

Packaged whale-watching tours are also offered by Via Rail from late July–early Oct. They include a 9-hour cruise on *Gobelet d'Argent*, plus 2 nights hotel and round-trip train from Montréal ($225), Québec City ($188) or Ottawa ($248) [Can]. Contact: Via Rail Canada Inc., Rail Travel Bureau, Central Station, Montréal, P.Q. H3N 3C3 Canada (Tel. 514-871-1331 or local Via or Amtrak office).

Occasional whale-watching tours on the St. Lawrence are offered by: (1) National Museum of Natural Sciences, Whale Watching Trips, Ottawa, Ont. K1A 0M8 Canada (Tel. 613-998-9281); (2) Gerard Iles, 2053 Vendome Ave., Montréal, P.Q. H4A 3M4 Canada (Tel. 514-484-8692); (3) Russ Kinne, No. Wilton Rd., New Canaan, CT 06840 USA (Tel. 203-966-4900 or 212-758-3420).

Ferries and Cruises

3 ferries on the St. Lawrence allow sightings of belugas, occasional minke, blue and fin whales, and harbor porpoises from mid-June–Nov. (1) Trois-Pistoles/Escoumins, a 1¼-hour seasonal crossing of the St. Lawrence, has the best chance of seeing blues. $5.25 [Can]. (Tel. 418-851-1436). For belugas and other whales, try (2) Rivière-du-Loup/Saint-Siméon, a 1¼-hour seasonal crossing of the St. Lawrence. $5.25 [Can]. (Tel. 418-867-1272); or (3) Baie-Ste-Catherine/Tadoussac, a free 5-minute ferry that crosses the Saguenay mouth year-round.

Weather/Sea Notes

Windy and cold on the water, though rarely rough seas. Rains occasionally. Can be hot and humid in July–early Aug. on shore lookouts. Snow arrives in Nov., sometimes as early as late Oct.

Museums

Musée de la Mer de Rimouski (Rimouski Marine Museum), Pointe-au-Père, P.Q.

La Halte Côtière de Pointe Noire (Pointe Noire Marine Center), Baie-Ste-Catherine, P.Q. (Tel. 418-237-4383). Contact: Société Linnéenne Saint-Laurent, C.P. 9880, Ste-Foy, P.Q. G1V 4C5 Canada (Tel. 418-653-8186).

More information

Tourisme-Québec, C.P. 20,000, Québec, P.Q. G1K 7X2 Canada (Tel. 514-873-2015).

Canada: Québec – North Shore (Côte-Nord)

Species

Common: blue whale (6), minke whale (2), fin whale (5), harbor porpoise (40). *Sporadic:* Atlantic white-sided dolphin (58), white-beaked dolphin (63), long-finned pilot whale (76), humpback whale (7), killer whale (75).

Lookouts

The old lighthouse at **1** Pointe-des-Monts is a great spot to watch and wait for blue whales. The blues, along with minkes and fins, have been seen as early as April and as late as the end of Nov., but best in early fall.

From Québec City, take Hwy. 138 about 320 miles to Godbout (beyond Baie-Comeau). 33 miles past Godbout, turn right on 7-mile road to lighthouse.

Tours

Since 1976, biologist Richard Sears and his colleagues have been researching whales along the north shore of the Gulf of St. Lawrence. Working out of a remote French-Canadian fishing village, the Mingan Island Cetacean Study has followed and photographed 10 species of whales. The focus has been the blue whale, and they have photographically identified individual blue whales using unique pigmentation patterns on their backs. Some blues return to the area in successive years, spending much of their year in the Gulf. Since 1981, Mingan Island Cetacean Study has offered 10-day programs in Aug.–Sept. which include several days watching whales from Zodiac inflatable boats, plus field trips to bird rookeries and other local wonders. $950 [US] plus air fare to Sept-Îles. Accommodations are not deluxe, but this is a rare opportunity to share in the excitement of research into the largest-ever animal. Contact: Mingan Island Cetacean Study, Box 518, Meriden, CT 06450 USA or Station de Recherche des Îles Mingan, C.P. 159, Sept-Îles, P.Q.

J. Michael Williamson / MICS

A blue whale raises its flukes as it dives in the Gulf of St. Lawrence.

G4R 4K3 Canada. These tours can also be booked through Oceanic Society Expeditions, Fort Mason Center, Bldg. E, San Francisco, CA 94123 USA (Tel. 415-441-1106).

Weather/Sea Notes
Windy and cold on the water though summer daytime temperatures from lookouts can be quite warm. Rain sometimes a factor.

More information
Association Touristique Régionale de Duplessis, Inc., 801 Boul. Laure, C.P. 156, Sept-Îles, P.Q. G4R 4K3 Canada (Tel. 418-962-0808).

Canada: Québec – Gaspé Peninsula (Gaspésie)

Species
Common: minke whale (**2**), fin whale (**5**).
Sporadic: humpback whale (**7**), blue whale (**6**), Atlantic white-sided dolphin (**58**), white-beaked dolphin (**63**), long-finned pilot whale (**76**), harbor porpoise (**40**).

Lookouts
Forillon National Park, located on the Gaspé Peninsula overlooking the Gulf of St. Lawrence, has several fair whale lookouts with the advantages of a national park: good campgrounds, hiking trails, visitor information and interpretation centers, and chances to see a variety of wildlife. Forillon National Park (about 10 miles from the airport and town of Gaspé) is a 660-mile drive north from Portland, Maine, or 440 miles east-northeast from Québec City. Hwy. 132 almost encircles the park along the water. Follow the signs to Cap Gaspé. The best area to look for whales is between Grand-Grève and Cap Gaspé, a 4-mile stretch of road (and parallel hiking trail) on Baie de Gaspé.

Although any spot here is good, the established lookouts (in order of popularity) are **1** Cap Gaspé, near lighthouse at the southeastern end of park; **2** Anse-aux-Sauvages, 2 miles from Cap Gaspé (parking); and **3** Anse-Saint-Georges, 3 miles from Cap Gaspé. All are well-marked lookouts (French: belvédère).

On the other side of the park, overlooking the Gulf of St. Lawrence, are 2 more possible whale sites: **4** Cap-des-Rosiers is on Hwy. 132 near lighthouse (French: phare); **5** Cap-Bon-Ami is 4 miles down a secondary road from Cap-des-Rosiers (parking; camping). For camping reservations and information about 3-times-daily summer boat cruises in park waters that regularly log fin and minke whale sightings, contact: Le Directeur, Parc National Forillon, C.P. 1220, Gaspé, P.Q. G0C 1R0 Canada (Tel. 418-368-5505).

The north coast of the Gaspé Peninsula, northwest of Forillon National Park, also has whale possibilities, at least for minke whales and harbor porpoises. Stop along the 110-mile-long stretch of Hwy. 132 from **6** Rivière-au-Renard (north edge of Parc Forillon) to Ste-Anne-des-Monts.

Tours

Seafarers, the Maine company sponsoring naturalist-led programs to see whales and sea birds in the Bay of Fundy, is planning its first trip to the Gaspé Peninsula for summer 1984. The 10-day itinerary will include visits to see the seabirds of Bonaventure Island and whales of Forillon National Park. About $100 [US] a day plus air fare. Seafarers, Box 428, RFD 1, Machias, ME 04654 USA (Tel. 207-255-8810).

Weather/Sea Notes

Lookouts cool and windy, but rarely cold during summer; fog and rain may be a factor.

More information

Association Touristique de la Gaspésie, C.P. 810, Carleton, P.Q. G0C 1J0 Canada (Tel. 418-364-7041).

Canada: British Columbia

Species

Common: gray whale (**1**), killer whale (**75**), Dall's porpoise (**45**).
Sporadic: minke whale (**2**), humpback whale (**7**), harbor porpoise (**40**), Pacific white-sided dolphin (**59**).
Rare: blue whale (**6**), fin whale (**5**), sei whale (**3**), Cuvier's beaked whale (**15**), sperm whale (**12**).

Lookouts

On the west coast of Vancouver Island, a 5-hour drive from Vancouver (including ferry) or a 4-hour drive from Victoria, migrating gray whales can be seen beginning in late Nov., but it's best in March–April. By June, the migrators have passed – all except 40–50 grays that spend their summers feeding along Vancouver Island. (They stay at least until the bulk of the gray whales returns from the Arctic in the fall and early winter *en route* to the Mexican calving lagoons.)

Good viewpoints in the Long Beach area, all of which have telescopes and are accessible by car: **1** Wickaninnish Centre at Wickaninnish Beach, 1½ miles off Hwy. 4 on the road to Tofino (see whale exhibit at centre); **2** Green Point, a short walk below campground on Long Beach off Hwy. 4; and **3** Radar Hill, less than a mile off Hwy. 4 at north end of Pacific Rim National Park.

Lookouts in the Long Beach Unit of Pacific Rim National Park that include ½- to 2-mile hikes on well-marked trails are

(from south to north off Hwy. 4 on the road to Tofino): **4** Wya Point at end of Half Moon Bay Trail off Willowbrae Trail; **5** Quisitis Point; **6** South Beach, at end of South Beach Trail, access from Wickaninnish Centre; **7** Box Island, access from Schooner Trail or north end of Long Beach; **8** Portland Point; and **9** Cox Point.

There are also many good gray whale lookouts along the **10** West Coast Trail (part of Pacific Rim National Park) between Bamfield and Port Renfrew (for experienced hikers only). During summer, Pacific Rim National Park provides free interpretive naturalist programs on whales (and other marine life) at Green Point and Box Island. To find out more, stop in at information center near Long Beach, 2 miles past Ucluelet turnoff on Hwy. 4, or write: Pacific Rim National Park, Box 280, Ucluelet, B.C. V0R 3A0 Canada.

On the Queen Charlotte Islands off northern B.C. (access via jet or ferry from mainland) from late April–early June, the gray whales pass **11** North Beach in the Rose Point/Rose Spit area of northeastern Graham Island in Tow Hill Provincial Park.

Less reliable, but possible in the summer, are killer whale sightings from the Gulf Islands (access by car on the B.C. Government ferry leaving several times a day from Tsawwassen, 22 miles south of Vancouver). They have been seen occasionally from **12** Mayne Island at Active Pass Lighthouse and from the **13** eastern tip of Saturna Island.

Tours

On northeastern Vancouver Island, most of a day's drive from Vancouver or Victoria, your best chance to see killer whales, minke whales and Dall's porpoises is aboard the 60-foot *Gikumi*. The 8-hour naturalist-guided cruises depart from the old mill town of Telegraph Cove most days from July–Sept. $48 [Can]/ person includes hearty lunch. Hotel or camping can be arranged. Contact: Bill Mackay or Jim Borrowman, Stubbs Island Charters Ltd., Box 303, Port McNeill, B.C. V0N 3J0 Canada (Tel. 604-928-3117/3185). Stubbs Island Charters also plans 6-day field photography tours that will include good orca opportunities.

A bull killer whale surfaces near the author's boat off northern Vancouver Island.

Tours aboard the *Gikumi* featuring killer whales may also be booked as a 3-day package from Swiftsure Tours of Victoria, starting at $225 [Can]. They also offer 2–3-day gray whale packages from late March–mid-April, starting at about $100 [Can]/day. All trips depart from Victoria and include whale watching by land, boat and air. Swiftsure Tours Ltd., 119-645 Fort St., Victoria, B.C. V8W 1G2 Canada (Tel. 604-388-4227).

Departing from Vancouver are 2-day guided excursions to see gray whales in late March–early April, and killer whales in Aug. $215 [Can] includes transport and lunches, but not accommodation. The tour organizers, Ecosummer Canada Expeditions, also offer guided kayaking tours that feature or include whale watching: (1) 8-day tours to killer whale waters of Johnstone Strait in Aug.; (2) 11-day west coast Vancouver Island tours in June that include visits with summer resident gray whales; (3) 14–15-day tours of the southern Queen Charlotte Islands from June through Aug. with incidental sightings of dolphins and various large whales. Prices start at $80 [Can]/day plus air charter to departure point. Experienced guides and naturalist interpreta-

tion. Contact: Ecosummer Canada Expeditions Ltd., 1516 Duranleau St., Vancouver, B.C. V6H 3S4 Canada (Tel. 604-669-7741).

More killer whale excursions to the **Johnstone Strait** area in Aug. are offered by (1) Biological Journeys, 1876 Ocean Dr., McKinleyville, CA 95521 USA (Tel. 707-839-0178); (2) Oceanic Society Expeditions, Fort Mason Center, Bldg. E, San Francisco, CA 94123 USA (Tel. 415-441-1106); (3) The University of British Columbia, Centre for Continuing Education, 5997 Iona Dr., Vancouver, B.C. V6T 2A4 Canada (Tel. 604-228-2181).

More gray whale excursions and day-trips to see gray whale summer residents and annual migration off **Pacific Rim National Park** are offered by (1) Sub-Tidal Adventures, 1192 Eber, Ucluelet, B.C. V0R 3A0 Canada (Tel. 604-726-7061); (2) Safari 11, Box 590, Tofino, B.C. V0R 2Z0 Canada (Tel. 604-725-3919); (3) Canadian Princess, Box 939, Ucluelet, B.C. V0R 3A0 Canada (Tel. 604-726-7771 or 598-3366); (4) Whitewater Adventures, Ltd., 105 W. 6th Ave., Vancouver, B.C. V5Y 1K3 Canada (Tel. 604-879-6701).

Additional gray whale charters available in **Ucluelet** and **Tofino** include: (1) Suncoast Charters, Box 490, Ucluelet, B.C. V0R 3A0 Canada (Tel. 604-726-7725); (2) Rosals Marine Charters, Ucluelet, B.C. V0R 3A0 Canada (Tel. 604-726-7119); (3) Bay-Shore Marina, Ucluelet, B.C. V0R 3A0 Canada (Tel. 604-726-7515); (4) Loudon Charters, Ucluelet, B.C. V0R 3A0 Canada (Tel. 604-726-4280); (5) Barkley Pacific, Box 188, Tofino, B.C. V0R 2Z0 Canada (Tel. 604-725-3284); (6) Seaforth Charters, Box 12, Tofino, B.C. V0R 2Z0 Canada (Tel. 604-725-3439).

Ferries and Cruises

Incidental sightings of killer whales and Dall's porpoises (less often humpbacks, minkes and harbor porpoises) on the B.C. Government ferries between Tsawwassen (22 miles from Vancouver) and Swartz Bay (19 miles from Victoria on Vancouver Island) and through the Gulf Islands, and on the 20-hour Port Hardy to Prince Rupert ferry. Sightings are logged year-round but July–Sept. is best. Ferries leave frequently every day. For schedules

and reservations contact: Tourism B.C. (604-387-1642) or B.C. Ferry Corp., INFORES, 1045 Howe St., Vancouver, B.C. V6Z 2A9 Canada (604-386-3431).

For Inside Passage cruises between Seattle and Alaska passing through killer whale and other whale areas, see Southeast Alaska.

Weather/Sea Notes

Winters wet and cool, summers dry and warm, but always carry rain gear. Southeast winds deliver clouds, rain and often instant gales from Sept.–May, but rarely in summer. In the normal summer pattern, westerly winds build every afternoon to 15–25 knots, with mornings often foggy. The trick is to maximize the viewing opportunity during the scant hour or 2 between the time the sun burns off the fog and the westerlies arise. Along eastern Vancouver Island, fog is not as prevalent and swells are shorter. Remember

A bull killer whale blows in Robson Bight, off northern Vancouver Island.

that on a hot July day, a sweater or even a coat is essential on the water. Whales are most plentiful in summer when, as well, viewing opportunities are best.

Oceanaria

Killer whales, belugas and Pacific white-sided dolphins at the Vancouver Public Aquarium, Stanley Park, Box 3232, Vancouver, B.C. V6B 3X8 Canada (Tel. 604-685-3364).

Killer whales at Sealand of the Pacific, 1327 Beach Dr., Victoria, B.C. V8S 2N4 Canada (Tel. 604-598-3373).

More information

Tourism B.C., 1117 Wharf St., Victoria, B.C. V8W 2Z2 Canada (Tel. 604-387-1642).

Canada: Manitoba

Species

Common: beluga (**34**).

Lookouts

Renowned for its polar bears that wander through town, Churchill also has belugas along the coastal coves and capes and in

the river mouth outside town. Access to Churchill is via jet or 30-hour train from Winnipeg that winds through boreal forest to the edge of the tundra. The belugas, arriving in June, depart late Aug., before the polar bears arrive. A good view point is **1** Cape Merry, a 1-mile walk along Cape Merry Centennial Parkway to the east bank of the Churchill River mouth. The river here is often thick with belugas. Across the river stands Prince of Wales Fort, built in the 18th Century by the Hudson's Bay Company. The Cape Merry site is on several $15–$20 [Can] local bus tours. Contact: (1) Churchill Wilderness Encounter, Box 9, Churchill, Man. R0B 0E0 Canada (Tel. 204-675-2729/2248); (2) North Star Bus Lines, Box 100, Churchill, Man. R0B 0E0 Canada (Tel. 204-675-2629); (3) The Great Canadian Travel Co., 712–504 Main St., Winnipeg, Man., Canada (Tel. 204-943-2039).

Tours

1-hour beluga tours leave **Churchill** harbor by boat. Daily, depending on weather and tides, from early June–Sept. 1. $15 [Can]/person. Contact: (1) Churchill Wilderness Encounter, Box 85, Churchill, Man. R0B 0E0 Canada (Tel. 204-675-2729; also has package tours from Winnipeg); (2) Sea North Tours, Box 222, Churchill, Man. R0B 0E0 Canada (Tel. 204-675-2195).

From **Winnipeg**, Via Rail has 7-day escorted tours during summer that include a beluga-watching trip in the Churchill River. Prices start at $1,175 [Can] for an upper berth. Contact: Via Rail Canada, Box 8116, 1801 McGill College, Floor 13, Montreal, P.Q. H3C 3N3 Canada (reservations through local offices of Via and Amtrak or through a travel agent).

From Winnipeg, several summer birding or general natural-history tours to Churchill take in belugas. The 5- to 11-day tours cost $100–$125 [Can]/day. Contact: (1) Canadian Nature Tours, FON Conservation Centre, 355 Lesmill Rd.,

Don Mills, Ont. M3B 2W8 Canada (Tel. 416-444-8419); (2) Questers Tours & Travel, Inc., 257 Park Ave. S., New York, NY 10010 USA (Tel. 212-673-3120); (3) Massachusetts Audubon Society, Lincoln, MA 01773 USA (Tel. 617-259-9500); (4) Wings, Inc., Box 974, Northeast Harbor, ME 04662 USA (Tel. 207-276-5077); (5) North America Nature Expeditions, Suite 104, 1776 Independence Ct., Birmingham, AL 35216 USA (Tel. 205-870-5550).

Biological Journeys plans its first Churchill tour for July 1984. Ronn Storro-Patterson is bringing hydrophones to listen to these "sea canaries" – as early whalers called the belugas. Contact: Biological Journeys, 1876 Ocean Dr., McKinleyville, CA 95521 USA (Tel. 707-839-0178). 707-839-0178).

Weather/Sea Notes

July and Aug. are warm months; average highs of about 60°F. and lows a few degrees above zero. Rough weather will cut visibility and cancel some tours. Allowances must be made for weather, but summers generally good with long hours of daylight.

Museums

Eskimo Museum, La Verendrye St., Box 10, Churchill, Man. R0B 0E0 Canada (Tel. 204-675-2252).

Interpretive Centre in Bayport Plaza, Churchill, has displays, films and slide shows of belugas. Contact: Parks Canada, Manitoba North Historical Sites, Box 127, Churchill, Man. R0B 0E0 Canada (Tel. 204-675-8863).

More information

Travel Manitoba, Dept. 3001, Winnipeg, Man. R3C 0V8 Canada (Tel. 204-944-3777).

Canada: Northwest Territories

Species

Common: beluga (**34**), narwhal (**33**), fin whale (**5**), minke whale (**2**).
Sporadic: bowhead whale (**10**), blue whale (**6**), humpback whale (**7**), sperm whale (**12**), northern bottlenose whale (**18**), harbor porpoise (**40**), killer whale (**75**), white-beaked dolphin (**63**).

Tours

Travel is often difficult and expensive in the 1.3-million-square-mile Northwest Territories, yet the chance of seeing belugas and narwhals, even the elusive bowhead, is beginning to lure whale watchers. Few trips are designed specifically for whale watchers, but many

naturalist-led wildlife tours feature whale sightings.

Canadian Nature Tours offers camping expeditions every summer. The tours meet in **Frobisher Bay** or **Resolute** (easy jet access). All expenses are covered in 5-day package tours at $1,150 [Can] and up. The Pond Inlet trip has the best chance to see a narwhal, plus possible belugas and more. The Somerset Island trip is sure to see belugas. Contact: Canadian Nature Tours, FON Conservation Centre, 355 Lesmill Road, Don Mills, Ont. M3B 2W8 Canada (Tel. 416-444-8419).

Sea kayaking with whales is a specialty of Ecosummer, a company that sponsors excellent tours in British Columbia and Alaska led by well-known biologists and anthropologists. An ongoing tour is "Northwest Passage by Kayak"; each summer another segment is traversed. Sightings of belugas, narwhals and possibly bowheads will be photographically and acoustically documented (with hydrophones). Graded moderate to strenuous, most trips involve hiking, carrying gear and 5–6 hours of paddling a day. Late July–Aug. About $2,500 [Can], including air charter from **Resolute Bay**, for 18 days. Contact: Ecosummer Canada Expeditions Ltd., 1516 Duranleau St., Vancouver, B.C. V6H 3S4 Canada (Tel. 604-669-7741).

Other escorted Arctic tours with wildlife

The Inuit still hunt the narwhal for food in the Northwest Territories.

possibilities can be arranged through (1) Bezal and Terry Jesudason, Box 200, Resolute Bay, N.W.T. X0A 0V0 Canada (Tel. 819-252-3875); (2) Jacopie Akpalialuk, Pangnirtung, N.W.T. X0E 0R0 Canada (Tel. 819-473-8847); (3) Steve and Norman Komoartuk, Pangnirtung, N.W.T. X0A 0R0 Canada (Tel. 819-473-8792).

At the other extreme from most of the above are luxury cruises, with naturalist guides, to remote areas, the **eastern Arctic** and **Hudson Bay** included. They promise sightings of most of the area's whales and dolphins, including narwhals and belugas. Landings are made in Zodiac inflatable boats. Itineraries change every year, but in 1983 there were 2 (30-day) excursions aboard the *M.S. Lindblad Explorer* to the Canadian Arctic, priced from $7,000–$15,600 [US]/ person depending on cabin, plus air fare to Halifax (or Reykjavik, Iceland). Contact: Salén Lindblad Cruising, Inc., 133 E. 55th St., New York, NY 10022 USA (Tel. 212-751-2300).

Weather/Sea Notes

Conditions vary widely by region. Average daily summer temperatures from 40s (F.) in the high Arctic to low 50s (F.) further south. Long (up to 24-hour) days of sun, but come prepared for rain and, on the water, it can get very cold. The Royal Canadian Mounted Police has a voluntary travel registration program for people venturing into the wilderness. Register at the RCMP detachment in the Northwest Territory community nearest to your point of departure.

More information
TravelArctic, Government of the Northwest Territories, Yellowknife, N.W.T. X1A 2L9 Canada.

Canada: Laws/Guidelines

In June 1982, "Cetacean Protection Regulations" were made under the Fisheries Act. The regulations prohibit the hunting of cetaceans in Canadian waters without a license. "Hunt" is interpreted much the same as "take" in the U.S. Marine Mammal Protection Act. To hunt means "to chase, shoot at, harpoon, take, kill, attempt to take or kill, or to harass cetaceans in any manner." Indians and Inuit are exempt if they are hunting for subsistence, but must have special permits for bowhead whales. Permits are also required to "hunt" cetaceans for "'scientific research or education". These regulations do not apply to belugas or narwhals, though separate regulations specify the manner in which belugas may be hunted and the number that can be killed, among other things. Belugas in the St. Lawrence are completely protected.

As for whale watching, the federal Department of Fisheries and Oceans recently attempted to formulate national guidelines to, in effect, define harassment and to ensure the safety of boaters. Besides the obvious, e.g., don't chase them and don't split up groups of whales, they recommend that boats stay 100 meters (300 feet) away and planes 300 meters (1,000 feet). When leaving a whale site, boats should start off smoothly and wait until 300 meters (1,000 feet) away before picking up speed.

The guidelines are subject to review and the Department of Fisheries and Oceans would like the comments of whale watchers and tour operators. To obtain a copy of the complete guidelines, contact: Director-General, Communications Directorate, Fisheries and Oceans, 240 Sparks St., Ottawa, Ont. K1A 0E6 Canada.

Greenland

Species
Common: minke whale (**2**), fin whale (**5**), humpback whale (**7**), sperm whale (**12**), beluga (**34**), harbor porpoise (**40**).
Sporadic: sei whale (**3**), narwhal (**33**), killer whale (**75**), long-finned pilot whale (**76**), northern bottlenose whale (**18**), white-beaked dolphin (**63**), Atlantic white-sided dolphin (**58**).
Rare: bowhead whale (**10**), right whale (**8**).

Tours
The 145-foot *M/V Nordbrise* makes 19 week-long cruises along the west coast from mid-May–mid-Sept. The mid-season **Disko Bay** cruise has the best whale possibilities. Captain and crew know area's fauna and flora. Prices from $1,750 [US] include air fare from Montreal. Contact: Greenland Cruises, Inc., 10 Park Ave., New York, NY 10016 USA (Tel. 212-683-1145).

Canadian Nature Tours has guided excursions to the west coast. Visitors stay in a small village hotel, making day-trips in a small boat or on foot. Whales are only part of these wildlife and cultural tours. Future dates and prices not set at press time. Contact: Canadian Nature Tours, FON Conservation Centre, 355 Lesmill Road, Don Mills, Ont. M3B 2W8 Canada (Tel. 416-444-8419).

Salén Lindblad Cruising and Society Expeditions often schedule a Greenland cruise during summer, sometimes together with visits to the Canadian Arctic (Salén Lindblad) or Norway and Iceland (Society Expeditions). Cruises are fairly certain to encounter whales and bow-riding dolphins. Ship naturalists will share their knowledge. 23–28 days from $7,250 [US] plus air fare. Contact: (1) Salén Lindblad Cruising, 133 E. 55th St., New York, NY 10022 USA (Tel. 212-751-2300); (2) Society Expeditions, 723 Broadway E., Seattle, WA 98102 USA (Tel. 206-324-9400 or 800-426-7794).

For students, the Ocean Research and Education Society sometimes studies humpback and other whales off the west coast of Greenland. These credit courses feature 6 weeks of sailing on a 144-foot, 3-masted barkentine called *Regina Maris*, plus 6 weeks of study in Gloucester, Massachusetts. $4,900 [US] includes living expenses at sea plus tuition. Contact: The Ocean Research and Education Society, Inc., 19 Harbor Loop, Gloucester, MA 01930 USA (Tel. 617-283-1475).

Weather/Sea Notes
Summer temperatures to low 50s (F.) with long days of sun, but weather can turn nasty in a hurry: wind, rain, high seas.

More information
Danish Tourist Board, Scandinavian National Tourist Offices, 75 Rockefeller Plaza, New York, NY 10019 USA (Tel. 212-582-2802).

Bermuda

Species
Common: humpback whale (**7**).
Sporadic: long-finned pilot whale (**76**).

Lookouts
Humpback whales, *en route* from the West Indies to northern waters, pass Bermuda's south coast from March–May with a peak in April. Any south shore headland on a calm day provides sighting opportunities. All are less than a ½-hour drive from main towns. (Note: no rental cars available; must use expensive taxis or rented mopeds/bicycles.) 3 of the best lookouts: **1** St. David's Head, from the cliffs at the end of Battery Rd. on the eastern end of Governors Island; **2**

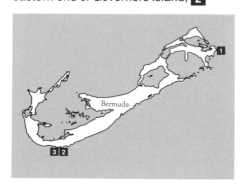

Gibb's Hill Lighthouse, off Lighthouse Rd. in Southampton Parish (from atop 117-foot lighthouse open to public); **3** Church Bay, also Southampton Parish, from headlands along South Rd. overlooking public beach.

Tours
Occasional 1- and 2-day humpback trips in April for members of the Bermuda Zoological Society (membership costs about $15 [US]/family). 2-day guided trips cost about $95 [US]. Contact: Bermuda Zoological Society, Box 145, The Flatts, Smith's 3, Bermuda.

Weather/Sea Notes
Warm in April from shore, but can be cold and rough at sea.

Museums
Skeleton of Cuvier's beaked whale and other whale and whaling displays at Bermuda Natural History Museum, Box 145, The Flatts, Smith's 3, Bermuda.

More information
Bermuda Dept. of Tourism, Suite 646, 630 5th Ave., New York, NY 10111 USA (Tel. 212-397-7700).

West Indies (Caribbean)

Species

Common: humpback whale (**7**), sperm whale (**12**), Atlantic spotted dolphin (**54**), bottlenose dolphin (**57**).
Sporadic: short-finned pilot whale (**77**), killer whale (**75**), fin whale (**5**), striped dolphin (**53**), spotted dolphin (**52**), common dolphin (**50**), spinner dolphin (**51**).

Tours

A chance to swim with a friendly pod of free-living Atlantic spotted dolphins east of Grand Bahama is the highlight of 3-, 4- and 5-day snorkeling trips aboard the 75-foot *M/V Impossible Dream*. April–Oct. About $100 [US]/day plus air fare to Hollywood, Florida. Contact: Oceanic Society Expeditions, Fort Mason Center, Bldg. E, San Francisco, CA 94123 USA (Tel. 415-441-1106); Seaventures International, Inc., Box 3271, Indialantic, FL 32903 USA (Tel. 305-723-9312).

At least 2 major "hot spots" for large and small cetaceans are accessible on extended sailing expeditions for students. Silver and Navidad banks, northeast of Dominican Republic, is a winter mating and calving area for humpback whales that spend their summers in the Northwest Atlantic. The Lesser Antilles, especially the Grenadines including St. Vincent, are also part of the humpbacks' winter range, plus an important area for sperm whales and various dolphins. Most expeditions include an "introduction" to the Bequia and other island whalers who still take a few small whales and dolphins and, occasionally, humpbacks and sperms from open boats.

(1) The Ocean Research and Education Society (ORES) has sail and study programs for students who want to help research whales and earn college credit. The non-profit ORES operates a 144-foot

Bernd Würsig

Common dolphins ride the bow of the Regina Maris.

barkentine called *Regina Maris* with several programs from Dec.–April to study humpback whales and other small cetaceans. Focus is on Silver and Navidad banks, but one trip also visits the Grenadines. Tuition for a 12-week sail and study semester is $4,900 [US] (includes living expenses for 6 weeks at sea, but not for 6 weeks at shore-based classroom in Gloucester). Occasional non-credit expeditions to Silver and Navidad banks to look at humpback whales cost about $700 [US] for 10 days–2 weeks. Excellent instructors. Contact: The Ocean Research and Education Society, Inc., 19 Harbor Loop, Gloucester, MA 01930 USA (Tel. 617-283-1475).

(2) The Ocean Research & Conservation Association (ORCA) offers several winter 7–14-day expeditions studying humpback and sperm whales and local whaling in the Grenadines. 16 participants plus up to 7 naturalists and crew sail aboard the 80-foot schooner *Scaramouche*. About $110 [US] per day, not including air fare. Contact: Great Expeditions, Box 46499, Station G, Vancouver, B.C. V6K 1R4 Canada (Tel. 604-734-4948).

(3) Sailing and exploring holidays throughout the Caribbean that often include dolphin and whale watching are offered by Ocean Voyages. 8–15-day cruises occur year-round, but winter in the Grenadines has the best whale possibilities. About $85 [US] a day, air fare extra. Contact: Ocean Voyages, Inc.,

1709 Bridgeway, Sausalito, CA 94965 USA (Tel. 415-332-4681).

Ferries and Cruises
More than 300 passenger ships sail the Caribbean year-round, including about 40 departing Florida in January. Tropical dolphins often visit the bow and sometimes large whales can be seen; on some cruise ships, the captain will announce sightings. For a complete list of Caribbean cruises, write: Caribbean Tourism Assoc., 20 E. 46th St., Rm. 1201, New York, NY 10017 USA.

Weather/Sea Notes
Tropical with regular trade winds and little rain. Can be cool and rough on the water.

Oceanaria
Bottlenose dolphins at Ocean Life Park Aquarium, Boca de Congrejos Isla, Villamar, Isla Verde, San Juan, Puerto Rico 00913 USA.

More information
Most Caribbean countries have tourist boards in New York, Toronto and London. A good source for all the Caribbean (including addresses of tourist offices for individual countries) is the Caribbean Tourism Assoc., 20 E. 46th St., Rm. 1201, New York, NY 10017 USA and (for. the Lesser Antilles including the Grenadines) the Eastern Caribbean Tourist Assoc., 220 E. 42nd St., New York, NY 10017 USA.

Mexico: The Lagoons of Baja California

Species
Common: gray whale (1), bottlenose dolphin (57).

Lookouts
Every year in late Dec., gray whales begin arriving at several large lagoons on the Baja California peninsula – the goal of a more than 5,000-mile journey from Arctic feeding grounds. In the lagoons, where the action lasts through mid-April, the gray whales calve and often mate, and can be observed from shore. Many lookouts can only be reached by desert trek or by sea. 2 good sites, however, are

on the road. Both are near the town of Guerrero Negro (hotels, trailer park), accessible via "Mexico 1", known officially as the Benito Juarez Hwy. This narrow hwy. has plenty of *vados* (flash flood run-off dips) and few solid shoulders, but if you stay on the road, drive less than 55 mph, and don't travel at night, it's fine. Guerrero Negro is 450 miles south of San Diego.

1 To view whales from shore in Laguna Guerrero Negro (Black Warrior Lagoon), take the turnoff to the town of Guerrero Negro, about 3 miles off Mexico 1. Just before entering town, the road

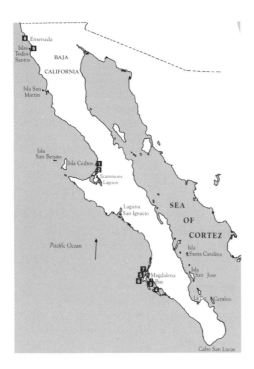

veers to the left and a ½-mile later is a stop sign. Turn right, and follow this road 6.8 miles to an abandoned pier. Years ago the lagoon here was dredged for ships that came to pick up salt from the area's evaporative salt works, and the activity drove the whales away. When loading was moved to a new dock (12 miles south), the whales came back. The whales swim close to the pier, passing with each tide change.

2 Another spot is "Nursery Inlet", part of Laguna Ojo de Liebre (Scammon's Lagoon). From Guerrero Negro, take road back to Mexico 1 and turn right (south); 5 miles later, a sign indicates "National Park of Gray Whales". The turnoff is a dirt road across the desert (4-wheel drive or high-clearance truck recommended). About 17 miles long, it passes many *salinas* (salt pans) on the way to a primitive campground. The slight rise overlooking the lagoon is the whale-watching spot.

At Bahia Magdalena, southern Baja, whale watching occurs: **3** near the grain elevators in San Carlos, access via Rt. 22, about 20 miles west of Ciudad Constitución (on Mexico 1); **4** at Punta Sterns, about a mile hike south of San Carlos; **5**

Baleen plates grow from the roof of the mouth of the gray whale.

Bottlenose dolphins chase fish onto the shore to catch them. This extraordinary behavior has been observed in Mexico and other places.

at Puerto Lopez Mateos (on Estero Soledad), from the fish cannery dock, access via dirt road running north off Rt. 22, 15 miles west of Ciudad Constitución; **6** on Estero Soledad, just south of Puerto Lopez Mateos (bottlenose dolphins sometimes chase fish onto the beaches here); **7** from Boca de Soledad north, access via short road and hike north from Puerto Lopez Mateos.

There are also many high lookouts on the first 80 miles of Mexico 1, the toll road between Tijuana and Ensenada, including **8** El Mirador turnoff, 20 miles north of Ensenada; **9** at Punta Banda Point, along road near la Bufadora, 13 miles northwest of Maneadero off Mexico 1 south of Ensenada. Gray whales can be seen migrating along the coast from Dec.–April, but are abundant from mid-Jan.–March.

Tours

Access to the lagoons is restricted, but a few commercial tours are permitted to operate in certain areas. **Laguna San Ignacio** is where curious gray whales known as "friendlies" often approach to be patted on the head. 7- to 10-day trips departing from San Diego on the 95-foot *Executive* (and other ships) cost about $135 [US]/day. Contact: Pacific Sea Fari Tours, 530 Broadway, Suite 1224, San Diego, CA 92101 USA (Tel. 619-226-8224).

Baja Expeditions Inc. acts as an outfitter for excursions to the southernmost lagoon, **Magdalena Bay**. Week-long cruises on the 80-foot *Don Jose* from Jan.–mid-March are $995 [US] plus air fare. Also a special whale-watching adventure: participants live on anchored raft, camping out, in well-travelled whale area. Week-long trips, Feb., in Magdalena Bay. Contact: Baja Expeditions, Inc., Box 3725, San Diego, CA 92103 USA (Tel. 619-297-0506).

More naturalist-led cruises and expeditions, some of which use the *Executive* or the *Don Jose*: (1) Baja Adventures, 16000 Ventura Blvd., Suite 200, Encino, CA 91436 USA (Tel. 213-906-1826); (2) Pacific Adventures Charter Service, Inc., 2445 Morena Blvd., Suite 200, San Diego, CA 92110 USA (Tel. 619-275-4253); (3) Nature Expeditions International, Box 11496, Eugene, OR 97440 USA (Tel. 503-484-6529); (4) Oceanic Society Expeditions, Fort Mason Center, Bldg. E, San Francisco, CA 94123 USA (Tel. 415-441-1106); (5) H&M Landing, 2803 Emerson St., San Diego, CA 92106 USA (Tel. 619-222-1144); (6) Fisherman's

Landing, 2838 Garrison St., San Diego, CA 92106 (Tel. 619-222-0391); (7) North America Nature Expeditions, Suite 104, 1776 Independence Court, Birmingham, AL 35216 USA (Tel. 205-870-5550); (8) California Pacific Expeditions, Box 2242, Alameda, CA 94501 USA (Tel. 415-521-7914); (9) Biological Journeys, 1876 Ocean Dr., McKinleyville, CA 95521 USA (Tel. 707-839-0178); (10) Smithsonian National Associate Program, A&I 1278, Washington, DC 20560 USA (Tel. 202-357-2477).

Weather/Sea Notes

Warm to hot and dry though may be cool at night. Cruises to lagoons can be cold and rough. Calmer in lagoons but afternoon winds can make life in a small boat unpleasant.

Laws/Guidelines

In January 1972, the Mexican president designated Laguna Ojo de Liebre (Scammon's Lagoon) a gray whale refuge – the first whale sanctuary anywhere. Today, 3 lagoons are protected – Laguna Guerrero Negro and Laguna San Ignacio, besides Scammon's – and the laws restrict boat activities to a few tour boats with special permits. Whale watching from shore is permitted. The ban on private boats in the lagoons lasts from the day the first whale arrives, usually about 15 December, to the day the last whale leaves, in mid-April.

More information

State Secretary of Tourism of Baja California, c/o Box 2448, Chula Vista, CA 92012 USA (Tel. 706-684-2126).

Mexico: Offshore West Coast/Sea of Cortez

Species

Common: fin whale (**5**), minke whale (**2**), blue whale (**6**), bottlenose dolphin (**57**), common dolphin (**50**), humpback whale (**7**), Bryde's whale (**4**), killer whale (**75**). *Sporadic:* gray whale (**1**), sperm whale (**12**), sei whale (**3**), short-finned pilot whale (**77**), long-finned pilot whale (**76**), false killer whale (**74**), Risso's dolphin (**70**), spotted dolphin (**52**), spinner dolphin (**51**), Pacific white-sided dolphin (**59**). *Rare:* cochito (**41**), pygmy sperm whale (**13**), Cuvier's beaked whale (**15**).

Tours

The number of species and relative abundance of whales and dolphins in this fairly accessible area, particularly the Sea of Cortez, is unrivaled. Access is through jet airports at Puerto Vallarta, on the west coast of the Mexican mainland, or La Paz, in southern Baja, though some tours sail from San Diego, making the several-day jog down along the Baja Peninsula part of the trip.

Several 7–11-day intensive whale tours are offered by Ronn Storro-Patterson and Ron LeValley of Biological Journeys, most of them aboard the 80-foot *Don Jose*: (1) "Blue Whales I" and "Blue Whales II" are 7-day cruises of the Sea of Cortez that depart from La Paz – a

chance to *live* with blue whales. About $1,000 [US] plus air fare. (2) "Whales, Whales, Whales" includes blue, fin and many other whales plus 2 days with grays in Magdalena Bay. Week-long March trip covers diverse whale habitats from lagoon to temperate waters to eastern tropical Pacific to Sea of Cortez. About $1,000 [US] plus air fare. (3) "West Coast Mexico: Humpback Whales" gives participants a chance to record humpback songs and learn about one of Mexico's hottest bird spots around San Blas. 2 week-long trips are offered in Dec. $950 [US] plus air fare to Puerto Vallarta. (4) "The Sea of Cortez" is an 11-day natural history cruise in May to include whales and sea birds plus daily hikes on the many islands. $1,350 [US] plus air fare. Contact: Biological Journeys, 1876 Ocean Dr., McKinleyville, CA 95521 USA (Tel. 707-839-0178/415-527-9622).

Baja Circumnavigated is the theme of Special Expeditions, Inc., with their deluxe cruises aboard the 143½-foot *Pacific Northwest Explorer*. High-profile naturalists and guest lecturers point out whales, seals, seabirds, including the gray whales of Magdalena Bay (and sometimes San Ignacio). The 2-week cruises are priced from $2,860 to $4,290 [US] and leave from San Diego,

A friendly gray whale engages in perhaps too friendly play in San Ignacio Lagoon, Mexico.

Jan.–mid-March. Contact: Special Expeditions, Inc., 133 E. 55th St., New York, N.Y. 10022 USA (Tel. 212-888-7980); or Exploration Cruise Lines, 1500 Metropolitan Park Bldg., Olive Way at Boren St., Seattle, WA 98101 USA (Tel. 206-624-8551).

Baja Expeditions, Inc., acts as an outfitter for charter groups: Sierra Club, Scripps Institute of Oceanography, University of California Extension, and American Cetacean Society. Whale and other natural-history cruises aboard the 80-foot *Don Jose* vary in length and are offered throughout the year. To join one of these groups or charter the boat, contact: Baja Expeditions, Inc., Box 3725, San Diego, CA 92103 USA (Tel. 619-297-0506).

Another outfitter with scheduled naturalist-led tours and charters available from late Dec.–April is Pacific Adventures Charter Service. The itinerary of the 95-foot-long *Executive* includes the offshore west coast, Sea of Cortez and Baja lagoons. Contact: Pacific Adventures Charter Service, 2445 Morena Blvd., Suite 200, San Diego, CA 92110 USA (Tel. 619-275-4253).

More naturalist-led cruises with whale-sighting opportunities (aboard *Executive, Don José*, and other ships) include: (1) Oceanic Society Expeditions, Fort Mason Center, Building E, San Francisco, CA 94123 USA (Tel. 415-441-1106); (2) Baja Adventures, 16000 Ventura Blvd., Suite 200, Encino, CA 91436 USA (Tel. 213-906-1826); (3) Nature Expeditions International, Box 11496, Eugene, OR 97440 USA (Tel. 503-484-6529); (4) Pacific Sea Fari Tours, 530 Broadway, Suite 1224, San Diego, CA 92101 USA (Tel. 619-226-8224).

Weather/Sea Notes

Sunny and hot, but pleasant on the water. The lower coastal areas semi-tropical. Rainy season May–Oct.; during fall sometimes strong southerly *chubascos*, windy rain-storms. Winter and spring ideal for whale watching.

More information

Delagación Federal, Plaza de la Constitución, Entre Belisario Dominguez y 5 de Mayo, La Paz, B.C., Mexico (Tel. 21199)

or Delagación Federal, Av. Guanojuato No. 375 Col. Cacho Edificio Longoria, Tijuana, B.C., Mexico (Tel. 53663).

Colombia: Interior

Species

Common: Amazon River dolphin (**37**), tucuxi (**47**).

Tours

From Leticia, Colombia's southernmost town bordering Peru and Brazil, naturalists Ronn Storro-Patterson and Ron LeValley lead 14-day river tours in June or July that include stops in all 3 countries. This undeveloped part of the Amazon Basin offers many birds (including horned screamers and hoatzins), fish (more species than the Atlantic Ocean), large mammals (jaguar, ocelot), and even primates (howler monkeys). Tucuxi and the Amazon River dolphin are only part of the wildlife parade, but important to Storro-Patterson. He describes Amazon River dolphins resting at the surface or sticking their long beaks out of water, the bright pink bodies contrasting with chocolate water. Tucuxi are quite active, racing around; and Storro-Patterson has recorded them "clicking" on his hydrophone as they chase fish up to the shore. Travel is by small boats and nights are spent in jungle camps and very rustic lodges. $1,400 [US] plus air fare. Contact: Biological Journeys, 1876 Ocean Dr., McKinleyville, CA 95521 USA (Tel. 707-839-0178).

Weather/Sea Notes

The humidity and heat is omnipresent; average annual temperature about 82°F.

More information

Colombian Government Tourist Office, 140 E. 57 St., New York, NY 10022 USA (Tel. 212-826-0660).

Brazil: Amazon River Basin

Species

Common: Amazon River dolphin (**37**), tucuxi (**47**).

Tours

See Colombia: Interior.

Many 1/2- to several-day boat tours of the Amazon leave from Manaus, a jungle city of 500,000. While not naturalist-led, these excursions do provide a taste of the jungle and its flora and fauna, including tucuxi and the Amazon River dolphin. One place near Manaus to see them is about 12 miles downstream to the muddy Amazon and blackish Rio Negro junction. For tours to the "Wedding of the Waters": (1) Amazon Explorers, Hotel Lord, Rua Marcilio Dias 217, Manaus, Amazonas, Brazil (Tel. 092-232-3101); (2) Tropical Hotel Manaus, Praia da Ponta Negra, Manaus, Amazonas, Brazil (Tel. 092-234-1165). Other agencies have offices in most hotels, or ask for reservation forms and information in lobby.

Ferries and Cruises

Tucuxi and the Amazon River dolphin can be seen from the twice-monthly government ENASA ferry between Manaus and Belém, a 4-day trip downstream to Belém or 5 days back to Manaus. Budget class starts at $30 [US], but bring a hammock; for $120 [US], first class includes private room, meals and access to upper decks, better for dolphin-watching. Contact: ENASA, Rua Marechal Deodoro, No. 61, Manaus, Amazonas, Brazil (Tel. 092-232-4280) or ENASA, Av. Presidente Vargas,

No. 41, Belém, Pará, Brazil (Tel. 091-223-3011).

For 21- to 25-day luxury tours of the Amazon basin – from Belém to Iquitos, Peru, 2300 miles upstream – there's the 130-passenger *World Discoverer*. Prices start at about $6,000 [US] for a twin, plus air fare. Contact: Society Expeditions, 723 Broadway E., Seattle, WA 98102 USA (Tel. 206-324-9400).

Weather/Sea Notes

Hot and humid. Best season for river excursions is July–Dec., the least rainy months. During rainy season, April–June, the Amazon triples its water volume and the width of the river goes from a low-water average of 1¼-miles up to 37 miles wide. Cetaceans become more dispersed, and it's harder to see them in the rain.

Brazil: Southeast

Species

Common: southern right whale (**9**), bottlenose dolphin (**57**).

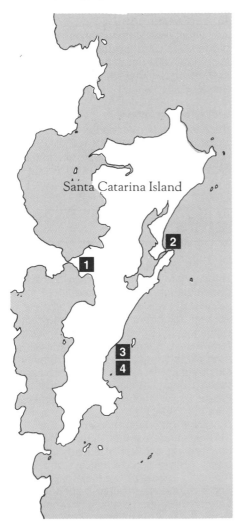

Santa Catarina Island

Lookouts

From July–Oct., the endangered southern right whale visits Santa Catarina Island, near Florianópolis, 433 miles south of São Paulo (access by air or good road from São Paulo). Set up a base at a hotel in Florianópolis or camp on the island. The lookouts: **1** on Barra da Lagoa, where whales approach within 100 feet of shore; from Florianópolis take the asphalt state road east about 5 miles across Santa Catarina Island and around Conceição Lagoon to the point where it opens into the sea; **2** Morro das Pedras, a high spot about 5 miles south of Florianópolis, also on the eastern side of the island, at the site of a Jesuit monastery (parking).

175 miles south of Florianópolis (80 miles northeast of Pôrto Alegre) is the resort town of Torres – a bottlenose dolphin lookout with a southern right whale spot

nearby. Torres is named after the basalt towers on the ocean that, from July–Nov., are a good place to scout for right whales. The basalt promontories are in the **3** State Park of Guarita, an easy walk from the town center. Nearby, in the **4** mouth of the Mambituba River, bottlenose dolphins live year-round.

Tours

No tours in southeast Brazil, but an environmental group based in Pôrto Alegre will guide whale watchers to Santa Catarina Island and Torres, at no charge. Group spokesman José Truda Palazzo Jr., recently co-authored a marine mammal protection bill for Brazil which, if approved, will be unique in Latin America, and more far-reaching than the U.S. Marine Mammal Protection Act. Palazzo is anxious to encourage interest in whales and whale watching. Contact: José Truda Palazzo Jr., Wildlife Protection Service, 24 de Outubro 1000/2301, Pôrto Alegre–RS 90000, Brazil (Tel. 22-31-91).

Ferries and Cruises

From the ferry/passenger boat between São José do Norte and Rio Grande, in the south of the state of Rio Grande Do Sul, bottlenose dolphins can be seen year round. The dolphins live in Lagoa dos Pa-

tos and 50 individuals have been photo-identified by Brazilian biologists Hugo P. Castello and Maria Cristina Pinedo. The passenger boat across the lagoon leaves every 1/2 hour and the car ferry twice daily. Poor winter weather makes sightings difficult; best time is Oct.–April.

Weather/Sea Notes

At Santa Catarina Island, daytime temperatures average a balmy 70°F. with almost no fog. Rain mostly in June–July. Waters are often clear and fairly calm.

At Torres, further south, it's cooler, waters are typically dark and winds are strong, particularly in whale season, though dolphins can be viewed during the pleasant summer, Nov.–April.

Laws/Guidelines

Any act of cruelty toward animals is forbidden by a national animal protection law. In practice this is not applied to marine mammals; that's why Palazzo's bill is needed.

More information

Brazilian Tourism Authority, 60 E. 42 St., Suite 1336, New York, NY 10017 USA (212-286-9600); Embratur, Praça Mauá, 7–10.°, Rio de Janeiro–20.000, Brazil (Tel. 021-21066).

Ecuador: Galapagos Islands

Species

Common: bottlenose dolphin (**57**), minke whale (**2**), spinner dolphin (**51**), fin whale (**5**).
Sporadic: sperm whale (**12**), Bryde's whale (**4**), sei whale (**3**), killer whale (**75**), Cuvier's beaked whale (**15**), humpback whale (**7**).

Tours

These remote volcanic islands, with their unique flora and fauna, inspired Darwin in the formulation of evolutionary theory. Today they continue to inspire all who visit. Whales and dolphins are part of the attraction, though few tour operators seek them out.

(1) "When we go to the Galapagos, the trips *are* oriented toward whales and dolphins," says Ronn Storro-Patterson, who

leads 13-day trips every July. Partner Ron LeValley, a bird man, provides a good balance. Previous expeditions have sighted Bryde's whales, minke whales, spinner dolphins and plenty of bow-riding bottlenose dolphins. $1,395 [US] plus air fare. Also, beginning in Nov. 1985, will be special Galapagos trips sailing from Costa Rica with 4 days in the Cocos Islands. Contact: Biological Journeys, 1876 Ocean Dr., McKinleyville, CA 95521 USA (Tel. 707-839-0178).

(2) Naturalist Ron Naveen, whose "Whales and Seabirds" tours off Maryland are highly rated, also leads up to 4 trips a year to the Galapagos. The 2-week trips concentrate on the major seabird and seal rookeries, but also spend much time on the water travelling between islands. Most of his cetacean sightings, in-

cluding sei whales, occur Feb.–June. 35–45-foot yachts are used with 6–10 people per trip. $2,026 [US] includes air fare from eastern US. Contact: Ron Naveen, 2378 Rt. 97, Cooksville, MD 21723 USA (Tel. 301-854-6262).

(3) 5 general natural-history tours a year are offered by Nature Expeditions International. Expedition naturalists are biologists or geologists. 10–20 participants spend 2 weeks cruising aboard comfortable, but not luxurious, yachts exploring 11 islands. $2,590 [US] plus air fare. Contact: Nature Expeditions International, Box 11496, Eugene, OR 97440 USA (Tel. 503-484-6529).

(4) Small sailboat expeditions for 4–10 people, guided by naturalist trained at local Darwin Station, are the specialty of Ocean Voyages. The 15–22-day trips covering most of the islands are for the adventurous. About $100 [US]/day plus air fare. Contact: Ocean Voyages, Inc., 1709 Bridgeway, Sausalito, CA 94965 USA (Tel. 415-332-4681).

To find out about more tours and cruises to the Galapagos, led by naturalists, contact: (5) Wilderness Travel, 1760 Solano Ave., Berkeley, CA 94707 USA (Tel. 415-524-5111); (6) American Museum of Natural History, Central Park W. at 79th St., New York, NY 10024 USA (Tel. 212-873-1440); (7) Society Expeditions, 723 Broadway E., Seattle, WA 98102 USA (Tel. 206-324-9400); (8) Questers Tours and Travel, Inc., 257 Park Ave. S., New York, NY 10010 (Tel. 212-673-3120); (9) Smithsonian National Associate Program, A&I 1278, Washington, DC 20560 USA (Tel. 202-357-2477); (10) Metropolitan Touring, Box 2542, Quito, Ecuador (Tel. 524-400); (11) Adventure Associates, 5925 Maple, Suite 116, Dallas TX 75235 USA (Tel. 214-257-6187); (12) Wings of the World Inc., Travel, 653 Mt. Pleasant Rd., Toronto, Ont. M4S 2N2 Canada (Tel. 416-482-1223); (13) Oceanic Society Expeditions, Fort Mason Center, Bldg. E, San Francisco, CA 94123 USA (Tel. 415-441-1106).

Weather/Sea Notes

Warm but not too hot, despite being on the Equator. The cool Humboldt Current helps keep the islands spring-like year round.

Laws/Guidelines

The Galapagos Islands are an Ecuadorian national park and its wildlife is fully protected.

Museums

Most tours to the Galapagos visit the biological research station at Academy Bay on Santa Cruz Island: Charles Darwin Research Station, Isla Santa Cruz, Galapagos, Ecuador.

More information

Dituris – The Ecuadorian Tourist Commission, Reina Victoria 514 y Roca, Box 2454, Quito, Ecuador.

Argentina

Species

Common: southern right whale (**9**), dusky dolphin (**62**), bottlenose dolphin (**57**). *Sporadic:* killer whale (**75**), long-finned pilot whale (**76**), Risso's dolphin (**70**), Burmeister's porpoise (**43**).

Lookouts

Península Valdés – the Patagonian cliffs where right whales come near shore to mate, calve and raise their young from mid-July–Nov. – is remote but accessible. About 750 miles south of Buenos Aires on National Rt. 3 (Ruta Nacional No. 3), it can also be reached by air through Tre-

lew. From Trelew, drive northeast about 45 miles to Puerto Madryn (where whales can sometimes be seen from the pier) and then take the asphalt road east to Península Valdés and many good cliffside lookouts, from 40–100 miles away: **1** Playa de las Ballenas, 8 miles south of Punta Norte on the open Atlantic; good for killer whales and southern elephant seals, too; **2** Reserva Faunística Provincial Caleta Valdés (Provincial Wildlife Reserve of Caleta Valdés); a narrow sea inlet where right whales sometimes seek shelter; on outer peninsula, south of Playa de las Ballenas; **3** Puerto

Pirámides, a town on the protected waters of Golfo Nuevo, halfway out peninsula to Punta Norte, where rights approach shore (sometimes can be seen from dining room of Argentine Automobile Club Inn); **4** Reserva Faunística Provincial Punta Pirámides (Provincial Wildlife Reserve of Punta Pirámides), a southern sea lion colony where female rights with calves often congregate; 5 miles south of Punta Pirámides; **5** Reserva Faunística Provincial Isla de los Pa-

Commerson's dolphins swim toward a whale-watching boat off Comodoro Rivadavia, Patagonia, Argentina.

jaros (Provincial Wildlife Reserve of the Island of the Birds), in Golfo San José, where right whales and dusky dolphins often pass near a tiny island covered with nesting seabirds; about 40 miles from Puerto Madryn; **6** Reserva Faunística Provincial Punta Norte (Provincial Wildlife Reserve of North Point), the site of a southern elephant seal breeding colony on the open Atlantic, with passing killer whales, dolphins and occasionally right whales; about 106 miles from Puerto Madryn.

Tours

Watching right whales from boats is restricted to Golfo Nuevo on the southwest side of Península Valdés. Local tours operate out of Puerto Madryn and Puerto Pirámides with qualified guides under regulations formulated by the Chubut Tourism and Conservation Direction. Contact: Dirección de Conservación del Patrimonio Turístico, 9120 Puerto Madryn, Chubut, Argentina.

22-day natural history tours of Patagonia that include 5 days on Península Valdés with right whales, sea elephants and sea birds, are offered by Questers Worldwide Nature Tours. Nov. tours catch whales just as they're leaving. $2,245 [US], plus about $1,300 for air fare from New York. Contact: Questers Tour & Travel, Inc., 257 Park Ave. S., New York, NY 10010 USA (Tel. 212-673-3120).

10- to 14-day marine mammal tours

Jorge Mermoz / courtesy Bernd Würsig

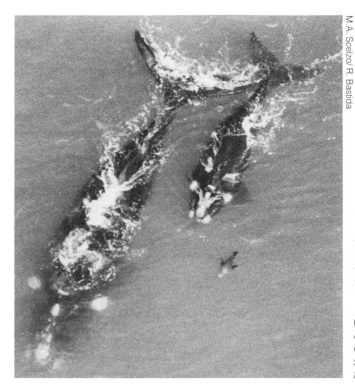

(Above) *Southern right whale mother and calf swim close to the surface off Peninsula Valdes, Argentina. Note the smaller sea lion beside them.*

(Below) *Photographic sequence of the action of a diving southern right whale's tail flukes.*

focusing on right whales in Sept. and Oct. are led by Ricardo M. Mandojana, Wurzburg AH, APO NY 09801 USA.

30-day whale/natural history tours are also given in Oct. by Biological Journeys, 1876 Ocean Dr., McKinleyville, CA 95521 USA (Tel. 707-839-0178).

Weather/Sea Notes
Cold, windy even from lookouts; can be rough on water. Whale season is southern winter and spring (July–Nov.) except for killer whales (March). Oct. is best month for whales and weather.

Laws/Guidelines
In Dec. 1974, the province of Chubut set aside Golfo San José as a permanent sanctuary for right whales. 1983 regulations restrict whale-watching boats to Golfo Nuevo with these stipulations: (1) boat drivers must turn off engines at 100 yards from whales; (2) boats may not approach whales in shallow water or (3) mothers with calves; (4) boats must have qualified guides on board (qualifications and responsibilities of guides are determined by Chubut Tourism Direction). For more information, contact the agencies that have devised regulations: (1) Dirección de Conservación del Patrimonio Turístico, 9120 Puerto Madryn, Chubut, Argentina; (2) Instituto Nacional de Investigación y Desarrollo Pesquero, Casilla de Correo 175, 7600 Mar del Plata, Argentina.

More information
Dirección Nacional de Turismo, Calle Suipacha 1111, Buenos Aires, Argentina (Tel. 31-2745).

Chile

Species
Common: sperm whale (**12**), Commerson's dolphin (**64**), Peale's dolphin (**60**), common dolphin (**50**).
Sporadic: blue whale (**6**), fin whale (**5**), sei whale (**3**), Bryde's whale (**4**), long-finned

A right whale's eye is the size of a grapefruit. Note the "eyebrow" callosity.

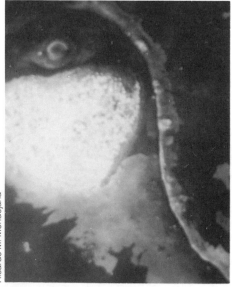

Ricardo M. Mondojana

pilot whale (**76**), bottlenose dolphin (**57**), Risso's dolphin (**70**), Burmeister's porpoise (**43**), hourglass dolphin (**61**), dusky dolphin (**62**), southern right whale dolphin (**69**), killer whale (**75**).
Rare: spectacled porpoise (**42**), black dolphin (**65**), southern bottlenose whale (**18**), Cuvier's beaked whale (**15**), humpback whale (**7**), southern right whale (**9**).

Tours
No whale-watching tours, but cruises through the Strait of Magellan offer good opportunities for the dedicated to see rare cetaceans found nowhere else in the world. The "Santa liners", a fleet of luxury 100-passenger, 20,000-ton cruise ships that carry some freight, operate year-round between Valparaiso, Chile, and Buenos Aires, Argentina – a 7-day trip. Though large whales may be seen offshore along the Chilean coast, the trip's highlight is the 36-hour passage through the Strait of Magellan. Naturalists sometimes come aboard during the passage and Chile's Institute of Patagonia has in the past enlisted passengers to record whale and dolphin sightings. Contact: Delta Lines, 2700 Stewart St., Tower, 1 Market Plaza, San Francisco, CA 94106 USA (Tel. 415-777-8300).

Sailing expeditions to southern Chile aboard the 40-foot *Equinoccio II* explore fjords and islets with whales, dolphins and extensive birdlife. 14 and 21 days, offered in Jan. and Feb. $1,275 and $1,775 [US], plus air fare. Contact: Ocean Voyages, Inc., 1709 Bridgeway, Sausalito, CA 94965 USA (Tel. 415-332-4681).

Weather/Sea Notes
Often rough and very wet especially through the Strait of Magellan. Some whales and dolphins are seen year-round but best season for weather is the austral summer. May still be cold and wet.

More information
Servicio Nacional de Turismo, CAS. 14082, Santiago, Chile (Tel. 60474).

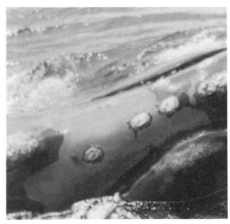

Francois Gohier

A southern right whale breaks the surface off Peninsula Valdes, Patagonia.

France: Mediterranean

Species
Common: striped dolphin (**53**), common dolphin (**50**), bottlenose dolphin (**57**). *Sporadic:* fin whale (**5**), Risso's dolphin (**70**).

Ferries and Cruises
The near-shore waters of the province of Var (from Marseille to Nice) are year-round haunts for several dolphin species, especially striped dolphins. During the summer, with a peak in July, fin whales feed in the offshore waters between Nice and Corsica (Corse). With dolphins, they are sometimes sighted from the car ferries between Nice and Bastia or Calvi on Corsica (5½–9 hours), and between Toulon or Marseille and Bastia or Calvi. 4th class deck fare is crowded during summer, but inexpensive and best for watching. Contact: Societé Nationale Maritime Corse-Méditerranée (SNCM), 3, ave. Gustave V, Nice, France (Tel. 89-89-89).

Weather/Sea Notes
Can be cool and choppy on the sea, but rarely cold and rough during summer.

Oceanaria
Killer whales and various dolphins at Marineland Côte D'Azur, avenue Mozart, 06600, Antibes, France (Tel. 93-33-49-49).

Museums
Many whale and dolphin exhibits at Musée National d'Histoire Naturelle, 57, rue Cuvier, Paris V[e], France.
  Musée Océanographique de la Rochelle, 28, rue Albert 1er, 17000 La Rochelle, France (Tel. 46-45-17-87).

More information
French Government Travel Office, 610 Fifth Ave., New York, NY 10020 USA (Tel. 212-757-1125).

Portugal

Species
Common: bottlenose dolphin (**57**), common dolphin (**50**), striped dolphin (**53**).

Lookouts
Dolphins live along the Costa da Galé

(south of Lisbon between Cabo Espichel and Cabo de Sines). Most are, however, well offshore, usually along the 50 fathom line. To see dolphins from land, visit the Rio Sado. In the Sado estuary lives a resident population of bottlenose dolphins –

phins come. Another area to sit and watch is across the river mouth on the beach at **3** Comenda. Access is from Setúbal on the secondary route west to the beach resorts of Figueirinha and Galapos. Comenda is the first beach at the mouth of the estuary. Most of the research on the dolphins is done in early fall. From earlier records, they are here in summer and perhaps other seasons too.

Ferries and Cruises
The short ferry from Setúbal to Tróia crosses the part of the estuary where dolphins are frequently seen.

Weather/Sea Notes
Idyllic conditions for dolphin watching and waiting, especially spring–early fall. With too much wind, visibility is cut.

the subject of recent studies by biologists A. M. Teixeira, R. Duguy, and E. Hussenot. They have begun individual photo-identification using nicks on the dorsal fins – a first for Europe. Driving south from Lisbon, take the main hwy. to the large city of Setúbal about 25 miles away. **1** Setúbal has a busy commercial harbor on the Rio Sado, yet it is sometimes possible to watch the dolphins bowriding on the ships as they approach. A better spot is at the **2** northern tip of the Peninsula de Tróia, which is only a short ferry from Setúbal. It is possible but unnecessary to take your car. Beside the ferry dock on the beach and looking back toward Setúbal is the place where the dol-

Laws/Guidelines
Dolphins are protected from harassment by recent laws in Portugal.

Museums
Vasco da Gama Aquarium, Avenida Mariginal, Dafundo, 1495 Lisboa, Portugal.

More information
Portuguese National Tourist Office, 548 Fifth Ave., New York, NY 10036 USA (Tel. 212-354-4403).
   Direcçao-Geral do Turismo, Avenida António Augusto de Aguiar, 86-1000 Lisboa, Portugal (Tel. 57-50-86).

Gibraltar

Species
Common: common dolphin (**50**), striped dolphin (**53**).
Sporadic: bottlenose dolphin (**57**).

Tours
For the past 4 years, ex-fisherman Mike Lawrence has been running 2¹/₂-hour dolphin tours almost daily from April–Nov. He encounters herds of up to 1,000 at a time. Tours depart mornings from Shep-

herd Marina. Cost £7.50 [UK]. Contact: Mike Lawrence, *Dolphin Safari*, Shepherd Marina, Gibraltar (Tel. 010-350-71914).

Weather/Sea Notes
Mornings cool on the water but usually calm; choppy by midday.

More information
Gibraltar Tourist Office, Cathedral Square, Box 303, Gibraltar.

Greece

Species
Common: common dolphin (**50**).
Sporadic: bottlenose dolphin (**57**), striped dolphin (**53**).

Tours
No scheduled tours but yacht charters to the islands regularly encounter dolphins. The thrill is seeing bow-riding dolphins in the spiritual home of whale watching, where Aristotle watched and wrote about his discoveries more than 2,000 years ago. One charter company recommended by Alaskans Jim and Nancy Lethcoe, who went dolphin watching the winter of 1982-3, is Iris Yacht Charters, 38, Akti Possidonos, Piraeus, Greece (Tel. 4173-690). There are many others; consult listings provided by travel agents, Greek Tourism offices, or found in special charter boat issues of *Yachting, Sail Magazine*, and *Cruising World*.

Ferries and Cruises
Numerous inter-island ferries, freight steamers and cruise ships have dolphin possibilities. The Greek Tourism offices or travel agents have detailed lists. Local ferries to the Cyclades and on to the Aegean islands along the Turkey coast, especially Rhodes, Samos and Lesbos (where Aristotle did his work), offer inexpensive tours through dolphin areas. Most depart Piraeus, outside Athens. Contact: Piraeus Central Port Authority (Tel. 4511-311).

Weather/Sea Notes
Subtropical in summer; mild winter, but can be cool to cold on the water.

More information
Greek National Tourist Organization, 645 Fifth Ave., Olympic Tower, New York, NY 10022 USA (Tel. 212-421-5777).

South Africa

Species
Common: southern right whale (**9**), bottlenose dolphin (**57**), Indo-Pacific humpbacked dolphin (**48**), dusky dolphin (**62**).
Sporadic: killer whale (**75**), common dolphin (**50**).

Lookouts
From May–Nov. with a peak in Sept., southern right whales visit the warm, shallow water bays from Table Bay (at Cape Town) east to Algoa Bay (at Port Elizabeth). Sites with good, elevated viewing spots include (from west to east): **1** Clifton on Rt. M6, 4 miles from Cape Town, overlooking Clifton Bay; **2** Llandudno off Rt. M6, north of Hout Bay; **3** Hout Bay, 12 miles south of Cape Town, including lookouts along Chapman's Peak Drive; **4** Simonstown, **5** Fish Hoek, **6** St. James, **7** near Steenbras River Mouth, and **8** around Koeël Bay – all on False Bay south of Cape Town; **9** Hermanus on Walker Bay from mountain viewpoint above town (excellent); **10** beside the old harbor and at De Kelders, on southeastern side of Walker Bay; **11** Cape Infanta, near the town of Infanta-on-River, about 150 miles east of Cape Town; **12** Mossel Bay.

Indo-Pacific humpbacked dolphins are even more common than bottlenose dolphins in Plettenberg Bay and may be observed year-round, close to shore (along with right whales, in season), from **13** the cliffs of Robberg, a rugged 3 1/2-mile-long peninsula that forms the southwest boundary of Plettenberg Bay. This spe-

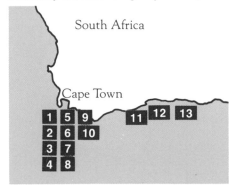

191

cial whale-watching spot has also yielded sightings of killer whales, common dolphins and rare pygmy right whales.

Weather/Sea Notes
Can be cool, though rarely cold from lookouts. Rough seas may preclude viewing opportunities. Avg. Sept. high temperature (during right whale peak) is 70°F.

Laws/Guidelines
Regulation 90, which became law Dec. 5, 1980, prohibits the catching or killing of whales and dolphins in South African waters. During the right whale breeding season, June 1–Nov. 30, boats or aircraft are requested to stay at least 300 yards away. For more information, contact: Dolphin Action and Protection Group, Box 156, Hout Bay 7872, Capetown, South Africa (Tel. 70-3182).

Oceanaria
Bottlenose and dusky dolphins at The Aquarium and Dolfinarium, Box 736, 2 West St., Durban, Natal, South Africa.

Bottlenose dolphins at Port Elizabeth Museum and Oceanarium, Beach Road, Humewood, Port Elizabeth 6000, South Africa.

More information
Satour, Private Bag X164, 0001 Pretoria, South Africa (Tel. 012-28-3800).

Sri Lanka

Species
Common: blue whale (**6**), sperm whale (**12**), Bryde's whale (**4**), spinner dolphin (**51**), bottlenose dolphin (**57**).
Sporadic: striped dolphin (**53**), spotted dolphin (**52**), Risso's Dolphin (**70**), Irrawaddy dolphin (**71**), Indo-Pacific humpbacked dolphin (**48**).

Lookouts
One of the world's hottest spots for large whales and dolphins was recently discovered off the east coast of Sri Lanka. In 1979, the International Whaling Commission established the Indian Ocean Whale Sanctuary. In 1981, the World Wildlife Fund/Netherlands sponsored an Indian Ocean study cruise to include 3 field seasons and, in early 1983, Trincomalee, Sri Lanka, became the base for the studies because of the abundance of large whales close to shore. The dolphins are there year-round; the large whales are at least seasonal residents. The most recent study occurred from Jan. to April and by the end of April, most of the large whales were gone. The best spot, called **1** Swami Rock, is about a mile northeast of Trincomalee, at a military site called Fort Frederick. Stand on the pillbox next to the Hindu temple and look east into the Bay of Bengal.

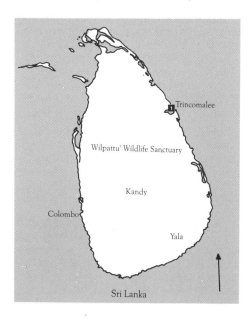

Tours
Whale watching on a limited scale from fish boats chartered on the spot began out of Trincomalee in early 1983. The Sri Lankan National Aquatic Resources Agency plans to monitor and regulate whale watching, weighing the interests of whale watchers, fishermen, scientists, and the whales, too.

Whale researcher Stephen Leatherwood is leading a 10-day expedition in March to view whales and dolphins from land, sea, and air. Contact: Oceanic Society Expeditions, Fort Mason Center,

Bldg. E, San Francisco, CA 94123 USA
(Tel. 415-441-1106).

Weather/Sea Notes
Tropical.

Laws/Guidelines
The National Aquatic Resources Agency
has recently designated the seas off Trincomalee as protected waters for whales.

Museums
Colombo National Museum, P.O.B. 854,
Albert Crescent, Colombo 7, Sri Lanka.

More information
Ceylon Tourist Board, Box 1504, 41, Glen
Aber Pl., Colombo 4, Sri Lanka (Tel.
89585); 609 Fifth Ave., Suite 308, New
York, NY 10017 USA (Tel. 212-935-0369).

*(Above) A sperm whale calf swims close to
its mother in the Indian Ocean off Sri Lanka.
Note the calluses on the dorsal fin. (Below) A
sperm whale group lies together at the
surface, their foreheads sticking out. The
meaning of this behavior is unknown.*

Japan

Species
Common: minke whale (**2**), Bryde's whale
(**4**), fin whale (**5**), sperm whale (**12**), short-
finned pilot whale (**77**), striped dolphin
(**53**), bottlenose dolphin (**57**), Pacific
white-sided dolphin (**59**), false killer whale
(**74**), Risso's dolphin (**70**).

Tours
Whale watching in Japan? "The possibilities are intriguing," says Ronn Storro-

Patterson of Biological Journeys. Most of
the whalers find their whales by watching
from the Japanese coast: Minke whales.
Bryde's whales. Sperm whales. The
sperms migrate north along the coast in
the spring and, as they parade past, the
whaling stations open one by one. Easily
accessible to whalers about 6 months of
the year, the sperms are also "there for
the watching," says Storro-Patterson. On
recent logistical visits to Japan, Storro-

Patterson has hired a fisherman to take him out to see whales. Now he's organizing the first commercial whale-watching tour to Japan, and the point, he says, is *not* to protest whaling, but just to charter a Japanese boat and watch whales, and get local publicity. "It might stimulate the curiosity of the Japanese toward these Americans who are willing to pay for the privilege of watching whales." Storro-Patterson admits that it could be a delicate situation but "I'd like to get the Japanese keyed up to the fact that whales are nice to look at." He doesn't plan to hire a whaling boat for the tour, but he foresees the day when the whaling boats, idle much of the year, are used to watch whales. Perhaps, he adds, the whalers could be relocated as whale-watching skippers. Far fetched? The International Whaling Commission moratorium on whaling is set for 1986 and the United States seems determined to "enforce" it with economic sanctions. These sanctions include banning fish imports and reducing fishing rights within the US 200-mile zone, both of which pose far greater economic threats to Japan than the end of whaling. The Japanese may soon be looking for something else to do with whales. For more information and a chance to participate in this pioneering whale-watching tour, contact: Biological Journeys, 1876 Ocean Dr., McKinleyville, CA 95521 USA (Tel. 707-839-0178).

Oceanaria

Several Japanese oceanaria may already be helping to ease Japan's transition from whaling to whale watching. Killer whales, short-finned pilot whales, and several species of dolphins, especially bottlenose dolphins, are on display.

Kamogawa Sea World, 1464-18 Higashicho, Kamogawa City, Chiba-Prefecture, 296, Japan.

Shirahama World Safari, Nishimuro-Gun, Shirahama, Wakayama-Prefecture, Japan.

Taiji Whale Museum, Taiji, Wakayama-Prefecture, Japan (oceanarium and whaling museum).

Izu-Mito Sea Paradise, Numazu-City, Shizuoka-Prefecture, Japan.

More information

For maps and general tourism information, contact: Japan National Tourist Organization at 6-6, Yurakucho 1-chome, Chiyoda-ku, Tokyo, Japan (Tel. 03-502-1461) or Rockefeller Plaza, 630 Fifth Ave., New York, NY 10111 USA (Tel. 212-757-5640).

Australia

Species

Common: humpback whale (**7**), southern right whale (**9**), bottlenose dolphin (**57**). *Sporadic:* minke whale (**2**), fin whale (**5**), blue whale (**6**), sperm whale (**12**), killer whale (**75**), long-finned pilot whale (**76**).

Lookouts

Migrating humpback whales (and other small cetaceans) can be seen migrating June–Oct. off the east coast: **1** at Cape Byron, off Pacific Hwy., north of Byron Bay in New South Wales, about 85 miles south of Brisbane; **2** from Pt. Lookout, near the lighthouse at the northeast tip of North Stradbroke Island, access via ferry on day-trip from Brisbane.

Southern right whales can be seen during winter (July–Sept.) as females move inshore to calve along the southern coast. Frequent sightings at **3** Logan's Beach near Warrnambool, 150 miles west of Melbourne, from whale-watching platform on high dune above beach visited by an estimated 50,000 whale watchers in 1982; and from the following Victoria locales on the south shore, less than 1½-hour drive from Melbourne: **4** Anglesea; **5** Point Lonsdale; **6** Inverloch.

Bottlenose dolphins can be seen almost every day from April–Oct. (infrequently from Nov.–March) at **7** Monkey Mia, a remote resort on Shark Bay, about 475 miles north of Perth. Since 1966, a group of up to 12 Monkey Mia dolphins have regularly approached swimmers, allowing themselves to be touched and fed, and sometimes playing games with swimmers.

To find out about recent local or seasonal abundance, particularly of right whales, contact State fisheries or wildlife

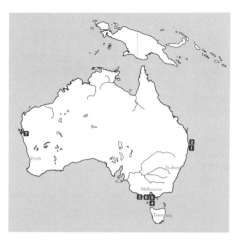

offices, or Australian National Parks and Wildlife Service, Head Office, G.P.O. Box 636, Canberra, A.C.T. 2601 Australia (Tel. 062-46-6211).

Weather/Sea Notes

Cool at winter lookouts on the south coast. Warm to hot year-round from east and west coasts (in whale areas near Brisbane and Monkey Mia).

Laws/Guidelines

Following the 1978 Frost Report – an independent inquiry into whales and whaling chaired by Sir Sydney Frost – Australia changed from a whaling country to one of the strongest advocates of cetaceans. The Whale Protection Act 1980 prohibits the killing, capturing, injuring of or interfering with cetaceans by all within the Australian Fishing Zone.

Oceanaria

Bottlenose dolphins at (1) Marineland of South Australia, Adelaide, South Australia 5024; (2) Warragamba Lion Safari, Sydney, New South Wales; (3) Pet Porpoise Pool Pty. Ltd., Coffs Harbour, New South Wales; (4) Atlantis Marine Park, Div. of Yanchep Sun City Pty. Ltd., Yan-

Rare melon-headed whales lie stranded on a beach at Moncton Island, Queensland, Australia.

chep, Western Australia; (5) King Neptune's Park, Port Macquarie, New South Wales.

Bottlenose dolphins, Indo-Pacific humpbacked dolphins, and a false killer whale at Sea World, Box 190, Surfers Paradise, Queensland 4217.

Museums

Whaling equipment and display at Whale World, formerly the Cheynes Beach Whaling Station, Frenchmans Bay, Albany, Western Australia 6334.

Whale displays at South Australian Museum, North Terrace, Adelaide, South Australia 5000.

National Museum of Victoria, 285–321 Russell St., Melbourne, Victoria 3000.

Killer whale skeleton and displays at Eden Killer Whale Museum, Imlay St., Box 304, Eden, New South Wales 2551.

More information

Australian Tourist Commission, Distribution Center, Box A-1, Addison, IL 60101 USA.

New Zealand

Species

Common: common dolphin (**50**), bottlenose dolphin (**57**), dusky dolphin (**62**), Hector's dolphin (**67**).
Sporadic: killer whale (**75**), minke whale (**2**), sei whale (**3**), Bryde's whale (**4**), fin whale (**5**), humpback whale (**7**), southern right whale (**9**), sperm whale (**12**), southern right whale dolphin (**69**), false killer whale (**74**), long-finned pilot whale (**76**), hourglass dolphin (**61**), Risso's dolphin (**70**).

Lookouts

On South Island, the Kaikoura coast along coastal Hwy. 1 south of Picton, offers occasional dolphin sightings year-round (dusky, common, bottlenose and maybe Hector's). Large whales are less likely, but possible. Best spot is **1** promontory at Kaikoura Head on Kaikoura Pe-

ninsula, near the site of a New Zealand fur seal colony.

Tours

There are no whale-watching tours, but big game fishing, sightseeing and yacht charters offer good dolphin and large whale possibilities within 5 or 10 miles of shore.

On North Island, in the Bay of Islands, fishing and sightseeing charters from Dec.–April are offered by Game Fishing Charters, Maritime Bldg., Paihia, Bay of Islands, New Zealand (Tel. Paihia 27-311). For sailboats: Rainbow Yacht Charters, c/o P.O. Opua, Bay of Islands, New Zealand (Tel. Paihia 27-269). Other good North Island whale areas accessible only by charter include Cavalli Islands, Poor Knights Islands, Hen & Chickens, and the volcanic White Island in Bay of Plenty. (Note: dusky, Hector's and southern right whale dolphins will not be seen in above locales as distribution is restricted to south of East Cape on North Island.)

On South Island, many of New Zealand's whales and dolphins, including duskies and Hector's, may be seen in the southern fiords in 3-million-acre Fiordland National Park. Many sightseeing cruises through Milford Sound and longer tours to Doubtful Sound and other fiords. A 2-hour Milford Sound launch trip is offered 3 times daily during (austral) summer through Fiordland Travel, Ltd. (Tel. Te Anau 859) or the THC hotel system (including the Milford Hotel). For more information: Fiordland National Park, Box 29, Te Anau, New Zealand (Tel. Te Anau 829).

In the **Marlborough Sounds** area, at the north end of South Island, good whale and dolphin possibilities (including sperm whales year round and humpbacks in winter) are offered by charter out of Picton. Southern Marine Charters, Box 246, Picton, New Zealand.

Wilderness tours that include launch trips through **Milford Sound** and to **Stewart Island** with whale and dolphin sightings are offered in Feb. Naturalist-led. 22 days. $1,875 [US], plus air fare. Wilderness Travel, 1760 Solano Ave., Berkeley, CA 94707 USA (Tel. 415-524-5111).

Ferries and Cruises

Some of the best whale and dolphin possibilities are aboard the 3⅓-hour South Island Ferry across Cook Strait between Wellington (departs Aotea Quay, north of city center) and Picton. 4–6 times daily, year-round. Reservations through travel agent or New Zealand Tourist Bureau (Tel. Wellington 725-399).

Another inexpensive ferry crosses Foveaux Strait from Bluff (27 miles from Invercargill) on South Island, to remote southern Stewart Island. 2½ hours; 3 days a week. Reservations through New Zealand Tourist Bureau.

Weather/Sea Notes

Climate varies from near-tropical in the north to cold temperate in the south. In general, austral summer is best for whale sightings but can be cold and rough on the water year-round, even on Cook Strait and Foveaux Strait ferry crossings.

Laws/Guidelines

The New Zealand Marine Mammals Protection Act of 1978 forbids harassment in New Zealand waters or by New Zealanders anywhere in the world.

Oceanaria

Common dolphins at Marineland of New Zealand, Private Bag, Napier, New Zealand (Tel. 58-493).

Museums

Cetacean exhibits at National Museum of New Zealand, Private Bag, Wellington, New Zealand (Tel. 04-859-609).

More information

New Zealand Government Tourist Office, Private Bag, Wellington, New Zealand, or Suite 1530, 10960 Wilshire Blvd., Los Angeles, CA 90024 USA (Tel. 213-477-8241).

Antarctica

Species

Common: minke whale (**2**), humpback whale (**7**), fin whale (**5**), sei whale (**3**), blue whale (**6**), sperm whale (**12**), killer whale (**75**), dusky dolphin (**62**), hourglass dolphin (**61**), Peale's dolphin (**60**).
Sporadic: southern right whale (**9**), Commerson's dolphin (**64**).
Rare: southern right whale dolphin (**69**), southern giant bottlenose whale (**16**).

Tours

Antarctica is the ultimate whale-watching destination. Yet with no support facilities – and a fragile ecosystem that cannot bear much tourism – the Antarctic remains inaccessible to all but a few scientists. 2 luxury cruise ships, however, have in recent years begun taking a limited number of visitors to the Antarctic Peninsula and McMurdo Base. Both ships carry high-profile scientists who act as guides. When whales are sighted, the ships slow down or stop, and sometimes whales or dolphins approach close. The 12–33-day cruises take place from late Nov.–early Feb. and most include visits to the old whaling station at South Georgia Island. Most passengers join the ships in Punta Arenas, Chile, on the Strait of Magellan. Cruises aboard *M/S World Discoverer* start at $3,990 [US] for a 12-day cruise; on *M/S Lindblad Explorer*, 21-day cruises start at $6,400 [US]. Air fare is extra. Contact: (1) Society Expeditions, 723 Broadway E., Seattle, WA 98102 USA (Tel. 206-324-9400 or 800-426-7794); (2) Salén Lindblad Cruising, 133 E. 55th St., New York, NY 10022 USA (Tel. 212-751-2300).

Appendix 1: Photographic Equipment, Clothing and Useful Items for Whale Watching

The best "equipment" for whale watching is a good pair of eyes, an unfettered mind and a lot of patience. But don't forget the basics: food, clothing, and shelter from the elements. On a remote cliff top or riding a cold and windy sea, a thermos of hot coffee or tea, for example, provides excellent company. There are also a few other items you may want to consider, depending on your interest in photography.

Key
Y = Yes
N = No
O = Optional

Items		Comments	FROM LAND/LOOKOUTS In the Tropics	In Temperate Regions	In Polar Regions	FROM CRUISE & OTHER LARGE SHIPS In the Tropics	In Temperate Regions	In Polar Regions	FROM SAILBOATS & SMALL BOATS In the Tropics	In Temperate Regions	In Polar Regions
Camera:	35mm single lens reflex	Because it's light and moderately priced.	Y	Y	Y	Y	Y	Y	Y	Y	Y
	Large format camera	If telephoto lenses and a tripod are used.	O	O	O	N	N	N	N	N	N
Lenses:	28mm-35mm	Wide-angle for very close approaches.	N	N	N	O	O	O	Y	Y	Y
	50 mm	Normal lens for close approaches.	Y	Y	Y	Y	Y	Y	Y	Y	Y
	105mm-135mm (or zoom)	Medium telephoto; 2nd most useful for shooting whales.	Y	Y	Y	Y	Y	Y	Y	Y	Y
	200mm-300mm (or zoom)	Long telephoto; probably most useful for whales.	Y	Y	Y	Y	Y	Y	Y	Y	Y
	400mm +	Very long telephoto; must use with tripod or mono-pod.	O	O	O	N	N	N	N	N	N
Filters:	UV or Skylight	To protect lens from spray (one for each lens).	Y	Y	Y	Y	Y	Y	Y	Y	Y
	Polarizing	To cut glare on the water.	O	O	O	O	O	O	O	O	O
Film:	Kodachrome 25 or 64	For color slides: fine grain with best color.	Y	Y	Y	Y	Y	Y	Y	Y	Y
	Ektachrome 200 or 400	For color slides: grainy but good with long telephotos.	O	O	O	Y	Y	Y	Y	Y	Y
	Kodak Plus-X or Ilford FP4	For black & white negatives: fine grain but low speed.	O	O	O	O	O	O	O	O	O
	Kodak Tri-X or Ilford HP-5 (also Ilford XP1)	For black & white negatives: still sharp but higher speed.	Y	Y	Y	Y	Y	Y	Y	Y	Y

Key
Y = Yes
N = No
O = Optional

Items		Comments	FROM LAND/LOOKOUTS			FROM CRUISE & OTHER LARGE SHIPS			FROM SAILBOATS & SMALL BOATS		
			In the Tropics	In Temperate Regions	In Polar Regions	In the Tropics	In Temperate Regions	In Polar Regions	In the Tropics	In Temperate Regions	In Polar Regions
Other:	Tripod	Find one that's portable yet sturdy and easy to set up.	Y	Y	Y	N	N	N	N	N	N
	Mono-pod	Good for fast shooting.	O	O	O	O	O	O	N	N	N
	Shoulder brace or gun stock	Holds camera with long telephoto lenses steadier.	O	O	O	O	O	O	O	O	O
	Blowbrush, lens paper, & cleaner	To keep lenses clean.	Y	Y	Y	Y	Y	Y	Y	Y	Y
	Soft dry cloth	To keep camera free from corroding salt spray.	Y	Y	Y	Y	Y	Y	Y	Y	Y
	Camera case (packsack, metal or fiberglass case)	Water-proof and large enough to carry accessories.	Y	Y	Y	Y	Y	Y	Y	Y	Y
	Nikonos underwater camera	Good all-weather camera but only useful for close approaches	N	N	N	O	O	O	O	O	O
Clothing:	Light cotton clothes	Light in weight and color.	Y	O	N	Y	N	N	Y	N	N
	Wool pants & shirt	Good for cold and damp weather.	N	O	Y	N	O	Y	N	O	Y
	Sweater	Often necessary on all but a tropical sea.	N	Y	Y	O	Y	Y	O	Y	Y
	Polar guard or down jacket (or parka)	Polar guard is better in wet climates.	N	N	Y	N	O	Y	N	O	Y
	Rain gear with hat or hood & rubber boots/wool socks	Seasonal need (some temperate climes in winter & polar summer).	N	O	O	N	O	O	N	O	O
	Wool hat or toque		N	O	Y	N	Y	Y	N	Y	Y
	Sun visor, baseball cap, or river guide cap	River guide cap provides best protection in the tropics.	Y	Y	O	Y	Y	N	Y	Y	N
	Thermal underwear		N	O	Y	N	O	Y	N	O	Y
	Mustang Floater coat or survival suit	For safety in case boat sinks or you fall overboard.	N	N	N	N	O	O	N	O	O
	Hiking boots		O	O	O	N	N	N	N	N	N
	Deck shoes or sneakers	Rubber-soled for grip.	O	O	N	Y	Y	O	Y	Y	N
	Gloves or mittens	Flexible gloves will allow photography.	N	O	Y	N	Y	Y	N	Y	Y

Key
Y = Yes
N = No
O = Optional

Items		Comments	FROM LAND/LOOKOUTS			FROM CRUISE & OTHER LARGE SHIPS			FROM SAILBOATS & SMALL BOATS		
			In the Tropics	In Temperate Regions	In Polar Regions	In the Tropics	In Temperate Regions	In Polar Regions	In the Tropics	In Temperate Regions	In Polar Regions
Etc.	Sunglasses	Use safety cord on boats.	Y	Y	Y	Y	Y	Y	Y	Y	Y
	Sun screen or lotion.	Use high-rated (#15) sun screen in the tropics.	Y	Y	Y	Y	Y	Y	Y	Y	Y
	Lip salve	With sun screen in the tropics.	Y	Y	Y	Y	Y	Y	Y	Y	Y
	Binoculars - 7x35, 7x50, or 8x40	Buy the best you can afford; rubber-encased if possible.	Y	Y	Y	Y	Y	Y	Y	Y	Y
	Telescope - 15x, 20x or higher magnification	Use with tripod.	O	O	O	N	N	N	N	N	N
	Plastic bags (small, see-through)	Cut lens-sized hole in bottom for shooting in the rain.	O	O	O	O	O	O	O	O	O
	Notebook with vinyl cover	To keep sighting information, sketches & notes (use soft lead pencil).	O	O	O	O	O	O	O	O	O
	Seasick medication	See Appendix 2 for detailed suggestions.	N	N	N	Y	Y	Y	Y	Y	Y
	Safety gear: life jackets, charts, etc.	This will be taken care of on big ships but check on small boats.	N	N	N	N	N	N	Y	Y	Y
	Maps, compass		Y	Y	Y	O	O	O	Y	Y	Y
	Snack, water, thermos, & other refreshments	May not be necessary to pack on large ships.	Y	Y	Y	O	O	O	Y	Y	Y

Note: ship or small-boat photography requires fast shutter speeds – 1/500 to 1/1000 of a second – to freeze the action, especially when ship, sea, and whales are moving, and telephoto lenses are used. Some photographers find high ASA film gives them more latitude. Others don't like the grainy color (or don't like working in black and white which does look good even with high ASA film); instead they wait for full sun, moderate seas and cooperative whales.

Appendix 2: **A Few Words about Seasickness**

When seasickness strikes, a true understanding of the alien and sometimes forbidding oceanic world of whales and dolphins is driven home with acute clarity. You can sometimes prevent this unpleasant "awareness", or ease it somewhat. Seasickness is caused by dissociation of stimuli coming to the brain. The eyes tell the brain one thing, but the inner ear disagrees. The brain valiantly tries to sort out the signals. Sometimes it doesn't succeed. Your stomach is the loser. Here's a summary of some of the medications available, as well as a few precautions and a recommended routine for day one at sea.

Marazine, *Dramamine*, *Bonine*, or *Gravol* are easily available in tablets or capsules. *Marazine* and *Gravol* are probably the most commonly used for the prevention and treatment of nausea and vomiting. Drowsiness is often an unwelcome side effect.

Transderm-V (generic name scopolamine) looks like a dime-sized Band-aid. It's worn on the hairless skin behind the ear. The drug, absorbed through the skin into the bloodstream, reduces the activity of nerve fibers in the inner ear which can disturb the balance mechanism. One "disc" lasts for 3 days, and doesn't cause drowsiness. About $3 for 2 discs.

Antivert is a prescription drug developed by the US Navy. Considered highly effective, it's available in tablets or suppositories.

The Stabilizer Wriststrap or "seasick strap" was recently developed by a New York doctor knowledgeable in acupuncture. An enthusiastic but often seasick sailor, Dr. Daniel Shu Jen Choy found that his nausea could be relieved by pressing a finger on an acupuncture point called the nei-kuan point, located on the inside of each wrist. But how does one keep pressing both wrists while sailing a boat? Dr. Choy fashioned a strap from a 9″ × ³/₄″ strip of white elastic, stitching pieces of velcro to each end to keep it tightly fastened around his wrist. In the center of the strap, he attached a hemispherical button to exert constant pressure on the point.

It's not difficult to find the nei-kuan point, though it's a good idea to practice putting on the strap before high seas arrive. The point is located between the 2 central or flexor tendons precisely 3 middle-finger widths up the arm from the wrist crease. The seasick strap worked for me sailing off Iceland in March and it may work for you. Tests show about a 70% success rate for sailors and it's almost as effective for treating nausea associated with chemotherapy and pregnancy. NASA is currently testing it on astronauts. The best thing about it is that it can be worn constantly and there are no side effects except a mark on the arm which fades in a few hours. Cost is $14.75 a pair (plus $1.50 postage). For more information, write to: Stabilization Medical Technology, Inc., Box 340, Broomall, PA 19008 USA. Or call 1-800-345-8112 (in PA: 1-800-662-2444).

The following precautions may also help prevent seasickness.

Start medication before the trip. 12 hours before with *Transderm-V*; ¹/₂ hour or more with tablets or capsules.

Come to the sea well rested and relaxed.

Eat lightly and avoid greasy food and alcohol before and during trip.

If once on the water you feel queasy, try munching on crackers, dry bread or rolls. Sip bubbly water, especially ginger ale.

Stay on deck, near the boat's center of gravity (usually over the engines). Breathe deeply. Keep your eyes on the horizon and go with the waves, bending your knees to reduce upper body movement instead of resisting the unfamiliar motion. Attitude is important. Feel the wind on your face and enjoy the power and exhilaration of the sea. Engage a shipmate in an interesting conversation – but not about seasickness! Keep yourself warm and comfortable but do not go below where it will be even harder for your eyes to comprehend the motion perceived by your inner ear.

Pray for whales. It's amazing that even in the roughest weather, few people are seasick when whales are sighted.

If all else fails, head for the *leeward* rail and get it over with.

Appendix 3: **Recording the Sounds of Whales and Dolphins**

Few whale-watching tours offer an opportunity to listen to whales. Yet to hear a whale is to approach it on its own terms. Living in a dark underwater world, cetaceans are sound creatures. They seem to communicate with each other and obtain most of the information about their world through sound.

It is surprisingly easy to make good recordings of whales and dolphins at sea. With many species, it is an easier and cheaper enterprise than photography. Whales can often be recorded at distances and in seas too rough for decent photography. They can also be recorded from shore.

Any good, small cassette recorder will do the job. Carry it inside a pack sack or camera bag to protect it from salt spray. Make sure you have the appropriate "line input" connection, so the tape recorder and hydrophone are compatible.

Finding a hydrophone (a special underwater microphone) is the hardest part. Try outlets specializing in marine electronics in large coastal cities (Boston, New York, Miami, Los Angeles, San Francisco, Seattle, Vancouver, Halifax).* If you have marine biologists or whale researchers in your area, or perhaps an oceanarium, approach them for local sources. Hydrophones range in price from $5 to $1,000. An inexpensive one can be fine but make sure it has a pre-amp (built-in or in a separate box) and that all the equipment works together. A pre-amp and, even, a hydrophone can be "home-built" if you have a friend knowledgeable in electronics. Some whale watchers have "invented" their own hydrophones by sticking a regular microphone in a condom – with passing results. Many others have used a plastic bag or other primitive housing and simply lowered a good microphone over the side, to its inevitable doom. A microphone designed for in-air recording is less than satisfactory underwater, especially when wet. Yet even hydrophones are susceptible to salt-water leaks. Keep a tube of silicon seal with you and use it on all hydrophone and cable connections *before* you hear the crackling bacon-in-hot-grease sound of a salt-water short.

To use: when you see whales (or enter a known whale area), stop the boat and shut off the engine. It is not necessary to be in good viewing range. Many researchers use hydrophones to *find* whales. Lower the hydrophone into the water to a depth of about 10 feet, or more if necessary, to eliminate surface noise. Most hydrophones are omnidirectional, i.e., they record sound from all directions. To cut the noise of ship traffic, it sometimes helps to make your hydrophone more directional. Position your boat between the offending motor noise and the whales. Lower the hydrophone on the whale-side of the ship, but not below the keel. Your ship will function as a sound shield. From land, unless the inshore water is deep, it may be necessary to set up a buoy – an inner tube anchored to the bottom works fine – with 25–50 yards of hydrophone cable leading back to your tape recorder. Sometimes it's sufficient to rig a long pole over the water with the hydrophone hanging down off the end.

Cetacean Recordings

Songs of the Humpback Whale, Capitol Records. SW-620.

Deep Voices. The Second Whale Record, Capitol Records. ST-11598.

Ocean of Song: Whale Voices, PET Records (Box 1102, Burbank, CA 91507 USA).

Northern Whales, Music Gallery Editions (30 Patrick St., Toronto, Ont. M5T 1V1 Canada).

Sound Communication of the Bottlenosed Dolphin, Biological System, Inc. (Box 26, St. Augustine, FL 32084 USA).

Sounds and Ultrasounds of the Bottle-nose Dolphin. Folkways Records.

*A good mail-order hydrophone with pre-amp and 30-foot cable is available for $100 from Lon A. Brocklehurst, Labcore Bio-acoustics, 3301 Capitol Ave., Tumwater, WA 98501 (Tel. 206-786-1622).

Appendix 4: **Reading List**

General

Alpers, A. 1961. *Dolphins. The Myth and the Mammal.* Houghton Mifflin Co., Boston. 268 pp., black and white photographs.

Brower, K. 1979. *Wake of the Whale.* Friends of the Earth/Dutton, New York. 161 pp., color and black and white photographs by W. Curtsinger.

Burton, R. 1980. *The Life and Death of Whales.* (Revised 2nd edition) Universe Books, New York. 185 pp., photographs.

Caldwell, D.K. and M.C. Caldwell. 1972. *The World of the Bottlenosed Dolphin.* J.B. Lippincott, Philadelphia. 157 pp., photographs.

Devine, E. and M. Clark. 1967. *The Dolphin Smile. Twenty-nine centuries of dolphin lore.* MacMillan and Co., New York. 370 pp., black and white photographs.

Ellis, R. 1980. *The Book of Whales.* Alfred A. Knopf, New York. 252 pp., color illustrations.

Ellis, R. 1982. *Dolphins and Porpoises.* Alfred A. Knopf, New York. 252pp., color illustrations.

Hoyt, E. 1981. *The Whale Called Killer.* E.P. Dutton, New York. 248 pp., color and black and white photographs.

Lilly, J.C. 1975. *Lilly on Dolphins: Humans of the Sea.* Anchor Press, Garden City, New York. 500 pp., black and white photographs.

McIntyre, J. 1974. *Mind in the Waters. A book to celebrate the consciousness of whales and dolphins.* Charles Scribner's Sons, New York. 240 pp., photographs and illustrations.

McNally, R. 1981. *So Remorseless A Havoc. Of Dolphins, Whales and Men.* Little, Brown and Co., Boston. 288 pp., black and white photographs, illustrations by P.A. Folkens.

Matthews, L.H. 1968. *The Whale.* Simon and Schuster, New York. 287 pp., illustrated.

Matthews, L.H. 1978. *The Natural History of the Whale.* Columbia University Press, New York. 219 pp., illustrated.

Melville, H. 1851. *Moby-Dick; or The Whale.* (Many publishers and editions) New York. 634 pp.

Norris, K.S. 1974. *The Porpoise Watcher: A naturalist's experiences with porpoises and whales.* W.W. Norton, New York. 250 pp., black and white photographs.

Ommanney, F.W. 1971. *Lost Leviathan.* Dodd, Mead and Co., New York. 280 pp.

Pryor, K. 1975. *Lads Before the Wind. Adventures in porpoise training.* Harper & Row, New York. 278 pp., black and white photographs.

Riedman, S.F. and E.T. Gustafson. 1966. *Home is the Sea for Whales.* Rand McNally and Co., Chicago. 264 pp., illustrated.

Scammon, C.M. 1874. *The Marine Mammals of the North-Western Coast of North America, Described and Illustrated: Together with an Account of the American Whale-Fishery.* J.H. Carmany and Co., San Francisco. (Reprinted 1968 by Dover, New York). 320 pp., illustrated.

Scheffer, V.B. 1969. *The Year of the Whale.* Charles Scribner's Sons, New York. 213 pp., illustrated.

Scheffer, V.B. 1976. *A Natural History of Marine Mammals.* Charles Scribner's Sons, New York. 157 pp., illustrated.

Wood, F.G. 1973. *Marine Mammals and Man: The Navy's Porpoises and Sea Lions.* Robert B. Luce, Washington, D.C. 264 pp., black and white photographs.

Regional and World Guides to Whales, Dolphins and Porpoises

Baker, A.N. 1983. *Whales & Dolphins of New Zealand and Australia.* Victoria University Press, Wellington, New Zealand. Color and black and white photographs and drawings.

Bennett, B., 1983. *The Oceanic Society Field Guide to the Gray Whale.* Legacy Publishing Co., San Francisco. 51 pp. Illustrated.

Haley, D. (editor) 1978. *Marine Mammals of Eastern North Pacific and Arctic Waters.* Pacific Search Press, Seattle. 256 pp., color and black and white photographs.

Katona, S.K., V. Rough, and D.T. Richardson. 1983. *A Field Guide to the Whales, Porpoises and Seals of the Gulf of Maine and Eastern Canada: Cape Cod to Newfoundland.* Charles Scribner's Sons, New York. 256 pp., black and white photographs and illustrations.

Leatherwood, S., R.R. Reeves and L. Foster. 1983. *The Sierra Club Handbook of Whales and Dolphins.* Sierra Club Books, San Francisco. 302pp., color illustrations, black and white photographs.

Watson, L. 1981. *A Sea Guide to Whales of the World.* Dutton, New York. 302 pp., color illustrations and photographs.

Appendix 5: **Glossary**

amphipod any of a large group of shrimp-like crustaceans, each about 1-2 inches long.

baleen a strong yet light substance made of keratin (the same protein in fingernails and hooves) which is found in 2 rows of comb-like plates growing down from the roof of the mouth of all baleen whales, also called Mysticetes. There are up to 960 baleen plates in a whale's mouth (300 on average, depending on species). The size of each plate ranges from 1-14 feet long and the color from white to tan-yellow to gray to black – depending on species. The baleen plates are used to strain plankton, small schooling fish and other organisms from the water (Syn. whalebone).

beak the elongated forward part of the head, especially in certain dolphins and beaked whales (Syn. snout).

biosonar clicking sounds used by odontocetes (toothed whales) and perhaps other whales to navigate and find food in their underwater world. Researchers have shown that dolphin biosonar can resolve extremely fine detail and that it is superior to man-made sonar. It may also be used for communication (Syn. echolocation).

blow the often visible expiration through the blowhole (Syn. spout).

blowhole the nostrils of a whale. Baleen whales have 2 blowholes situated side by side; toothed whales have 1 blowhole.

bonnet the large callosity of right whales found at the crest or top of the head. A term first used by whalers, it resembles the type of head-gear worn by women of an earlier century.

bow rider a dolphin that travels alongside the bow or front of a ship, keeping pace with it.

breach the action of a whale as it jumps clear of the water (Syn. leap).

bristles the filter fibers that form the fringe along the edge of each baleen plate.

bubble cloud large circular patch of tiny bubbles produced by feeding humpback whales.

bubble net a ring of single bubbles produced by feeding humpback whales to encircle prey (Syn. bubble ring).

bubble stream a continuous stream of bubbles that may stretch for several hundred yards underwater. Associated with aggressive behavior in humpback whales, bubble streams may have other uses. Other whales and dolphins sometimes make bubble streams when they vocalize underwater.

callosity an irregular, crusty protuberance of horny material called keratin found in patches on the head of all right whales.

cape the dark dorsal surface of some cetaceans; has the appearance of a cape.

cetacean a member of the animal order called Cetacea consisting of whales, dolphins and porpoises.

chevron the pale gray mark behind the head on the back of fin whales. Also, any chevron-shaped mark on a whale's back, flank or cape.

clicks or click train brief pulses of sound repeated at varying rates and used for echolocation or biosonar.

copepod any of a small subclass of minute crustaceans that baleen whales eat, especially in warmer waters.

crustacean any of a large class called Crustacea consisting of mostly aquatic arthropods having a hard shell, such as shrimps, crabs, barnacles, lobsters, etc.

dorsal fin raised cartilaginous part of some cetaceans situated on the back and often clearly visible when a cetacean surfaces for air.

dorsal surface the back or upper side of a cetacean.

echolocation see biosonar.

estrous condition of being "in heat".

euphausiid any of a group of shrimp-like pelagic crustaceans, each about an inch long (Syn. krill).

eye patch area of whitish pigment situated above and behind each eye of a killer whale (called post-ocular patch by some researchers). Also, the dark area around the eyes of many dolphins.

falcate recurved or curved-back shape.

finning the action of a whale slapping a flipper against the water while lying on its side (Syn. flippering, flipper slap, flipper lob, flipper flapping).

fins the flippers or side fins of a whale (Syn. flippers, pectoral fins).

flippering see finning.

flippers the pectoral or side fins of a whale (Syn. fins, pectoral fins).

flukes the tail fin of a whale (Syn. tail, tail flukes).

head knobs see tubercles.

head-up see spy-hop.

krill planktonic crustaceans and larvae, usually euphausiids, eaten by baleen whales.

lag a dolphin belonging to the genus *Lagenorhynchus*.

lobtailing the action of a whale slapping its flukes against the water (Syn. loptailing, lobbing its tail, tail lobbing).

median ridge the raised line that bisects a whale's head from the lips to the blowholes.

melon the bulbous forehead of odontocetes (toothed whales).

mysticete a member of the suborder of Cetacea called Mysticeti, the suborder of baleen whales. Mysticeti comes from the Greek words meaning "mustached sea monsters" (Syn. baleen whale).

notch the V-shaped indentation dividing the rear edge of the flukes of many cetaceans (Syn. median notch).

odontocete a member of the suborder of Cetacea called Odontoceti, the suborder of toothed whales. Odontoceti comes from the Greek words meaning "toothed sea monsters" (Syn. toothed whale).

pectoral fins the flippers or side fins of a whale (Syn. flippers, fins).

pelagic oceanic; living or occurring in the open ocean.

pigmentation pattern the arrangement of coloration in skin tissue which allows certain species of baleen whales to be individually identified.

pod a group of whales; in killer whales, a permanent association of up to about 40 whales.

rorqual a member of the baleen whale family called Balaenopteridae.

rostrum forward extension of the upper jaw.

saddle the gray patch just behind the dorsal fin of a killer whale; also the middorsal area on any cetacean.

scrimshaw an artistic engraving on whalebone or whales' teeth, commonly sperm whales' teeth.

sexual dimorphism physical differences between the male and female of a species that enable it to be easily sexed.

sounding to whalers, the descent of the whale after it has been harpooned; to whale watchers and researchers, the deep descent of the whale after a series of shallow respiration dives.

spar see spy-hop.

spout see blow.

spy-hop the action of a whale raising its head out of the water (Syn. bob, head-up, spar).

tail lash the action of a male humpback directing its tail flukes at another male in competition for females; bloody head knobs and, occasionally, torn flukes are the result.

tail print the slick or patch of calm water left at the surface after a whale dives; a whale's "footprint" (Syn. tail slick, fluke wash).

tail stock the narrowing, rear part of a whale between the tail flukes and the rest of the body (Syn. peduncle).

throat grooves the pattern of pleats in the throat unique to rorquals. The pleats allow the throat to expand during feeding to accommodate large quantities of fish and krill in a single gulp.

tubercles small bumps on the head of a humpback whale (Syn. head knobs); also refers to bumps on the back of a finless porpoise used to carry young.

ventral surface the belly or underside of a cetacean.

whalebone see baleen.

Index